GRE® Exam

Verbal Workbook

Sixth Edition

Other Kaplan Books on Graduate School Admissions

Get into Graduate School

Kaplan GRE Exam: Comprehensive Program

Kaplan GRE Exam: Premier Program

Kaplan GRE Math Workbook

Kaplan GRE Exam Subject Test: Biology

Kaplan GRE Exam Subject Test: Psychology

Kaplan GRE Exam Vocabulary in a Box

Kaplan GRE Exam Vocabulary Prep

GRE® Exam
Verbal Workbook
Sixth Edition

PUBLISHING

New York

© 2008 Kaplan, Inc.

Published by Kaplan Publishing, a division of Kaplan, Inc.
1 Liberty Plaza, 24th Floor
New York, NY 10006

Printed in the United States of America

August 2008
10 9 8 7 6 5 4

ISBN-13: 978-1-4195-5219-9

Kaplan Publishing books are available at special quantity discounts to use for sales promotions, employee premiums, or educational purposes. Please email our Special Sales Department to order or for more information at kaplanpublishing@kaplan.com, or write to Kaplan Publishing, 1 Liberty Plaza, 24th Floor, New York, NY 10006.

Table of Contents

Updates to the GRE..viii

How to Use This Book...xi

PART ONE: GETTING STARTED

Chapter 1: About the GRE CAT...3

    What's on the GRE?..3

    How Is the GRE Scored?...5

    How Do I Register?...5

    How Does the CAT Format Work?...5

    How Should I Attack the Verbal Section?..6

    How Do I Move Around on the CAT?...8

    Pros and Cons of the GRE CAT..9

PART TWO: VERBAL PRACTICE TESTS

Chapter 2: GRE Sentence Completion..13

    The Four Fundamentals...13

    The Kaplan Four Step Method for Sentence Completion...................16

    Practice Set..18

    Answers...19

    Sentence Completion: Test 1...21

    Answers...23

    Sentence Completion: Test 2...27

    Answers...29

    Sentence Completion: Test 3...33

    Answers...35

    Sentence Completion: Test 4...39

    Answers...41

    Sentence Completion: Test 5...45

    Answers...47

Chapter 3: GRE Analogies...51

    The Four Fundamentals..51

    The Kaplan Four-Step Method for Analogies..54

    Practice Set..56

    Answer Key...57

    Analogies: Test 1..59

    Answers..60

    Analogies: Test 2..63

    Answers..64

    Analogies: Test 3..67

    Answers..68

    Analogies: Test 4..71

    Answers..72

    Analogies: Test 5..75

    Answers..76

Chapter 4: GRE Antonyms...79

    The Four Fundamentals..79

    The Kaplan Four-Step Method for Antonyms..82

    Practice Set..84

    Answer Key...85

    Antonyms: Test 1..87

    Answers..88

    Antonyms: Test 2..91

    Answers..93

    Antonyms: Test 3..95

    Answers..97

    Antonyms: Test 4..99

    Answers..101

    Antonyms: Test 5..103

    Answers..105

Chapter 5: GRE Reading Comprehension...107

    The Four Fundamentals..107

    The Kaplan Four-Step Method for Reading Comprehension...............................111

    Practice Set..112

    Answer Key...114

    Reading Comprehension: Test 1..115

    Answers..118

Reading Comprehension: Test 2 121

Answers 124

Reading Comprehension: Test 3 127

Answers 130

Reading Comprehension: Test 4 133

Answers 136

Reading Comprehension: Test 5 139

Answers 142

PART THREE: ANALYTICAL WRITING

Chapter 6: Strategies for GRE Writing 147

What to Expect 147

The Four Basic Principles of GRE Writing 147

The Kaplan Five-Step Method for the Analytical Writing Measure 149

The Issue Essay 150

The Argument Essay 153

Practice Essays 157

GRE Analytical Writing Scoring 158

GRE Writing Style 159

PART FOUR: VOCABULARY BUILDER

Chapter 7: Increasing Your GRE Vocabulary 163

Before You Get Started 163

Basics of Vocabulary Building 164

Parts of Speech 164

Chapter 8: Top GRE Words 167

200 Top GRE Words in Context 168

Chapter 9: GRE Word Groups 207

Chapter 10: Word Root List 217

Introduction to the Word Root List 217

Chapter 11: Opposite Drills 235

Opposite Drill Answer Keys 257

Chapter 12: GRE minidictionary 279

A Special Note for International Students 317

Updates to the GRE

Instead of one major overhaul as originally planned the Educational Testing Service (ETS) will introduce revisions to the Graduate Record Examination (GRE) gradually, beginning with two new question types—one math, one verbal—that were introduced into the computer-based GRE in November 2007. On Test Day, you may see just one sample of the new math question type, just one sample of the new verbal question type, OR you won't see either question at all.

For the time being, these new question types do not count toward your score. As of this printing, ETS has not announced a timeline for when these new types will count toward your score.

THE NEW VERBAL SECTION QUESTION TYPE—TEXT COMPLETION

Although Sentence Completion questions with more than one blank space are found in the GRE exam, the new Verbal question type—Text Completion—is a more complex version.

In this new Text Completion question type, you will be asked to select one entry for each blank from the corresponding column of choices, and it may include as many as three blanks within one question.

Just as with the Sentence Completion questions, this new question type tests your vocabulary and your ability to understand the context in which words are used. The principles and strategies you use for the Sentence Completion questions can be applied to the Text Completion question type. Here is a sample question:

> As a result of the (i) _____ pace of life, urban living (ii) _____ many young professionals the opportunity to (iii) _____ their lives with a sense of constant excitement.

Blank (i)	Blank (ii)	Blank (iii)
(A) intrinsic	(D) instigates	(G) eschew
(B) ephemeral	(E) affords	(H) inter
(C) frenetic	(F) arrogates	(I) imbue

Answer: C, E, and I

Use the clues given in the sentence to determine which word belongs in each blank. Starting with the first, you are looking for an adjective that would best describe urban living and that is similar to *constant excitement*.

Choice (A) means inherent, which doesn't fit the context of the phrase, and (B) means fleeting or brief—again, an inapt description of the pace of urban life; therefore, choice (C) is correct. The second blank requires a word that means to be made available or to give the opportunity. Therefore, choice (E) is correct. One meaning of *afford* is to offer or impart. The final blank requires a word that tells what young professionals have the opportunity to do. Choice (G) means to avoid and choice, (H) means to bury, so they are incorrect. Young professionals are not likely to choose urban living to avoid constant excitement, therefore (I), which means to permeate, is the correct answer.

STAY ON TOP OF THE LATEST DEVELOPMENTS

As ETS makes further announcements, you can depend on Kaplan to provide you with the most accurate, up-to-the-minute information. You can get updates by visiting us at Kaptest.com/NEWGRE.

Good Luck!

kaptest.com/publishing

If there are any important late-breaking developments—or any changes or corrections to the Kaplan test preparation materials in this book—we will post that information online at **kaptest.com/publishing**. Check to see if there is any information posted there for readers of this book.

kaplansurveys.com/books

What did you think of this book? We'd love to hear your comments and suggestions. We invite you to fill out our online survey form at **kaplansurveys.com/books**. Your feedback is extremely helpful as we continue to develop high-quality resources to meet your needs.

How to Use This Book

Kaplan has prepared students to take standardized tests for more than 70 years; longer than the GRE has even been around. Our team of researchers and editors know more about preparation for the GRE than anyone else, and you'll find their accumulated knowledge and experience in this book.

The GRE is a standardized test, and so, while every test is not identical, every test covers the same content in essentially the same way. This is good news for you; it means that by studying the material in this book, you can prepare for exactly the kind of questions you can expect to encounter on Test Day.

The main focus of this book is in reviewing the verbal concepts you need to get a good score on the GRE. Strategic reviews, exercises, and practice sets with explanations will help you brush up on the verbal skills you'll need for test day.

If possible, work through this book a little at a time over the course of several weeks. There is a lot of information to absorb, and it's hard to do it all at once. Cramming just before the test is not a good idea. You probably won't absorb much information if you pack it in at the last minute.

The GRE Verbal Workbook is divided into four sections, each serving its own very important purpose. With careful review and practice, the content and strategies contained in this book will help you to score your best on the GRE.

Getting Started

The first thing you need to do is find out exactly what to expect on the GRE. In part one of this book, we'll provide you with background information on the Verbal Section of the test, what it covers, and how it's organized. The GRE is only available in a computerized version. We will show how this version of the GRE differs from the more traditional paper-and-pencil test.

GRE Verbal Practice Tests

Once you have the big picture, you will need to focus more specifically on the test content. Part two of this book does just that. It gives you a complete tour of the Verbal question types that you will see on Test Day. There's a chapter for each of the four major content areas: Sentence Completion, Analogies, Antonyms, and Reading Comprehension. And each chapter provides tips for mastering the question type at hand, including the Kaplan Method, which gives you time-tested strategies for approaching a question type, and plenty of testlike examples to practice on.

Analytical Writing

This section provides you with information about the GRE Analytical Writing Measure. It contains descriptions and examples of the two types of essay question types, the Issue Essay and the Argument Essay, as well as tips for successfully completing each. This chapter also presents the Kaplan Method for the Writing Section, as well as guided practice in using it to complete some sample essays. The section ends with some practice essay prompts as well as a scoring guide that will enable you to see how your practice essays measure up to the ETS scoring rubric.

Vocabulary Builder

Since vocabulary is the most important skill on the verbal portion of the GRE, the last portion of the this book contains material to help you to build your vocabulary skills. There is a list of the words that appear most frequently on the GRE, and tips for learning words in groups and for using word roots to determine a word's meaning. If vocabulary isn't one of your particular strengths, start studying this material immediately and consult it periodically as you continue to study.

| PART ONE |

Getting Started

Chapter 1: **About the GRE CAT**

Before we start preparing for the Verbal section of the GRE, let's take a look at the big picture. In this chapter, we'll discuss the content and structure of the GRE. We'll also explain strategies for making the computer-adaptive (CAT) format of the exam work to your advantage.

WHAT'S ON THE GRE?

The Graduate Record Examination (GRE) is a computer-based exam that is administered by Educational Testing Service (ETS). The Verbal section is 30 minutes long and is made up of four question types: Sentence Completions, Antonyms, Analogies, and Reading Comprehension. The Quantitative section is 45 minutes long and is made up of three question types: Problem Solving, Quantitative Comparison, and Graphs. The Analytical Writing Measure is 75 minutes long and consists of two essays. (You will be required to write these on the computer.) In addition, there can be up to two unscored experimental sections. A short break is given between each section.

Verbal Questions

There are about six Sentence Completion questions. In each of these, one or two words from a sentence is missing. You must select an answer choice that best fits those blanks. The heart of Sentence Completions is not grammar or vocabulary; rather, Sentence Completions test your ability to recognize the author's intent, and find the best words to fit this meaning.

 RUSSIAN ROULETTE

Don't try to figure out which section of your test is experimental. Even if you guess right, it can hurt your score. If you guess wrong. . . .

There are about eight Analogies questions. In each of these you are given a pair of words. You must determine the relationship between these pairs and choose the pair of words from the answer choices that has the same relationship. While Analogies test vocabulary to some extent, they are really testing your ability to form a strong connection between words. Fortunately, the same types of relationship show up on the GRE over and over again.

There are about nine Antonym questions. Here you are given a word and must choose its opposite from among the answer choices. Antonym questions mainly test your vocabulary skills. Kaplan provides you with two ways to improve your performance on these questions: first by showing you which words are most likely to appear on the test, and second by giving you techniques to enable you to find the correct answer even if you do not know the meaning of all the words in the question.

PREDICTABLE

The GRE tests the same principles over and over. Every GRE is virtually the same as every other one because the format is consistent from year to year to yield dependable results.

The Verbal section will contain two or three reading comprehension passages (each approximately 200–300 words) with two to four questions based on each. The passages are written in difficult, often technical prose adapted from books and journals in the broad areas of the humanities, the social sciences, and the natural sciences. You shouldn't take the reading comprehension challenge lightly. The reading skills you developed in college and use for your personal pleasure are ill-suited to success on the GRE. Reading comprehension requires a commitment to a different, more aggressive kind of reading. We'll explain these new reading techniques in the chapter on reading comprehension.

Quantitative Questions

Quantitative Comparisons are a "fixed-format" question type, meaning that each of the four answer choices has a specific definition. (You may remember this question type from the SAT.) You'll see about 15 Quantitative Comparison questions. In each you must compare two quantities and decide which is the larger, or if you have enough information to make this judgment. This is one of the most difficult question types on the GRE, but also one where your effort and a well-considered strategy yield great rewards.

You'll see approximately ten Problem Solving questions in the classic five-answer-choice format. The concepts and skills tested are taken from the broad areas of arithmetic, algebra, and geometry—essentially the math we all studied in high school. This doesn't mean, however, that the GRE rewards you solely for your knowledge of that material. The most successful test takers organize available data and efficiently utilize an arsenal of math tools and test-taking strategies.

You'll see about two graph sets, each of which will be followed by two or three questions. The graphs that show up on the GRE are those that are most commonly used in everyday life: bar, line, and pie charts, which are often combined with information tables. The most successful test takers will learn how to read a graph so that they can focus on the data that they need and not waste time with all the extraneous data that a graph provides.

Analytical Writing Section

The Analytical Writing section allows schools to evaluate your academic writing ability. The Analytical Writing section must be written on the computer. You will use a simple word processing program. The essays will then be sent to graders who will determine your Analytical Writing score at a later date.

The writing assessment consists of two timed essay sections. The first is what ETS calls an "Issue" essay. You'll be shown two essay topics—each a sentence or paragraph that expresses an opinion on an issue of general interest. You'll be asked to choose one of the two topics, and then you'll be given 45 minutes to plan and write an essay that communicates your own view on the issue. Whether you agree or disagree with the opinion provided is irrelevant: What matters is that you back up your view with relevant examples and statements.

The second of the two writing tasks is the "Argument" essay, which is somewhat different. This time, you will be shown a paragraph that argues a certain point. You will then be given 30 minutes to assess the argument's logic. As with the "Issue" essay, it won't matter whether you agree with the information provided.

HOW IS THE GRE SCORED?

The official score report you receive, and which ETS will send to the graduate schools you choose, will contain five separate scores: both a scaled score and a percentile score for the Quantitative and Verbal sections of the test (the scaled score lies on a 200-800 scale), and your score on the Analytical Writing section. (See chapter 6 for details on how the Writing section is scored.) You'll receive your unofficial Quantitative and Verbal scores on the computer immediately after you take the exam. Some schools will look at your scores for all three sections, while others will look at scores for only one or two. Check with the schools in which you are interested before you start studying. Also bear in mind that while some programs only look at one or two scores, applications for financial aid may be dependent on all your GRE scores.

Each of these scores will be accompanied by a percentile ranking, showing the percentage of test takers who scored below you. An improvement in your percentile ranking can often mean the difference between choosing from the top graduate programs and from less prestigious programs.

 **NUMBERS GAME**

You can't score higher than 800 or lower than 200 on either the Verbal or the Quantitative section. The Writing section is scored separately on a scale from 0–6.

HOW DO I REGISTER?

The GRE is administered at many special computerized testing centers six days a week during regular business hours. To register to take the GRE, go to www.gre.org. You can download the most recent *GRE Information and Resource Bulletin*, which is published by ETS every summer for the forthcoming academic year.

HOW DOES THE CAT FORMAT WORK?

The CAT format takes some getting used to—in fact, it's pretty weird at first. Here's how it works. You will see only one question at a time. Instead of having a predetermined mixture of basic, medium, and hard questions, the computer will select questions for you based on how well you are doing.

The first question will be of medium difficulty. If you get it right, the second question will be selected from a large pool of questions that are a little harder; if you get the first question wrong, the second will be a little more basic.

If you keep getting questions right, the test will get harder and harder; if you slip and make some mistakes, the test will adjust and start giving you easier problems, but if you answer them correctly, it will go back to the hard ones. Ideally, the test gives you enough questions to ensure that scores are not based on luck. If you get one hard question right, you might just have been lucky, but if you get ten hard questions right, then luck has little to do with it. So the test is self-adjusting and self-correcting.

Because of this format, the GRE CAT is very different structurally from the paper-based test. After the first problem, every problem that you see is based on how you answered the prior problem. That means you cannot return to a question once you've answered it, because that would throw off the sequence. Once you answer a question, it's part of your score, for better or worse. That means you can't skip around within a section and do questions in the order that you like.

Another major consequence of the CAT format is that hard problems count more than easy ones. It has to be this way, because the very purpose of this adaptive format is to find out at what level you reliably get about half the questions right; that's your scoring level.

Imagine two students: one who does ten basic questions, half of which she gets right and half of which she gets wrong, and one who does ten very difficult questions, half of which she gets right and half of which she gets wrong. The same number of questions have been answered correctly in each case, but this does not reflect an equal ability on the part of the two students.

In fact, the student who answered five out of ten very difficult questions incorrectly could still get a very high score on the GRE CAT. But in order to get to these hard questions, she first had to get medium-difficulty questions right.

What this means for you is that no matter how much more comfortable you might be sticking to the basic questions, you definitely want to get to the hard questions if you can, because that means your score will be higher.

HOW SHOULD I ATTACK THE VERBAL SECTION?

In the chapters that follow, we'll cover techniques for answering various types of questions that you can expect to see on the Verbal section of the GRE. But you'll also need strategies for managing a section as a whole. Here are some strategies for attacking a section of the GRE CAT.

Be Systematic

THE ART OF USING SCRATCH PAPER

Developing a systematic, organized way to use your scratch paper will help you save time and eliminate mistakes.

Because it's so important to get to the hard questions as early as possible, work systematically at the beginning of a GRE CAT section. Use scratch paper to organize your thinking. If you eliminate choices, cross them off and guess intelligently. Invest the necessary time to try to answer the first few questions correctly. You must, however, leave enough time to mark an answer for every question in the section. You will be penalized for questions you don't reach.

Draw a Grid

If crossing off answer choices on paper tests really helps to clarify your thinking (using a process of elimination), you may want to consider making a grid on your scratch paper before you begin the CAT. Use it to mark off answer choices that you have eliminated, as shown below. That way you can tell at a glance which answer choices are still in the running. If you end up using it often, it'll be worth the ten seconds it takes to draw a simple grid, like this one:

A	✗	✗		✗		✗			✗		✗		
B		✗	✗	✗				✗	✗	✗	✗		✗	
C					✗				✗					✗
D	✗		✗		✗			✗		✗		✗		
E	✗	✗		✗			✗			✗				

Pace Yourself

Of course, the last thing you want to happen is to have time called before you've done half the questions. It's essential, therefore, that you pace yourself, keeping in mind the general guidelines for how long to spend on any individual question or passage.

No one is saying that you should spend, for instance, exactly 90 seconds on every Antonym question. But you should have a sense of how long you have to do each question, so you know when you're exceeding the limit and should start to move faster. You'll develop this sense if you time yourself while working on practice GRE questions.

Stop the Clock

The timer in the corner can work to your advantage, but if you find yourself looking at it so frequently that it becomes a distraction, you should turn it off for 10 or 15 minutes and try to refocus your attention on the test, even if you lose track of time somewhat. The CAT rewards focus and accuracy much more than it does speed.

Don't Waste Time on Questions You Can't Do

We know that foregoing a possibly tough question is easier said than done; we all have the natural instinct to plow through test sections, answering every question as it appears. But it just doesn't pay off on the GRE CAT. If you dig in your heels on a tough question, refusing to move on until you've cracked it, you're getting in the way of your test score. Like life itself, a test section is too short to waste on lost causes.

 **IT'S SUPPOSED TO BE TOUGH**

No matter how good you are at standardized tests, the CAT is designed to find the level at which you find questions hard. Thus, everybody should think the CAT is difficult.

Remain Calm

It's imperative that you remain calm and composed while working through a section. You can't allow yourself to be rattled by one hard question or Reading Comprehension passage to the degree that it throws off your performance on the rest of the Verbal section. Expect to find some difficult questions, but remember, you won't be the only one encountering difficult problems. The test is designed to challenge everyone who takes it. Having trouble with a difficult question isn't going to ruin your score, but getting upset about it and letting it throw you off track will. When you understand that part of the test maker's goal is to reward those who keep their composure, you'll recognize the importance of not panicking when you run into challenging material.

HOW DO I MOVE AROUND ON THE CAT?

Let's preview the primary computer functions that you will use to move around on the CAT. ETS calls them "testing tools," but they're basically just boxes that you can click with your mouse. The screen below is typical for an adaptive test.

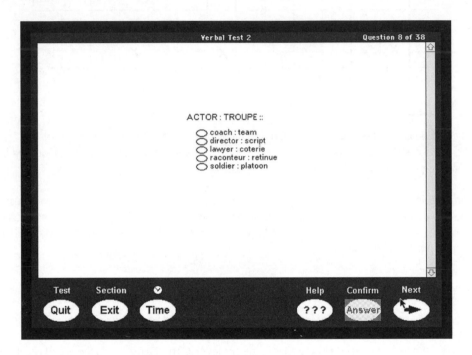

Here's what the various buttons do.

The *Time* Button

Clicking on this button turns the time display at the top of the screen on and off. When you have five minutes left in a section, the clock flashes and the display changes from Hours/Minutes to Hours/Minutes/Seconds.

The *Exit* Button

This allows you to exit the section before the time is up. If you budget your time wisely, you should never have to use this button—time will run out just as you are finishing the section.

 NO SKIPPING AROUND

You can't skip questions on the GRE CAT; you have to answer every question you get. But you do get more time per question on the CAT than on the formerly offered paper-and-pencil test.

The *Help* Button

This one leads to directions and other stuff from the tutorial. You should know all this already, and besides, the test clock won't pause just because you click on Help.

The *Quit* Button

Hitting this button ends the test.

The *Next* Button

Hit this when you want to move on to the next question. After you press Next, you must hit Confirm.

The *Confirm* Button

This button tells the computer you are happy with your answer and are really ready to move to the next question. You cannot proceed until you have hit this button.

The Scroll Bar

Similar to the scroll bar on a Windows-style computer display, the scroll bar is a thin, vertical column with up and down arrows at the top and bottom. Clicking on the arrows moves you up or down the page you're reading.

PROS AND CONS OF THE GRE CAT

There are both good and annoying things about the GRE CAT. The following are a few things you should be thankful for or watch out for as you prepare to try your luck on the test.

Eight Good Things about the CAT

1. There is a little timer at the top of the computer screen to help you pace yourself (you can hide it if it distracts you).
2. There will be only a few other test takers in the room with you—it won't be like taking it in one of those massive lecture halls with distractions everywhere.
3. You get a pause of five minutes between each section. The pause is optional, but you should always use it to relax and stretch.
4. You can sign up for the CAT two days before the test, and registration is very easy.
5. The CAT is much more convenient for your schedule than the pencil-and-paper exam was. It's offered at more than 175 centers three to six days a week (depending on the center) all year long.
6. The CAT gives you more time to spend on each question than you got on the paper-based test.
7. You can see your scores before you decide which schools you want to send them to.
8. Perhaps the CAT's best feature is that it gives you your scores immediately and will send them to schools just 10 to 15 days later.

📖 NO DISTRACTIONS

One advantage of the GRE CAT is that it gives you the chance to work methodically on one question at a time with no other questions there to distract you.

Seven Annoying Things about the CAT

1. You cannot skip around on this test; you must answer the questions one at a time in the order the computer gives them to you.

2. If you realize later that you answered a question incorrectly, you can't go back and change your answer.

3. If the person next to you is noisy or distracting, the proctor cannot move you or the person, since your test is on the computer.

4. You can't cross off an answer choice and never look at it again, so you have to be disciplined about not reconsidering choices you've already eliminated.

5. You have to scroll through reading comprehension passages, which means you won't be able to see the whole thing on the screen at once.

6. You can't write on your computer screen the way you can on a paper test (though some have tried), so you have to use the scratch paper they give you, which will be inconveniently located away from the computer screen.

7. Lastly, many people find that computer screens tire them and cause eyestrain—especially after four hours.

PART TWO

Verbal Practice Tests

Chapter 2: **GRE Sentence Completion**

Of all the GRE Verbal question types, Sentence Completions are probably the most student-friendly. Unlike Analogies and Antonyms, Sentence Completions provide you with a context to help you figure out tough vocabulary. And unlike Reading Comprehension questions, they only require you to read one sentence at a time. As the name suggests, Sentence Completion questions test your ability to complete sentences that are missing one or two key words by selecting the appropriate answer choice.

The directions for this section look like this:

> **Directions:** This sentence has one or more blank spaces. Each blank indicates that a word or phrase has been omitted. Of the five following words or sets of words, choose the one word or set that, when inserted in the sentence, best fits the meaning of the entire sentence.

The difficulty of the sentence completions you will see on the GRE depends on how many questions you get right. If you perform well on the Verbal Section, you will find that the later sentence completions you encounter involve tougher vocabulary and more convoluted logic.

THE FOUR FUNDAMENTALS

To improve your skill in answering GRE sentence completions, you'll need to familiarize yourself with the basic principles for approaching them—and you'll need some practice. The Four Fundamentals below will help you to increase your skills and confidence as you approach Test Day. And with skills and confidence, you'll be able to earn points on the GRE!

Every Clue Is Right in Front of You

Each sentence contains a few crucial clues that help you to determine the meaning of the missing word(s). Clues in the sentence limit the possible answers, and finding these clues will guide you to the correct answer.

What are the important clues in the following question?

1. Although she earned her fame for her striking murals, the artist felt that her sculpture merited greater _____.

    ① disdain
    ② acclaim
    ③ deliberation
    ④ viewing
    ⑤ publicity

Here, the word *although* is a classic structural clue. It tells you that you can expect a change of direction in the sentence. The first half tells you that the artist became famous as a muralist, but that she thought her sculpture deserved more BLANK. The word *although* tells you that she must think her sculptures are even better than her murals, and that they merit more praise, or *acclaim.*

Look for What's Directly Implied and Expect Clichés

We're not dealing with poetry here. These sentences aren't excerpted from the works of Toni Morrison or William Faulkner. The correct answer is the one most directly implied by the meanings of the words in the sentence. Very often, for example, the definition of the missing word is provided in the sentence:

2. Because Gould's theory has been neither completely rejected nor completely accepted by the scientific community, its status remains _____ .

    ① repudiated
    ② sanctioned
    ③ quizzical
    ④ preferable
    ⑤ debatable

Here, choice (5), *debatable,* means "neither completely rejected nor completely accepted."

Sometimes you can choose the correct answer because the missing words are part of familiar-sounding phrases or because they simply sound right in the context of the sentence:

3. The increasing acceptance of the notion that the news media is not a(n) _____ commentator upon events, but rather, a mouthpiece for the vested interests of its powerful owners, demonstrates the public's growing _____ large corporations.

    ① disinterested...mistrust of
    ② meddlesome...suspicion of
    ③ official...apprehension of
    ④ impartial...satisfaction with
    ⑤ manipulative...confusion with

In the above example, the correct answer, choice (1), works because the phrases *disinterested commentator* and *growing mistrust of* simply *sound* correct.

Look for "Structural Road Signs"

Some words such as *since, however,* or *because*—give clues to the structure of the sentence that will point you to the right answer. The following are road signs found in GRE CAT sentence completions:

Straight-Ahead Road Signs

These make one part of the sentence support or elaborate on another part. They continue the sentence in the same direction. Examples include *and, similarly, in addition, since, also, thus, because, ; (semicolon),* and *likewise.*

Detour Road Signs

These words indicate a change in the direction of the sentence. They make one part of the sentence contradict or qualify another part. Examples include *but, despite, yet, however, unless, rather, although, while, unfortunately,* and *nonetheless.*

Watch Out for Common Wrong-Answer Types

If you get stumped on any GRE CAT Sentence Completion, you can still earn points by using the process of elimination. Do this by ruling out as many wrong answer choices as you can, and then picking from the remaining choices. Here are some common wrong answer types to look out for:

Half-Right/Half-Wrong

In a sentence that contains two blanks, one of the two words provided in a given answer choice fits while the other one doesn't. Make sure that both words fit the context of the sentence!

Au Contraire

In a sentence that contains one blank, the word in the given answer choice means exactly the opposite of the word you're looking for.

Clunkers

The word(s) in a given answer choice simply do not sound right in the context of the sentence.

 FILL IN THE BLANK

When working through a Sentence Completion question:

- Look for clues in the sentence
- Focus on what's directly implied
- Pay attention to "structural road signs"

MORE STRATEGIES FOR SENTENCE COMPLETION QUESTIONS

Look for Keywords: *Keywords are descriptive words or phrases that clue you in to the missing words in a sentence. Unlike road signs, where a small set of words tells you a sentence's direction, keywords will reflect its theme, give you a sense of its logic, or provide clues to the author's intent. For example, if "ambivalent" is a keyword in the sentence, and it's followed by a negative sentiment, it is likely pointing to a positive word in the answer choices.*

Paraphrase Long or Complex Sentences: *You may encounter a sentence that, because of its length or structure, is hard to get a handle on. When faced with a complex sentence like this, put it in your own words. If you can sum up 44 words in 14, it's easier to find the right answer.*

Use Word Roots: *If you can't figure out the meaning of a word, take a look at its root to try to get close to its meaning. (In the back of this book, you'll find the Latin and Greek roots of many common GRE words.) Etymology can often provide clues to meaning, especially when you couple a root definition with the word in context.*

Pick up a copy Kaplan's GRE guide to get more practice for the Verbal Section question types and to see examples of these tips in action.

Drill

In the following examples, test your knowledge of Sentence Completion road signs by selecting the word that most correctly completes the sentence:

1. The singer's lyrics were quite lovely, but her vocal tone was extremely (harsh, melodious).
2. Fred was so annoyed with his publicist that he repeatedly (praised, lambasted) him in public.
3. Because Mabel had the reputation of being a mediocre cook, most believed her chances of winning the bake-off were (good, slim).
4. Despite the fact that the racehorse's performance in recent competitions had been disappointing, the oddsmakers were predicting a (win, disappointment) at the Derby.
5. Many felt the rules for the scholarship competition had been unfair and, furthermore, the judges were (biased, fair).
6. Although they appear quite cuddly, brown bears actually pose a large (threat, attraction) to tourists.

THE KAPLAN FOUR-STEP METHOD FOR SENTENCE COMPLETION

Now that you have learned the basics, you're ready to learn Kaplan's strategic approach to Sentence Completions on the GRE CAT. Approaching Sentence Completions in a systematic manner is the best way to avoid common pitfalls and improve your score.

❶ **Read the whole sentence.**
- Look for road signs to help you determine what type of word you're looking for.
- If the sentence is long or clumsy, rephrase the sentence in your own words.

❷ **Predict an answer.**

- In two-blank questions, try to predict for both blanks.

- Use the road signs and logic you found in Step 1 to determine the direction in which the sentence is heading.

❸ **Scan the answer choices, choosing the one that best fits your prephrase.**

- Look for those that match your prediction.

- Eliminate answer choices that don't come close to your prediction.

- On two-blank sentences, work with one blank at a time, eliminating answer choices as you go.

❹ **Read your selected answer choice back into the sentence.**

- If it makes sense, you have a winner.

- If it doesn't make sense, go back to the answer choices and find one that works better.

- If you get stuck, eliminate answer choices that you know are wrong and guess among the remaining choices.

Try It Out

Let's apply the Kaplan Four-Step Method for Sentence Completions to an example.

4. We will face the idea of old age with _____ as long as we believe that it invariably brings poverty, isolation, and illness.

① regret

② apprehension

③ enlightenment

④ veneration

⑤ reverence

❶ Let's begin by reading the whole sentence strategically. Immediately note the structural clue *as long as.* This phrase will tell us what to expect when we prepare to fill in the blank. The sentence tells us that old age brings *poverty, isolation,* and *illness.* Naturally, therefore, we would face it with something like "fear."

❷ Now it's time to predict our answer. As we decided in Step 1, we should look in the answer choices for a word that means *fear.*

❸ Here's where we scan the answer choices and look for one that best fits our predicted answer. *Apprehension* means "fear," so choice (2) is our best answer. But let's eliminate some answers that we know are wrong, just to be sure. Choice 1, *regret,* is tempting, but you feel regret for something that has already happened, not for something you will face in the future. *Veneration* and *reverence* both mean "great respect," so we can eliminate choices 4 and 5, too.

❹ Now we'll plug our answer into the sentence: *We will face the idea of old age with apprehension as long as we believe that it invariably brings poverty, isolation, and illness.* This sentence certainly makes sense, so we have found our winner

PRACTICE SET

Now try the following Sentence Completion questions on your own, using the Kaplan Four-Step Method. Time yourself: Give yourself a maximum of 30–45 seconds to do each example.

1. Despite much informed _____, the relationship between sunspot cycles and the earth's weather remains _____.

   ① argument . . . decisive
   ② confusion . . . tenuous
   ③ conjecture . . . ambiguous
   ④ evidence . . . clear
   ⑤ analysis . . . systematic

2. As a consequence of the Antarctic's _____ climate, the only forms of plant life to be found in the continent's interior are a few _____ lichens and mosses that cling to the frozen rocks.

   ① frigid . . . hardy ✗
   ② extreme . . . mysterious
   ③ harsh . . . luxuriant
   ④ freezing . . . complex
   ⑤ changing . . . tiny

3. Conflict between generations may be a problem that has persisted for centuries, but the nature and intensity of the conflict obviously _____ in response to changes in social and economic conditions.

   ① increases
   ② disappears
   ③ declines
   ④ varies ✗
   ⑤ wanes

Think about how you solved these Sentence Completion questions. To maximize your score, it's important to start practicing the techniques we covered in this chapter. On the pages that follow, you'll find sets of GRE Sentence Completion practice questions that will help you to hone your skills with this question type. Try these practice sets under testlike conditions, moving from one question to the next at a rapid pace. Complete, strategic explanations to all of these questions follow so that you can check your answers and learn the most efficient means for completing each question correctly.

ANSWERS

Testlike Questions

1. (2)
2. (5)
3. (1)

Drill

1. harsh
2. lambasted
3. slim
4. win
5. biased
6. threat

Practice Set

1. (3)
2. (1)
3. (4)

SENTENCE COMPLETION: TEST 1

Time: 10 Questions/10 Minutes

Directions: Each sentence has one or more blank spaces. Each blank indicates that a word or phrase has been omitted. Of the five following words or sets of words, choose the one word or set that, when inserted in the sentence, best fits the meaning of the entire sentence.

1. Male sperm whales are normally ____ creatures; however, when they are jealously guarding their territory, they have been known to ____ ships.

   ① docile . . . attack
   ② aggressive . . . strike
   ③ large . . . assault
   ④ peaceful . . . ignore
   ⑤ powerful . . . assail

2. The ____ genius of the late Glenn Gould is apparent in this imaginative ____ for piano of Wagner's "Siegfried Idyll," which the composer originally scored for full orchestra and presented to his wife Cosima on her birthday.

   ① ineluctable . . . diminution
   ② exceptional . . . music
   ③ incommensurate . . . homage
   ④ unmistakable . . . adaptation
   ⑤ brilliant . . . celebration

3. Opponents of affirmative action by quota, the practice of hiring on the basis of race or sex as well as ____, maintain that both the hired and the rejected suffer ____ when not judged on their abilities alone.

   ① loyalty . . . prejudice
   ② status . . . nepotism
   ③ competence . . . injustice
   ④ creed . . . indignity
   ⑤ dexterity . . . degradation

4. An ancient and mythopoeic neurological disorder, epilepsy is ____ in part by the sensation of intense and altered consciousness doctors call an "aura," which ____ the epileptic seconds before a seizure.

   ① neutralized . . . overcomes
   ② characterized . . . grips
   ③ obviated . . . afflicts
   ④ enhanced . . . debilitates
   ⑤ diagnosed . . . proselytizes

5. Although the European Economic Community was established to ____ the economic growth of all its member nations equally, some express ____ at what they claim is their unfair burden in maintaining the organization.

   ① regulate . . . favoritism
   ② retard . . . vehemence
   ③ promote . . . resentment
   ④ measure . . . irritation
   ⑤ aid . . . wrongfulness

6. Those who make up their minds that life should be a succession of triumphs are soon enlightened by ____ reality; even money can ____ the truth only briefly.

   ① stark . . . defuse
   ② bland . . . quench
   ③ dread . . . encourage
   ④ limpid . . . hold back
   ⑤ harsh . . . stave off

KAPLAN

7. In 1921, Antioch College adopted a policy requiring students to _____ beyond their stacks of books and contribute their talents to the working world in order to earn their bachelor's degrees.

   ① rise
   ② venture
   ③ probe
   ④ excel
   ⑤ strut

8. The candidate announced, to the _____ of her devoted campaigners, that unless her performance in the polls improved she would _____ the race.

   ① consternation . . . withdraw from
   ② bewilderment . . . abstain from
   ③ mortification . . . continue
   ④ delight . . . step out of
   ⑤ awe . . . renounce

9. The _____ private contributions for disease research creates _____; the money goes for research into the best-publicized disease, which is not always the most serious or widespread one.

   ① lack of . . . a reallocation
   ② need for . . . a nuisance
   ③ infirmity in . . . a debt
   ④ colloquialism of . . . a paradox
   ⑤ indispensability of . . . a disparity

10. Her charisma was a double-edged sword; in her friends, it aroused both admiration and _____.

    ① envy
    ② laudation
    ③ equanimity
    ④ obstinacy
    ⑤ affection

ANSWERS AND EXPLANATIONS

1. Choice (1)

❶ The first blank here will be filled with a word that describes what type of creatures male sperm whales *normally* are. The "detour" road sign *however* between these clauses indicates that a contrasting point will be made. What we learn in the first clause will be different from that in the second. So, these whales are normally something, but sometimes can be different. A clue in the second clause helps us figure this one out. In the second clause, we learn that something happens when the whales are *jealously guarding their territory.* They probably act aggressively or violently when guarding their territory, so the first blank will be a contrast to this. It must suggest that the whales are not normally violent. The second blank will be filled with a word that tells us what the whales do to ships when they are guarding their territory.

❷ A good prephrase for this answer would be, "These whales are normally peaceful creatures; *however,* when guarding their territory, they have been known to sink ships."

❸ Starting with the first blank, two choices look good right away, (1) and (4). Choice (1) also looks good for the second blank, while the second word in (4) is the opposite of what we need. We'll hold onto (1) and quickly check the others. In choice (2), the words are not contradictory. An *aggressive* whale would normally *strike* ships. We need a pair of words that is opposite in meaning. Choices (3) and (5) can be eliminated because each is a descriptive word that relates to the whale's physical characteristics rather than to its temperament.

❹ *Male sperm whales are normally* docile *creatures; however, when they are jealously guarding their territory, they have been known to* attack *ships.*

2. Choice (4)

❶ There are several good clues to work with in this sentence. The first blank describes a type of genius that is *apparent* in Gould's work, so the first blank will be a positive word reinforcing the notion of *genius.* The second blank is described as being *imaginative* and *for the piano.* Later in the sentence we find that originally, the piece was scored for *a full orchestra.* Gould must have changed it, in an imaginative way, so it would be for piano only.

❷ A good prephrase here would be, "Gould's amazing genius is apparent in this imaginative version of the musical piece."

❸ The first blank seems easier to work with, so we'll start there. Choices (2), (4), and (5) have strongly positive words for the first blank. For the second blank we predicted "version." Of these three choices, only (4), *adaptation*, is a good match for the second blank. This is probably our answer. Choices (2) and (5) can be eliminated because the second word in each does not convey the meaning at the end of the sentence that a change had been made. Choices (1) and (3) don't work because the first word in each is not positive. *Ineluctable* means "inevitable," which is not very positive in this context, and *incommensurate* means "inadequate," which is not positive at all.

❹ *The* unmistakable *genius of the late Glenn Gould is apparent in this imaginative* adaptation *for piano of Wagner's "Siegfried Idyll," which the composer originally scored for full orchestra and presented to his wife Cosima on her birthday.*

3. Choice (3)

❶ For the first blank, there are a couple of clues to pay attention to. It falls in a part of the sentence set off with commas. This means that the phrase is defining what *affirmative action by quota* is. The road sign *as well as* right before the blank tells us that there is a basis upon which people are being hired other than race or sex. Since the end of the sentence states that people suffer when *they are not judged on their abilities alone,* the third quality, the first missing word must mean "their abilities alone." The second blank will have a negative connotation, since the opponents believe that people *suffer* from it.

❷ A prephrase of this answer might be, "Opponents of affirmative action by quota, hiring based on race or sex as well as abilities, feel that everyone suffers discrimination when not judged on just their abilities."

❸ Our prediction for the first blank is more definitive, so we'll start there. The only answer that comes close to our prediction is choice (3). Both the first and second words fit perfectly, so this looks like the right answer. We'll scan the other choices just to be sure. We can rule the others out quickly because none of the words for the first blank in choices (1), (2), (4), or (5) means "their abilities alone."

❹ *Opponents of affirmative action by quota, the practice of hiring on the basis of race or sex as well as* competence, *maintain that both the hired and the rejected suffer* injustice *when not judged on their abilities alone.*

4. Choice (2)

❶ The clues in this sentence are subtle. Don't be distracted by the hard word *mythopoeic*, which means "giving rise to myths." It does not affect the direction in which the sentence is going; in fact, the whole first part of the sentence before the first comma is irrelevant. The part of the sentence with the first blank tells us that doctors have noted that an "aura" accompanies epilepsy. So the first blank must link the "aura" to the condition. The part of the sentence around the second blank tells us that an "aura" does something to the epileptic before a seizure; we can assume that it will be something bad, so the second blank should be negative.

❷ A good prephrase for these blanks would be, "Epilepsy is discovered or diagnosed or accompanied in part by an aura that effects the epileptic seconds before the seizure."

❸ The second blank is more precise here. Unfortunately, all of the answer choices work in the second blank except (5). We'll eliminate (5) and evaluate the others closely. Now that (5) is out, the only answer that is logical for the first blank is choice (2), *characterized.* Choices (1) and (4) do not make sense for the first blank; nor does (3), *obviated,* which means "to prevent."

❹ *An ancient and mythopoeic neurological disorder, epilepsy is* characterized *in part by the sensation of intense and altered consciousness doctors call an "aura," which* grips *the epileptic seconds before seizure.*

5. Choice (3)

❶ The road sign *although* at the beginning of this sentence acts as a "detour." It signals a change in direction between the first and second halves of the sentence. In the first part, we're told that the goal is to do something to the growth of all of the member nations equally. No doubt this is a positive word; an organization would not be established to hinder the growth of all the members of the group. The second blank tells us that some nations believe they unfairly bear a greater burden for running the organization and are expressing some type of feeling about this. The second blank must be a negative word that has to do with what they are feeling.

❷ A prephrase for this sentence might be, "Although the EEC was established to encourage the growth of all its members, some express anger or discontent or dismay that they share more of a burden for the organization."

❸ We'll start with the first blank since it's more precise. Right away the positive words in choices (3) and (5) look good for the first blank. For the second blank, (3) works much better than (5). It is logical that the members would express *resentment* over the *unfair burden,* while it would be redundant to say they express *wrongfulness* over the injustice. Something that is *unfair* is, after all, "wrong." We'll hold onto (3) and check the others. Choice (2) can be eliminated right away because it is negative. The ECC would not want to *retard* the growth of its members. Choices (1) and (4) are neither positive nor negative, so neither would be a good choice, unless nothing else worked, which is not the case here.

❹ *Although the European Economic Community was established to* promote *the economic growth of all its member nations equally, some express* resentment *at what they claim is their unfair burden in maintaining the organization.*

6. Choice (5)

❶ The first blank describes the word *reality,* and we learn that this type of reality makes people reconsider their idealistic belief that life is only a *succession of triumphs.* Since they expect something overly optimistic, the reality of the situation will be a letdown for them. The word describing reality will, therefore, have a negative meaning. A "straight-ahead" road sign, a semicolon, connects these two clauses. Consequently, the second clause will reinforce the same concept found in the first. In the second clause, the *truth* is that this overly optimistic belief is unrealistic. Money will have some type of impact on the truth *only briefly,* we're told. Since money has this effect only briefly, and then the harsh truth will set in, this clause must be suggesting that money will "put off" or "hide" the truth for only a short time.

❷ A prephrase of this answer might be, "Idealistic people are soon faced with grim reality; even money can hide or help them avoid the truth only briefly."

❸ The first blank is more concrete, so we'll start with it. Choices (1) and (5) look the best for the first blank. Choice (1) doesn't work for the second blank, though, because defuse would mean that the truth will be calmed or lessened by money. Money doesn't just *defuse* the truth for a while. It actually covers up the truth. So, (5) works much better for both blanks. We'll hold onto it and check the rest. We can eliminate choices (2) and (4), since the first word in each is not negative. Due to the second blank, choice (3) can be eliminated, because it doesn't convey the meaning that money can only hide the truth for a while.

❹ *Those who make up their minds that life should be a succession of triumphs are soon enlightened by a* harsh reality; *even money can* stave *off the truth only briefly.*

7. Choice (2)

❶ The two clues to figuring out the correct answer here are the word *beyond* right after the blank and the general meaning of the sentence. There are some words that won't sound right with the preposition beyond, so any choice that makes logical sense, stating that the students are going beyond regular studies, must be double-checked with beyond.

❷ Any word that means "going beyond" will work here.

❸ The choice that looks good right away is (2), *venture,* which means "brave the unknown," because it has the meaning we want and sounds fine with the word *beyond* following it. We'll hold onto it and quickly check the others. Choice (1) doesn't work because the correct idiomatic expression is "rise above," not *rise beyond.* Plus, there is no indication in the sentence that the school thinks one experience is superior, or above, the other. Both are necessary to graduate. Choices (3) and (5) do not work well. To probe something is to examine it. We usually say "probe into" something and not *probe beyond it.* The notion that the students would *strut beyond* their studies has a negative connotation, so that doesn't work. The school would certainly want them to do something positive. Choice (4) can be eliminated because it is not idiomatically correct. Students wouldn't *excel beyond* their studies. The school would probably want them to excel at both, in any case.

❹ *In 1921, Antioch College adopted a policy requiring students to* venture *beyond their stacks of books and contribute their talents to the working world in order to earn their bachelor's degrees.*

8. Choice (1)

❶ The road sign *unless* tells us that a "detour" or contrast is coming in the sentence. Therefore, we can predict that unless her performance improves, she would have to do something different from what she is doing now. This would no doubt not be what her campaigners would want to hear, since they support her and would want her to win. The second blank will describe a change from what she is doing now, campaigning, and the first blank will be a somewhat negative word describing how her followers will feel if she stops campaigning.

❷ A good prephrase for this sentence would be, "The candidate announced, to the dismay of her campaigners, that unless things got better she would drop out of the race."

❸ Starting with the second blank (since our prediction has less room for change in it), we can narrow it down to choices (1) and (4) right away. The first word in choice (1) looks good, too, so we'll hold onto this one and check the others. Choice (4) can be eliminated because the first word is positive. Choice (2) is out because it is not idiomatically correct. We don't say that someone would *abstain from* a race, and most likely, the campaigners would not be filled with *bewilderment* or confusion about this announcement. There would be no reason for them to feel bewildered if she decided to quit when she was behind in the polls. They would be disappointed, but not bewildered. Choice (3) does not make sense because the second word, *continue,* would not be a contrast with what she is doing now. Choice (5) can be eliminated because the first word is positive.

❹ *The candidate announced, to the* consternation *of her devoted campaigners, that unless her performance in the polls improved she would* withdraw *from the race.*

9. Choice (5)

❶ Since both blanks occur in the first of two clauses, it's most likely the second clause that will provide most of the clues we need. We should note immediately that the two clauses are joined by a semicolon, a "straight-ahead" road sign, which tells us that the two sentences will be consistent in meaning. The ideas in both will be similar and support each other. In the second clause, we learn that privately contributed money is given to the *best publicized* cause, not always to the one that is *most serious.* This would be a real problem for researchers. If they had enough money, they would no doubt work on the most serious problems first, no matter what cause the public donated to. Instead, their research priorities are determined not by need but by popular support. It must be that contributions are limited, and the researchers are forced to spend time on the popular causes first.

❷ A prephrase of this answer could be, "The need for private contributions creates a problem for researchers."

❸ Three choices, (1), (2), and (5), look pretty good for the first blank. Choice (1) does not work because the words for the second blank are not supported by the original sentence. There is no indication in the first or second clause that the money is being *reallocated*, or simply "shifted," from one cause to the other. It is being given to one cause and not to the other. The second word in choice (2), *nuisance*, is not strong enough, given what we know. *Nuisance* makes it sound like this is a minor issue, when in fact we were told that the money does not go to the *most serious or widespread* disease. This would be more than a minor issue. In choice (5), *disparity* is a much better choice for the second blank, since it indicates an unfair situation. This looks like pretty good answer as for both blanks, but we'll check the remaining choices to be sure. Choices (3) and (4) can be eliminated because the words for the first blank do not express the need for or reliance upon private contributions.

❹ *The* indispensability *of private contributions for disease research creates a* disparity; *the money goes for research into the best-publicized disease, which is not always the most serious or widespread one.*

10. Choice (1)

❶ A major road sign here is the semicolon between the two clauses, signaling a continuation or consistency between the two parts. If her *charisma* is a *double-edged sword,* then it has contrasting points—good aspects and bad aspects. The clause after the semicolon will elaborate on or give an example of these conflicting sides. In the second clause, we find that even in those who like her, her charisma arouses admiration, which would be the good side of the sword, and something else, which must be the bad side. This blank must be filled in with a negative word.

❷ A prephrase here might be, "Her charisma provoked both admiration and dislike in her friends."

❸ Only two choices here have negative meanings, (1) and (4). Choice (1) makes the most sense, since charisma could easily invoke envy in others, and that would definitely be a negative side to her charisma. Choice (4), *obstinacy,* is negative but means "stubbornness"; this answer does not make sense in the sentence. Choice (1) looks like the right answer; the remaining three choices can be ruled out because they are positive in meaning. Choice (2), *laudation,* means "praise"; (3), *equanimity,* means "even-tempered"; and (5), *affection,* has a very positive meaning.

❹ *Her charisma was a double-edged sword; in her friends, it aroused both admiration and* envy.

SENTENCE COMPLETION: TEST 2

Time: 10 Questions/10 Minutes

Directions: Each sentence has one or more blank spaces. Each blank indicates that a word or phrase has been omitted. Of the five following words or sets of words, choose the one word or set that, when inserted in the sentence, best fits the meaning of the entire sentence.

1. The composition of that painting is so _____ and direct that the casual observer might think that it did not require much _____.

   ① regimented . . . talent
   ② complex . . . skill
   ③ beautiful . . . feeling
   ④ simple . . . thought
   ⑤ emotional . . . consideration

2. Filmed on a ludicrously _____ budget and edited at breakneck speed, Melotti's documentary nonetheless _____ the Cannes critics with its trenchancy and verve.

   ① low . . . disappointed
   ② inflated . . . distracted
   ③ uneven . . . amused
   ④ disproportionate . . . appalled
   ⑤ inadequate . . . surprised

3. The _____ of the desert explains why so many Egyptian mummies are still intact, whereas humidity of the tombs in tropical rain forests supports the agents of decay so that few Aztec mummies have _____.

   ① heat . . . survived
   ② aridity . . . endured
   ③ anhydration . . . decayed
   ④ barrenness . . . proliferated
   ⑤ seclusion . . . surfaced

4. They _____ until there was no recourse but to _____ a desperate, last-minute solution to the problem.

   ① berated . . . try
   ② delayed . . . envision
   ③ procrastinated . . . implement
   ④ debated . . . maintain
   ⑤ filibustered . . . reject

5. The Wankel Rotary Engine was an engineering marvel that substantially reduced automobile exhaust emissions, but because it was less fuel-efficient than the standard piston-cylinder engine, it was _____ in the early 1970s when _____ pollution gave way to panic over fuel shortages.

   ① needed . . . disillusionment with
   ② conceived . . . attention on
   ③ modified . . . opinion on
   ④ abandoned . . . preoccupation with
   ⑤ discarded . . . interest in

6. Friendship, no matter how _____, has its boundaries; _____ advice, when thrust insistently upon one, is rarely an act of friendship, regardless of the adviser's intent.

   ① cool . . . contradictory
   ② enjoyable . . . obverse
   ③ intimate . . . unsolicited
   ④ distant . . . marital
   ⑤ special . . . desired

7. Anarchists contend that government is by
definition the repression of natural human desire,
and their _____ rivals concur; it is over the _____ of
this definition that the two groups battle.

① sympathetic . . . phraseology
② perennial . . . semantics
③ ideological . . . implications
④ fascistic . . . expression
⑤ fiercest . . . etiology

8. Despite generous helpings of _____ from a group
of _____ critics, this iconoclastic poet's three
volumes have sold steadily.

① zeal . . . hidebound
② mockery . . . obscure
③ tedium . . . respected
④ abuse . . . ineffectual
⑤ vitriol . . . influential

9. Because the different components of the film
industry were "vertically" oriented—arranged
so that all _____, from production to projection,
were held by one company—it was _____ that
monopolistic practices would arise.

① opportunities for control . . . inevitable
② burdens of business . . . understandable
③ exercises of power . . . appropriate
④ means of solicitation . . . predictable
⑤ perquisites of commerce . . . unsavory

10. From the _____ that the peasants tried to conceal
as they knelt before the body of the dictator's son,
I concluded that, far from affection, it was _____
that had brought them to the wake.

① hatred . . . sarcasm
② reticence . . . violence
③ diligence . . . adulation
④ trepidation . . . fear
⑤ sorrow . . . patriotism

ANSWERS

1. Choice (4)

❶ The "straight-ahead" road sign *and* after the blank tells us that the missing word and the word *direct* will support each other. They both describe the composition of a painting, and the correct choice will be consistent with the word *direct*. For the second blank, there are a couple of clues to notice. We're told that the *casual observer* might think something about the painting. You wouldn't expect a casual observer to be very thorough or perceptive. The casual observer might mistakenly assume that the way the painting seemed initially, with its *direct* composition, indicates that it didn't require much from the artist.

❷ A prephrase of this answer is easier for the first blank, but several words would work in the second. A partial prephrase might be, "The composition is so simple and direct that the casual observer might think it didn't require much from the artist."

❸ Choice (4) immediately looks good because the first word is a perfect match. The second word, *thought*, makes sense, too, so we'll hold onto this one while we check the others. Choice (2) can be eliminated because the first word, *complex*, is contrary to *direct*. These two words could not be joined by a "straight-ahead" road sign like *and*. Choices (1), (3), and (5) are not good for the first blank because each of these words does not support or elaborate upon the meaning of direct, which is what we expect since the two words will be joined by *and*. Something that is *regimented*, *beautiful*, or *emotional* may or may not be "direct." There is no clear connection.

❹ *The composition of that painting is so* simple *and direct that the casual observer might think that it did not require much* thought.

2. Choice (5)

❶ The first blank describes what type of budget the film had. The road sign *and* after the word *budget* tells us that the budget and the rate at which it was edited are equal elements in the sentence. In other words, one is not positive while the other is negative. They would both be positive or both be negative. Consequently, since the editing was done at a hectic pace, the budget must have been restricted in some way. The road sign *nonetheless* acts as a detour and indicates that what you would expect after reading the first part of the sentence does not prove to be true. There must be a shift in direction for the second blank. Instead of the negative reaction you would expect from the first part of the sentence, a positive word must describe the critics' responses. The critics must have liked the film even though the budget and editing were done under severe constraints.

❷ A prephrase for this answer would be, "Filmed on a low budget and edited quickly, the film nonetheless was received well by the critics."

❸ Starting with the first blank because it is more precise, we are immediately drawn to choices (1) and (5). Although in choice (1) *low* works perfectly for the first blank, *disappointed* in the second blank is contrary to the sense of the sentence. Choice (5) looks good for both blanks. We'll hold onto it and check the others. Choices (2) and (4) can be eliminated because the second word in each is negative. The second word in choice (3), *amused*, looks good, but the first word doesn't make sense in describing the budget. How could a budget be *ludicrously uneven*?

❹ *Filmed on a ludicrously* inadequate *budget and edited at breakneck speed, Melotti's documentary* nonetheless *surprised the Cannes critics with its trenchancy and verve.*

3. Choice (2)

❶ For the first blank, we are looking for a word that describes a desert and explains why the mummies are still intact. After the comma, we find an important road sign that acts as a detour. The word *whereas* indicates that the Egyptian conditions are different from those described after the road sign, which is where we learn about the conditions found in tropical rain forests. So, the road sign *whereas* indicates that the first blank will be the opposite of humid. Likewise, the second blank tells us about Aztec mummies, which we know will be the opposite of what is true of Egyptian mummies. If the Egyptian mummies are still intact, then Aztec mummies must not have survived.

❷ A good prephrase of this sentence is, "The dryness of the desert explains why Egyptian mummies are still around, whereas the humidity in tropical rain forests explains why so few Aztec mummies have survived."

❸ Both of our predictions are pretty precise, so we can start with either one. Looking for a word that means "dryness" for the first blank directs us to choices (2) and (3). Both *aridity* and *anhydration* mean "lacking in moisture," but the second word in choice (3), *decay*, is the opposite of what we're looking for. We need a word that means "survived." Choice (2), *endured*, is perfect. We'll hold onto (2) and check the others. The first word in choices (1), (4), and (5) eliminates these answers. All of these words may be true of the desert, but none of them mean "dry."

❹ *The* aridity *of the desert explains why so many Egyptian mummies are still intact, whereas the humidity of the tombs in tropical rain forests supports the agents of decay so that few Aztec mummies have* endured.

4. Choice (3)

❶ The meaning of this sentence itself is the best clue here for the missing words. We learn that they did something until only one option remained open to them, a desperate, last-minute solution. They must have waited or put off their work until they had no recourse.

❷ A prephrase for this sentence could be, "They delayed until there was no choice but a last-minute solution to solve the problem."

❸ Starting with the first blank because our prediction is pretty definite, choices (2) and (3) look good. We can eliminate (2) because the second word, *envision,* that is, "predict or foresee," does not convey the meaning of a solution. The second word in choice (3), *implement,* means "execute or achieve," so choice (3) works well for both blanks. We'll hold onto it and check the others. Based on the first word, choices (1), (4), and (5) can be eliminated. Of these three only (5), *filibustered,* suggests delaying, but even it has a more specific meaning that is not applicable here. To filibuster is to interrupt or delay something from occurring by engaging in activities such as long speeches and discourse.

❹ *They* procrastinated *until there was no recourse but to* implement *a desperate, last-minute solution to the problem.*

5. Choice (4)

❶ This is a fairly long sentence whose omissions occur toward the end. Take the sentence apart, paraphrasing what each phrase means, and pay close attention to the

first few lines, which will have to tell us how to fill in the blanks. The road sign *but because* after the first comma is critical in directing us to the right answer. But indicates that a detour is coming, and the word *because* tells us that an explanation will be given. The second part of the sentence will contrast with the first and will tell us why it is so. In the first part, we learn that the engine was a *marvel* that reduced pollution. However, it was not *fuel-efficient.* The word because tells us that the lack of fuel efficiency led to something, unlike the fact that the engine was so marvelous. The fact that it reduced pollution must not have been important anymore, since there was a *panic over fuel shortages.*

❷ A prephrase for this sentence would be, "The engine was rejected or modified in the 1970s, when concern with pollution gave way to panic over fuel shortages."

❸ Working with the first blank, choices (3), (4), and (5) look good. While *modified* in the first blank of choice (3) makes sense, the second phrase, *opinion on,* is too broad. We're not told if it was a positive or negative opinion that gave way or what direction it gave way to. This answer, then, is not precise enough and would not warrant modifying the engine. In choice (4), if a *preoccupation with* pollution gave way to panic over fuel shortages, that would explain why the engine was no longer valued. This is a much stronger word choice than *opinion on.* This looks like the best answer, but we'll check the others to be sure. The second word in choice (5) does not fit well in the context. A mere loss of *interest in* pollution would not explain abandoning a marvelous engine. We can eliminate choices (1) and (2) based on the first word in each, since neither of them suggests that the engine was rejected or changed in anyway.

❹ *The Wankel Rotary Engine was an engineering marvel that substantially reduced automobile exhaust emissions, but because it was less fuel-efficient than the standard piston-cylinder engine, it was* abandoned *in the early 1970s when* preoccupation *with pollution gave way to panic over fuel shortages.*

6. Choice (3)

❶ The semicolon between these two sentences acts as a "straight-ahead" road sign. It tells us that the second thought will be a continuation of, or will support, the first thought. The basic meaning of the first sentence is that friendship has its limits no matter what. The first blank must be filled in with something that reinforces the notion of having limits in all cases. The second sentence tells us that advice that is thrust upon someone cannot be considered an act of friendship. The second blank will be filled in with a word that describes advice that is *thrust insistently* on someone—advice that is not asked for.

❷ A prephrase for this sentence would be, "All friendship, no matter how close, has boundaries; unwanted advice, when thrust upon someone, is rarely a sign of friendship."

❸ Choice (3) looks good right away because the first word, *intimate*, matches our prediction of *close*, and the second word, *unsolicited*, is perfect, too. We should check the other answers quickly just to be sure, though. Choices (1) and (4) can be eliminated because the first word in each is the opposite of *close*. The first word in choices (2) and (5) might be all right if nothing else were better, but both can be eliminated on the basis of the second word in each. Obverse means "inside out or upside down," which doesn't make sense in this context, and *desired* is the opposite of what we are looking for.

❹ *Friendship, no matter how* intimate, *has its boundaries;* unsolicited *advice, when thrust insistently upon one, is rarely an act of friendship, regardless of the adviser's intent.*

7. Choice (3)

❶ For the first blank, we are looking for a word that will describe *rivals*. To determine what is in the second blank, we must read for the context of both clauses. Since the two clauses are joined by a semicolon that acts as a "straight-ahead" road sign, we know that the two ideas will support each other or continue a similar thought. In the first clause, we are given anarchists' view of government, which their rivals agree with. The second clause tells us where the two rival groups differ.

❷ This would be a hard one to prephrase, so we should go directly to the choices looking for words that are in line with the context of the sentences.

❸ Since the first blank describes rivals, we can eliminate choice (1) because rivals are unlikely to be *sympathetic*. The second word in choice (2) rules out this answer because it is inconsistent with the sentence. *Semantics* means "the meaning of words." They could not agree on the definition if they disagreed about the meaning

of the words in the definition. Choice (3) is the best answer so far. Both words make sense in the sentence because *ideological* rivals would be ones that disagree on the philosophy of whatever they are in disagreement about. It would make sense, then, that they would differ in opinion about something important, like the *implications* of the definitions. We'll hold onto this one and check the last two. In (4), the second word, *expression*, means "the way something is stated." We know that the rivals agree on the definition, yet this answer would suggest that they disagree about how it is stated. How it's stated and its definition are too closely related for them to agree on one and disagree about the other. Choice (5) is out because *etiology* is the study of causes, and it doesn't make sense that they would disagree about the causes of the definition.

❹ *Anarchists contend that government is by definition the repression of natural human desire, and their* ideological *rivals concur; it is over the* implications *of this definition that the two groups battle.*

8. Choice (5)

❶ The word *despite* is a "detour" road sign that tells us that there is a change or a contrast later in the sentence. Despite something from the critics, the poet's work sold steadily. The critics must not have favored the poetry, which would explain why it would be surprising that the work still sold well. For the first blank, we would look for a word that suggests the critics' disapproval. The second blank is harder to figure out. We know the word will describe the critics, but many words, both positive and negative, could work here. We will just have to evaluate the meaning of each of the choices to which we narrow it down.

❷ A good prephrase, for the first blank at least, would be, "Despite negative responses from some type of critics, the poetry sold well."

❸ Starting with the first blank, since it is more precise, choice (5) seems to be just right. *Vitriol* means severe criticism, which would work in the first blank, and *influential* in the second blank explains why it's surprising that these type of critics' responses did not negatively impact the sales of the book. Still, we should run through the other answers quickly. From the first word, we can eliminate choice (1) because zeal is positive, and we need a negative word. Choice (3) does not fit well in the first blank either, because *tedium* may be defined as boredom. Receiving boring responses from the critics does not entail that the responses were negative. Choices (2) and (4) can be eliminated because of the second word in each. It is not logical that the response of *obscure* or *ineffectual* critics would explain the contrast suggested by the word *despite*. If the critics have no influence, it would not be surprising that the books sold well. We're looking for a word that would justify the road sign *despite*.

❹ *Despite generous helpings of* vitriol *from a group of* influential *critics, this iconoclastic poet's three volumes have sold steadily.*

9. Choice (1)

❶ The comma after the first blank is an important clue that tells us what type of word we are looking for. Because it is set off with commas, the phrase *from production to projection* simply renames the word in the preceding blank. This phrase describes every aspect of the film industry, so the correct word will, too. Since all of these components were *held by one company,* it makes sense that a monopoly would eventually arise. In the second blank, we're looking for something that expresses the fact that monopolies were bound to arise.

❷ A good prephrase of this answer would be, "Because the different components were arranged so that all aspects of the business were held by one company, monopolistic practices were bound to arise."

❸ Predictions for both of these blanks are pretty definite, but the second is a little more precise, so we'll start there. Choice (1) looks good right away because *inevitable* means that it was bound to happen, which was our prediction for the second blank. *Opportunities for control* works well in the first blank, too. This one looks good. We'll hold onto it and check the others. Choices (3) and (5) can be eliminated because the second word in each does not convey the meaning that something would have to happen. Choices (2) and (4) can be eliminated because the words for the first blank, *burdens of business*

and *means of solicitation,* are not logical in the overall context. Having control of all of the components of the film industry would certainly not be burdens, nor would all of them act as a means of soliciting.

❹ *Because the different components of the film industry were "vertically" oriented—arranged so that all* opportunities for control, *from production to projection, were held by one company—it was* inevitable *that monopolistic practices would arise.*

10. Choice (4)

❶ The first blank will describe something that the peasants tried to conceal as they knelt before the body of the dictator's son. This doesn't sound like a very positive situation. They are kneeling and we know that they live under a dictatorship, so it is likely that the peasants are being required to do this. The second part of the sentence supports this theory. We learn that *far from affection,* something else brought them to the wake. Consequently, we're looking for a negative word in both blanks.

❷ Many words would work in these blanks, so we'll just have to evaluate each choice carefully looking for two negative words that fit in this context.

❸ Starting with the second blank since we have a little more information to work with there, choice (4) looks like the best answer. It makes sense that *fear* would bring them to the wake of the dictator's son. The first word, *trepidation,* also fits the sentence, since it means "apprehension." We'll hold onto this one and check the others. Choice (1) can be eliminated because there is no indication in the sentence that the peasants are concealing *sarcasm,* and they would not show this if they felt something as extreme as *hatred.* Likewise, the second word in choice (2), *violence,* is not suggested from the clues. Choices (3), *adulation,* and (5), *patriotism,* are positive. We're looking for something negative here.

❹ *From the* trepidation *that the peasants tried to conceal as they knelt before the body of the dictator's son, I concluded that, far from affection, it was* fear *that had brought them to the wake.*

SENTENCE COMPLETION: TEST 3

Time: 10 Questions/10 Minutes

Directions: Each sentence has one or more blank spaces. Each blank indicates that a word or phrase has been omitted. Of the five following words or sets of words, choose the one word or set that, when inserted in the sentence, best fits the meaning of the entire sentence.

1. Despite the increased attention _____ juvenile delinquency, a _____ in crimes committed by juveniles has been seen.

   ① allotted to . . . dip
   ② offered to . . . proliferation
   ③ given to . . . rise
   ④ spent on . . . decrease
   ⑤ withdrawn from . . . growth

2. Much of the Beatles' music, as evidenced by "All You Need Is Love," was characterized by a superficial _____ subtly contradicted by an inherent, deeper cynicism.

   ① competence
   ② world-weariness
   ③ liveliness
   ④ naiveté
   ⑤ gloss

3. During their famous clash, Jung regarded Freud ambivalently, attacking the father of modern psychoanalysis even as he _____ him.

   ① enlightened
   ② chastened
   ③ revered
   ④ despised
   ⑤ preferred

4. Hers was not a quick but a thorough intelligence; however _____, she came to _____ all things touching her life.

   ① unmindfully . . . embrace
   ② desperately . . . appreciate
   ③ slowly . . . jettison
   ④ methodically . . . discern
   ⑤ ploddingly . . . understand

5. Considering the _____ era in which the novel was written, its tone and theme are remarkably _____.

   ① enlightened . . . disenchanted
   ② scholarly . . . undramatic
   ③ superstitious . . . medieval
   ④ permissive . . . puritanical
   ⑤ undistinguished . . . commonplace

6. The Colonel believed that even a minor _____ the rules could not go _____ if he were to maintain discipline.

   ① disrespect for . . . unfelt
   ② infraction of . . . unpunished
   ③ alteration of . . . unrewarded
   ④ deviation from . . . unappreciated
   ⑤ adherence to . . . unobserved

7. Feuds tend to arise in societies that _____ centralized government; when public justice is difficult to enforce, private recourse is more _____.

   ① espouse . . . acceptable
   ② affirm . . . objectionable
   ③ dislike . . . satisfying
   ④ reject . . . brutal
   ⑤ lack . . . effective

8. He must always be the center of attention; he would rather be criticized than _____.

   ① ignored

   ② selfish

   ③ remembered

   ④ praised

   ⑤ different

9. Part of a person's immediate response to pain is determined not only by his _____ emotional state but also by his _____ previous painful experiences.

   ① frightened . . . fears from

   ② permanent . . . scars from

   ③ particular . . . lack of

   ④ current . . . memories of

   ⑤ recent . . . denial of

10. Greek philosophers tried to _____ contemporary notions of change and stability by postulating the existence of the atom, _____ particle from which all varieties of matter are formed.

    ① personify . . . a mutating

    ② reconcile . . . an indivisible

    ③ simplify . . . a specific

    ④ eliminate . . . an infinitesimal

    ⑤ confirm . . . an interesting

ANSWERS

1. Choice (3)

❶ The "detour" road sign *despite* at the beginning of this sentence helps us figure this one out. Because *despite* indicates that the two parts of the sentence are contrasting with each other, we know that *despite the increased attention* on this issue, something has happened. You would expect that with increased attention, there would be fewer crimes committed by this group. However, the word *despite* indicates that what we might expect does not prove to be true. We're looking for the opposite of what we would normally expect given these circumstances.

❷ A good prephrase for this one would be, "Despite increased attention on juvenile delinquency, an increase in crimes has been seen."

❸ Working with the second blank since it is more specific, choices (2), (3), and (5) look good. After considering the first blank, though, only choice (3) makes sense. The first word in choice (2), *offered*, is not strong enough. Simply offering attention to this issue does not tell us whether or not attention was actually given. We need something more definitive in the first blank to indicate that the expected cause and effect was not realized. Choice (5) can be eliminated since the first word, *withdrawn*, is the opposite of what we're looking for. We'll hold onto (3) and check the remaining two. Choices (1) and (4) are inappropriate, since the second word in each doesn't have a contrasting meaning to the first clause. We must have a contrast because of the word *despite* in the first clause.

❹ *Despite the increased attention* given to *juvenile delinquency, a* rise *in crimes committed by juveniles has been seen*.

2. Choice (4)

❶ The "detour" road sign *contradicted* tells us that the blank will be opposite in meaning to *cynicism*— something like innocence.

❷ A good paraphrase would be, "The Beatles' music was characterized by a superficial innocence subtly contradicted by an inherent, deeper cynicism."

❸ Choice (4) looks good right away because naiveté means "innocence." None of the other choices comes close to being opposite in meaning to *cynicism*.

❹ *Much of the Beatles' music, as evidenced by "All You Need Is Love," was characterized by a superficial* naiveté *subtly contradicted by an inherent, deeper cynicism*.

3. Choice (3)

❶ The key word to figuring out which answer should go in the blank is *ambivalently*. An ambivalent attitude is one that contains both positive and negative feelings. We know that the negative side of Jung's attitude is that he attacked Freud. However, even as he attacked Freud, Jung did something that must have been positive in order to have shown ambivalence toward Freud. We're looking for something positive for this blank.

❷ Many positive words would work here, so it would be hard to prephrase an answer. Instead, we should go directly to the choices and evaluate each one carefully given the context of the sentence.

❸ Choice (3) looks good right away since revered is a very positive word. We'll hold onto it and check the others. Choices (2) and (4) can be eliminated because they are negative. Choice (1) is out because it doesn't really make sense in the context of the sentence. If Jung *enlightened* Freud, it might have a positive effect on Freud, but it is impossible to say whether this would have a positive or negative impact on Jung. Choice (5) is not a good answer because it sounds idiomatically incorrect to say *even as he preferred him*.

❹ *During their famous clash, Jung regarded Freud ambivalently, attacking the father of modern psychoanalysis even as he* revered *him*.

4. Choice (5)

❶ The road sign *but* in the first clause indicates that her intelligence has two contrasting qualities: It is not *quick*, yet it is *thorough*. Since the two clauses are joined by a semicolon, a "straight-ahead" road sign, we know that the second will support or elaborate upon the first. There is more information available on the second blank; if we look there, we see that of the two qualities, the latter one, her thoroughness, is what is being described. The first blank must reflect the other quality, slowness.

❷ The first blank can be prephrased, but the second is not as precise. A working paraphrase could be, "Her intelligence was not quick, but it was thorough; however slowly, she would come to understand all things eventually."

❸ Since the prediction for the first blank is more precise, we should start there. Choices (3) and (5) look good because the first word in each matches our prediction. Looking at the second blank, choice (3) can be eliminated. It would not make sense that she would *jettison*, or get rid of, all things in her life. Choice (5) looks good for both blanks. We'll hold onto it and check the others. We can eliminate choices (1) and (2), because the first word in each does not relate to how slowly she thinks. Similarly, we can eliminate choice (4), because *methodically* does not tell us how slowly the thinking is done, just the manner in which it is done.

❹ *Hers was not a quick but a thorough intelligence; however* ploddingly, *she would come to* understand *all things touching her life.*

5. Choice (4)

❶ The most helpful approach to figuring out what should go in each of these blanks is to pay attention to the overall context. Two words are especially important here—*considering* at the beginning of the sentence and *remarkably* before the second blank. Thinking about how these words are typically used, we can determine that the two words will be opposites of each other. "Considering that the era is a certain way, it's remarkable or surprising that the theme and tone are something different." So, we know we're looking for opposites.

❷ Many different options are available for these blanks, so it would be hard to prephrase an answer here. We just have to be sure that the answer we select contains two opposite or contrasting words.

❸ Scanning the choices, the two words in (4) appear to have the contrasting, opposing connotation we're looking for. (*Puritanical* means "prudish and straight-laced.") We'll hold onto it and check the others. Choices (1) and (2) can be eliminated because there is no definite connection between the two. There is no specific relationship, opposite or otherwise, between *enlightened* and *disenchanted*, nor between *scholarly* and *undramatic*. Choices (3) and (5) can be eliminated because in each the words are closely related, not opposites of each other. During *medieval* times, superstitious beliefs were commonplace, and *undistinguished* and *commonplace* mean virtually the same thing.

❹ *Considering the* permissive *era in which the novel was written, its tone and theme are remarkably* puritanical.

6. Choice (2)

❶ After the second blank, we read that the Colonel wants to maintain discipline. From that context, we can determine that breaking the rules will not be tolerated.

❷ A good prephrase here would be, "Even a minor breaking of the rules could not go unpunished."

❸ Looking for words that match what we predicted, choice (2) immediately jumps out. We should look at the others, though, just to be sure. Choices (3) and (4) are illogical, because an *alteration* in the rules would not be *unrewarded* by a strict disciplinarian, nor would a *deviation* from the rules be *unappreciated.* Choice (1) can be eliminated because a *disrespect* for rules would definitely be felt, not *unfelt*, by a disciplinarian. Choice (5) does not make sense, either, because there is no reason that *adherence* must be observed in order to maintain discipline.

❹ *The Colonel believed that even a minor* infraction *of the rules could not go* unpunished *if he were to maintain discipline.*

7. Choice (5)

❶ The semicolon between these clauses is a "straight-ahead" road sign that indicates a close connection between the two. The first clause tells us that *feuds tend to arise* in societies that feel a certain way about *centralized government.* In the second clause, we learn more about these societies—*public justice is difficult to enforce* in them. These societies must not have strong, centralized governments. This helps us with the first blank. The *private recourse* mentioned at the end of the second clause is referring to *feuds,* since a feud is a fight or dispute between factions or families that tends to be a private matter. So, feuds, or private recourse, tend to occur in these societies.

❷ A prephrase of this answer might be, "Feuds tend to arise in societies that do not have centralized governments; when public justice is unavailable, private recourse is more common."

❸ Choice (5) looks like a good answer right away because *lack* is very close to our prediction, and *effective* would make sense in this context, too. We'll check the others just to be sure. Choices (1) and (2) can be eliminated, because the first word in each would mean that these societies are in favor of centralized government. We're looking for the opposite of this. Choice (3) can be eliminated since a *dislike* of centralized government would not in itself make public justice *difficult to enforce.* We need a stronger word in the first blank that would explain why public justice is not an option for these societies. Moreover, we don't know whether or not private recourse is more *satisfying* when public justice is hard to enforce. Choice (4) can be eliminated because even though the first word, *reject,* is a good selection, the second word, *brutal,* is unsupported in the sentence. We do not know that the recourse is "more brutal" in these societies than in others. We only know that the recourse tends to be private rather than public.

❹ *Feuds tend to arise in societies that* lack *centralized governments; when public justice is difficult to enforce, private recourse is more* effective.

8. **Choice (1)**

❶ The semicolon between these clauses acts as a "straight-ahead" road sign that tells us that these two ideas are closely related or elaborate upon each other. Since the blank is in the second clause, we'll look to the first for direction. There we discover that this person requires lots of attention. The second clause will be consistent with this notion; it explains just how much he needs this attention. What would he rather be criticized for than have happen? Not getting any attention.

❷ A prephrase here could be, "He'd rather be criticized than ignored."

❸ Choice (1) meets our prediction, but we'll look at the others just to be sure. Scanning the other choices quickly now that we have one that looks perfect, we see that all of the remaining options do not support the first part of the sentence. None of these other choices reinforce the idea that he always has to be the center of attention.

❹ *He must always be the center of attention; he would rather be criticized than* ignored.

9. **Choice (4)**

❶ The road sign that helps us in this sentence is the words *not only . . . but also,* which indicate that more than one thing determines *response to pain.* The word in the first blank will describe an emotional state, and the second will relate to actual, previous *experiences.* One is based on feelings, and the other on actual events. The road sign tells us that the two words will contrast with each other in some way.

❷ It would be difficult to predict the many different pairs that could fill these blanks. We will just have to evaluate the choices carefully, looking for words that contrast with each other.

❸ Choices (1) and (2) can be eliminated because these words are too similar to warrant the not only . . . but also contrast. These pairs of words are basically saying the same thing. In choice (3) *particular* works well, but *lack of* previous experiences doesn't make sense. Choice (4) makes sense in the context and has a contrasting meaning that supports the use of the *not only . . . but also* phrase, contrasting current emotions with memories of previous experiences. We'll just check the next answer to be sure that choice (4) is the one we want to select. Choice (5) doesn't work because the *recent* emotional state is not very logical and *denial of* previous experiences definitely doesn't make sense. Why would the recent emotional state, and not the current one, have an influence? And denying a previous experience would also mean that it would not have an influence on the person responding to pain.

❹ *Part of a person's immediate response to pain is determined not only by his* current *emotional state but also by his* memories *of previous painful experiences.*

10. **Choice (2)**

❶ These philosophers were trying to do something with the *notions of change and stability.* The first thing we should notice is that change and *stability* are starkly opposing ideas. Therefore, they must have been doing more than just trying to understand change and stability, which really wouldn't be that difficult anyway. They must have been trying to rationalize something about both of them. The first blank, then, will be filled with a word that expresses what they were trying to resolve about change and stability. The way they tried to do this was to hypothesize about the existence of a *particle* that could explain both change and stability. We're told that this particle is the atom from which all varieties of matter are formed, which would include both changing and stable things. The second blank will describe the atom in some way.

❷ The first blank is easier to prephrase, such as "Greek philosophers tried to resolve notions of change and stability," for the first part of the sentence, and we'll just carefully evaluate the choices for the second blank.

❸ Choice (2) is the only one in which the first word reflects the content of the sentence. *Reconcile* (which means "settle a dispute") is the perfect description of trying to rationalize the simultaneous existence of opposing forces. The second word looks good, too. We'll hold onto it, and check the others. Choices (1), (3), (4), and (5) can be eliminated on the basis of the first word in each. There is no suggestion in the sentence that any of these things is what the philosophers wanted to do.

❹ *Greek philosophers tried to* reconcile *contemporary notions of change and stability by postulating the existence of the atom,* an indivisible *particle from which all varieties of matter are formed.*

SENTENCE COMPLETION: TEST 4

Time: 10 Questions/10 Minutes

Directions: Each sentence has one or more blank spaces. Each blank indicates that a word or phrase has been omitted. Of the five following words or sets of words, choose the one word or set that, when inserted in the sentence, best fits the meaning of the entire sentence.

1. To an untrained eye the horse appeared to be very _____, whereas in actuality it was _____ and unmanageable.

   ① beautiful . . . reckless
   ② gentle . . . wild
   ③ calm . . . indolent
   ④ spirited . . . energetic
   ⑤ friendly . . . languid

2. The modern detective novel grew out of Gothic fiction when nineteenth-century authors began to propose _____ rather than supernatural explanations for seemingly _____ occurrences.

   ① earthly . . . everyday
   ② complex . . . scientific
   ③ rational . . . mysterious
   ④ religious . . . . miraculous
   ⑤ literary . . . mundane

3. Though scientific discoveries are often disproved shortly after they've been accepted as fact, scientists still seem to leap to hasty conclusions, _____ that the _____ nature of what can be called "fact" has not eroded their confidence.

   ① proving . . . undeniable
   ② demonstrating . . . illusory
   ③ showing . . . predictable
   ④ denying . . . distinctive
   ⑤ admitting . . . volatile

4. It was an ingrained concept of Soviet doctrine that another world war was _____ and a great many Soviet domestic and foreign policies and practices were designed to ensure that if any nation _____ the war, it would be the Soviet Union.

   ① impossible . . . won
   ② survivable . . . prevented
   ③ coming . . . commanded
   ④ avoidable . . . instigated
   ⑤ inevitable . . . survived

5. Many believe that jazz improvisation is a creation of the 20th century, but it is _____ that improvisation has its _____ in the figured-bass techniques of the 17th and 18th centuries.

   ① unlikely . . . roots
   ② possible . . . past
   ③ arguable . . . origin
   ④ proven . . . future
   ⑤ interesting . . . unity

6. Whales hurt none in their peaceful migrations through the earth's seas, yet are savagely hunted by man, who _____ superior need.

   ① assumes
   ② perpetuates
   ③ retains
   ④ assimilates
   ⑤ manifests

KAPLAN

7. The meaning of this line seems clear: The poet, though not denigrating the concept of ____, nonetheless emphasizes the importance of man's role in humanity in the ____.

   ① independence . . . abstract
   ② community . . . extreme
   ③ unity . . . synthesis
   ④ perfection . . . majority
   ⑤ individuality . . . aggregate

8. His unbridled curiosity led him to explore every field of ____, yet his ____ stances kept him at odds with the devout society he so wanted to be acknowledged by.

   ① science . . . interesting
   ② interest . . . common
   ③ thought . . . unorthodox
   ④ hope . . . heretical
   ⑤ study . . . optimistic

9. Because of his inherent ____, Harry steered clear of any job that he suspected could turn out to be a travail.

   ① impudence
   ② insolence
   ③ eminence
   ④ indolence
   ⑤ imminence

10. Victorien Sardou's play *La Tosca* was originally written as a ____ for Sarah Bernhardt, and later ____ into the famous Puccini opera.

   ① role . . . reincarnated
   ② biography . . . changed
   ③ metaphor . . . edited
   ④ present . . . fictionalized
   ⑤ vehicle . . . adapted

ANSWERS

1. Choice (2)

❶ The road sign *whereas in actuality* indicates a contrast—however the horse appeared, it was really the opposite. From the end of the sentence we know that the horse was *unmanageable,* so the first blank will contain a descriptive word that contrasts with unmanageable. The second blank will be filled with a descriptive word reinforcing a negative quality like *unmanageable.*

❷ A good prephrase for this would be, "Although the horse appeared calm or manageable, it proved to be something negative."

❸ Since our prediction is more precise for the first word, we'll start there. Choices (2) and (3) will both work well for the first blank. The second word in choice (2) is consistent with the context. It is logical to say that the horse is both *wild* and *unmanageable.* Choice (3), however, does not make sense in the second blank, because indolent means "lazy." There is no indication that the horse is lazy, and the two words, *indolent* and *unmanageable,* are not similar enough to be joined by the road sign *and.* We'll throw out (3) and hold onto (2) while we quickly check the rest. Choice (1) can be ruled out because a *beautiful* horse could be either manageable or not manageable. *Beautiful* would not justify the word *although* at the beginning of the sentence. Choice (4) can be eliminated because we are looking for contrasting words in these blanks, and *spirited* and *energetic* are very similar in meaning. Choice (5) doesn't work because *languid* means "weak" or "sluggish." A weak or sluggish horse would most likely be manageable, not unmanageable, and there is no contrasting meaning at all between *friendly* and *languid.*

❹ *To an untrained eye the horse appeared to be very* gentle, *whereas in actuality it was* wild *and* unmanageable.

2. Choice (3)

❶ The context of this sentence is what leads us to the right answer here. We can figure out what type of word should go in the first blank because of the phrase *rather than supernatural explanations.* That tells us that the word for the first blank means "not supernatural." As for the second blank, we know that previously *supernatural* causes were blamed for this type of occurrence, so it must be a type of occurrence that does not seem normal.

❷ A good prephrase of this answer would be, "Authors began to propose natural rather than supernatural explanations for seemingly abnormal occurrences."

❸ Choice (3) seems just right. Both words fit our prediction, so we'll hold onto it and check the others. In choice (1), the first word, *earthly,* looks good, but the second word, *everyday,* doesn't fit. We need a word for the second blank that means abnormal. *Everyday* would be the opposite of what we need. Choices (2), (4), and (5) can be eliminated because the first word in each is too different from what we're looking for. None of these qualities—*complex, religious,* or *literary*—is suggested in the sentence.

❹ *The modern detective novel grew out of Gothic fiction when nineteenth-century authors began to propose* rational *rather than supernatural explanations for seemingly* mysterious *occurrences.*

3. Choice (2)

❶ Paraphrasing long sentences will help you to cut to their essentials. Here we learn that even though discoveries are disproved quickly, scientists still jump to conclusions. What does that indicate about the scientists? It must not bother them that what is supposed to be "fact" is indeed likely to change. After all, they continue leaping to hasty conclusions even though it is common that their discoveries are disproved.

❷ This would be a difficult one to prephrase. Many words could go in each blank, so we must evaluate the choices carefully and be sure that both words work in the context of the sentence.

❸ Choice (1) can be eliminated because the second word, *undeniable,* is inconsistent with the notion that the facts are changing, and that what we know about them now may not be accepted later. Choice (2) looks good for both blanks, so we'll hold on to it for now. Choice (3) is out because *predictable* is the opposite of what this sentence is saying about scientific knowledge. It's not predictable; it's constantly changing. Choice (4) is illogical in the context. The scientists are still following the same pattern of jumping to conclusions. This answer suggests that their confidence has been eroded, which is proven to not be the case in the rest of the sentence. Choice (5) is incorrect because it's not logical to say that the scientists are *admitting* that they are wrong to jump to conclusions. Why would they still do it, if they admit it's wrong? Even if you thought this might work, another choice, (2), fits much better.

❹ *Though scientific discoveries are often disproved shortly after they've been accepted as fact, scientists still seem to leap to hasty conclusions,* demonstrating *that the* illusory *nature of what can be called "fact" has not eroded their confidence.*

4. Choice (5)

❶ The second part of this sentence helps us fill in the first blank about what was *an ingrained concept of Soviet doctrine.* Just before the second blank, we hear definitive things about the war. We're told that the Soviets believed that if any nation did something during or before or after the war, they wanted it to be the Soviet Union. Since they wanted this thing for their own country, no doubt it was positive. They must have anticipated that there would be another world war, and it makes sense that if they anticipated another war, they would want to be the ones to come out on top. This helps us fill in the second blank.

❷ A prephrase of this answer would be, "The Soviets believed that another war was unavoidable, so they wanted to ensure they did not lose it."

❸ Choice (5) is the only one in which both words seem to be in line with what we've predicted. We'll hold onto it, and check the others. Starting with our prediction for the first blank, which is more precise, we can eliminate choices (1) and (4). These choices express the opposite meaning of what we're looking for. Choices (2) and (3) do not make sense when paired together. Just because a war is *survivable* doesn't mean they would necessarily want to *prevent* it. Likewise, just because a war was *coming,* there would be no reason for them to think they could *command* it. And how would one country command the entire war anyway? They could command their side of the war, but nothing else.

❹ *It was an ingrained concept of Soviet doctrine that another world war was* inevitable, *and a great many Soviet domestic and foreign policies and practices were designed to ensure that if any nation* survived *the war, it would be the Soviet Union.*

5. Choice (3)

❶ The road sign *but* after the comma indicates that a detour is coming. So, there will be a change or contrast from the first part of the sentence. At the beginning of the sentence, we're told that *many* think jazz

improvisation first occurred in the 20th century. The second part of this sentence where we find the two blanks will no doubt dispute this belief.

❷ A good prephrase of this answer would be "but it is believed that improvisation has its beginnings in the 17th and 18th centuries."

❸ Beginning with the choices for the second blank, choices (1) and (3) are our closest matches. Choice (1) can be eliminated because the first word, *unlikely,* is the opposite of what we're looking for. Choice (3) seems to fill both blanks well. We'll hold onto it, and check the others. Choice (2) is out because it is idiomatically incorrect to say that improvisation had its past in the 17th or 18th centuries. Choice (4) doesn't work because the second word, *future,* is illogical. The future cannot be in the past. Choice (5) also doesn't make sense because the second word, *unity,* is unsupported in the sentence. We're not looking for information on the characteristics of jazz; instead, we need something that indicates when jazz improvisation originated.

❹ *Many believe that jazz improvisation is a creation of the 20th century, but it is* arguable *that improvisation has its* origin *in the figured-bass techniques of the 17th and 18th centuries.*

6. Choice (1)

❶ From this sentence we know that the whales are *peaceful,* yet are *savagely* hunted. From this tone, we can assume that the author disapproves of the situation. The blank, then, will be filled with something that suggests man's *superior* need is not a real one.

❷ A prephrase for this sentence might be, "The whales are savagely hunted by man, who argues for superior need, or believes he has superior need."

❸ Choice (1) looks good because assumes matches the tone and content of this sentence. We'll hold onto it, and check the others. Choice (2) does not work because there is nothing in the sentence that tells us how long this has been going on. And it sounds like a justification for hunting, which the author would oppose. Choices (3) and (5) can be ruled out because they are not consistent with the author's tone. The author thinks it is bad that the whales are hunted. The author would not agree that man *retains* or *manifests* superior need. Both of these answers imply that man has a right to hunt the whales. Choice (4), *assimilates,* is not logical in this context. What would the phrase *man assimilates superior need* mean?

❹ *Whales hurt none in their peaceful migrations through the earth's seas, yet they are savagely hunted by man, who* assumes *superior need.*

7. Choice (5)

❶ The key to finding an answer here is the road sign *nonetheless,* which signals contrasting ideas in the two clauses. Because it is in the first part of the sentence, the word for the first blank will contrast with the phrase the *importance of man's role in humanity,* found after the road sign *nonetheless.*

❷ It would be very difficult to prephrase an answer to this sentence, so we just have to keep in mind that the two words will be contrasting and that the first one will relate to "man's role in humanity."

❸ Choices (1), (2), and (4) can be eliminated because there is no contrast between the two words in each. None of the words in these pairs really has any specific relationship to each other when it comes to meaning. Choice (3) can be eliminated; these words reflect a similar meaning rather than a contrasting one. Since *aggregate* in choice (5) means "the whole," there is a clear contrast with the first word, *individuality.* Here's our answer.

❹ *The meaning of this line seems clear: The poet, though not denigrating the concept of* individuality, *nonetheless emphasizes the importance of man's role in humanity in the* aggregate.

8. Choice (3)

❶ The "detour" road sign *yet* between these clauses tells us that there will be a change in direction in this sentence. We are told that his *unbridled curiosity* resulted in his exploration of every field, which is a positive thing. The change in direction comes when, after the word *yet,* we find out something negative. He wanted to be acknowledged by society, a society we are told was *devout.* The second blank, describing his stances, must be filled with a word that would not be acceptable to a devout society. Since *devout* means "devoted to religion," the word will have to mean "antireligious." For the first blank, any word that conveyed the idea that he explored many different subjects would work.

❷ We can make a pretty definite prephrase for the second blank in this sentence, but the first blank could be filled with various words. A partial prephrase would be, "Yet his sacrilegious stances kept him at odds with a devout society."

❸ Checking the second word, we are immediately drawn to choices (3) and (4), both of which have the meaning of "against accepted religious beliefs." Choice (3) looks good for both blanks because *every field of thought* conveys the idea of a wide array of subjects. Choice (4) doesn't work for the second blank because *field of hope* doesn't relate to the breadth of his explorations but more to expectations; besides, it's not really clear what the phrase *every field of hope* is meant to signify. Choice (3) seems correct, but let's review the others. There is no reason in choice (1) that his *interesting* stances would be objectionable to a devout society, and *field of science* is too limited. He may have explored much more than just science. In choices (2) and (5), *interest* and *study* work for the first blank, but *common* and *optimistic* don't make sense for the second. A *devout society* would not necessarily reject a *common* or *optimistic* stance.

❹ *His unbridled curiosity led him to explore every field of thought, yet his* unorthodox *stances kept him at odds with the devout society he so wanted to be acknowledged by.*

9. Choice (4)

❶ The blank in this sentence is going to be filled with a word that describes Harry's personality. We discover what his personality is like when we read that he doesn't want a job that will be a *travail.* Since *travail* means hard work, something that is extremely difficult, then we know that the missing word will reflect that disposition. Harry doesn't like to work hard.

❷ A good prephrase here would be, "Due to his laziness, Harry avoided jobs that might be a travail."

❸ Choice (4), *indolence,* is perfect because it means "laziness," but we'll look at the others to double-check this answer. Choices (1) and (2), *impudence* and *insolence,* are incorrect because they both describe someone who is disrespectful and cocky. We don't know that Harry is either one of these. He just doesn't like to work. Choice (3), *eminence,* means "high rank" or "high repute," neither of which work here. It doesn't make sense that Harry's *eminence* would make him want to avoid work. Choice (5), *imminence,* can be eliminated because it refers to something that is about to happen. There is no logical connection between imminence and travail.

❹ *Because of his inherent* indolence, *Harry steered clear of any job that he suspected could turn out to be a travail.*

10. **Choice (5)**

❶ To correctly complete this sentence, we must note that *La Tosca* was first written as a play and then made into an opera. This helps us to determine what type of word should go in the second blank. The second blank will explain that the play was changed or adapted to become an opera. The first blank is harder to work with. The play was written for the actress Sarah Bernhardt to do something, but it's unclear exactly what that might be, so we'll have to look to the choices for the second word.

❷ A prephrase of this one would be easy for the second blank but harder for the first. We should look for a sentence like, "The play was written as something for Sarah Bernhardt, and later changed or adapted into the famous opera."

❸ Choice (5) immediately looks good because of the word *adapted* in the second blank, which we had

predicted. Even though the first word, *vehicle,* may seem odd at first, it makes sense after you realize that it's not the idea of transportation that is meant here but *vehicle* in the sense of a play that was created as a means for displaying a specific actor's talents. Both words will work, so we'll hold onto this answer and check the other choices. Choice (1) can be eliminated because *reincarnated* suggests the rebirth of something living, and *role* is also inappropriate since an entire play would not be written as a role for one person. Choice (2) is acceptable for the second word, but the first, *biography,* doesn't fit. Sardou could write a biography of Bernhardt, but not one for her. Choice (3) can be eliminated because *metaphor* would not work for the first blank, since a metaphor is a poetic device used to describe something; meanwhile, *edited* for the second blank does not accurately represent the changes necessary to make a play into an opera. Much more must be done to this play than simply editing. For choice (4), the first word, *present,* is fine, although the play might be an unusual gift, but the second word, *fictionalized,* is wrong. Changing a story from a play into an opera does not change it from being based on reality (nonfiction) to being fictionalized.

❹ *Victorien Sardou's play* La Tosca *was originally written as a* vehicle *for Sarah Bernhardt, and later* adapted *into the famous Puccini opera.*

SENTENCE COMPLETION: TEST 5

Time: 10 Questions/10 Minutes

Directions: Each sentence has one or more blank spaces. Each blank indicates that a word or phrase has been omitted. Of the five following words or sets of words, choose the one word or set that, when inserted in the sentence, best fits the meaning of the entire sentence.

1. First published in 1649, Pacheco's ____ treatise contains not only chapters outlining iconography and technique, but also commentary on contemporary painters that now ____ our most comprehensive information on these artists, as well as the most thorough discussion available on Baroque aesthetics.

   1. inconsequential . . . comprises
   2. invaluable . . . constitutes
   3. historical . . . lacks
   4. superficial . . . supports
   5. important . . . excludes

2. Very little is known of the writer Theophilus; however, from his eclectic writings, we can ____ that he was well ____.

   1. assume . . . educated
   2. understand . . . disciplined
   3. appreciate . . . respected
   4. expect . . . exposed
   5. acknowledge . . . received

3. Because he was highly regarded as a theoretical ____ throughout his career, it is somewhat surprising that today he is remembered ____ for a poem he wrote on painting.

   1. artist . . . primarily
   2. practitioner . . . exclusively
   3. painter . . . possibly
   4. writer . . . surreptitiously
   5. mathematician . . . only

4. Her systematic approach to scientific research was often rewarded in her ____ life, but it proved disastrous when her ____ mind examined every flaw in her friends and family, preventing her from truly appreciating others.

   1. career . . . disorganized
   2. private . . . analytical
   3. public . . . fragile
   4. professional . . . methodical
   5. family . . . orderly

5. Because law and custom require that a definite determination be made, a judge is forced to behave as if a verdict is ____, when in fact the evidence may not be ____.

   1. negotiable . . . persuasive
   2. justified . . . accessible
   3. unassailable . . . insubstantial
   4. incontrovertible . . . admissible
   5. self-evident . . . conclusive

6. The author presumably believes that all businessmen are ____, for her main characters, whatever qualities they may lack, are virtual paragons of ____.

   1. clever . . . ingenuity
   2. covetous . . . greed
   3. virtuous . . . deceit
   4. successful . . . ambition
   5. cautious . . . achievement

KAPLAN

7. Personal correspondence is often a marvelous reflection of the spirit of an age; the subtle _____ of Swift's epistles mirrored the eighteenth-century delight in elegant _____.

   ① profundity . . . ditties
   ② poignancy . . . pejoratives
   ③ contempt . . . anachronisms
   ④ provinciality . . . pomposity
   ⑤ vitriol . . . disparagement

8. Ginnie expects her every submission to be published or selected for performance, and this time her _____ is likely to be _____.

   ① candor . . . dispelled
   ② anticipation . . . piqued
   ③ enthusiasm . . . dampened
   ④ optimism . . . vindicated
   ⑤ awareness . . . clouded

9. His opponent found it extremely frustrating that the governor's solid support from the voting public was not eroded by his _____ of significant issues.

   ① exaggeration
   ② misapprehension
   ③ discussion
   ④ selection
   ⑤ acknowledgment

10. Our spokesperson seems to be uncertain of our eventual victory but _____ facing the alternative, as if merely admitting the possibility of defeat would lead to the dreaded thing itself.

   ① unsure of
   ② complacent when
   ③ fearful of
   ④ certain of
   ⑤ helped by

ANSWERS

1. Choice (2)

❶ The first blank in this sentence will describe Pacheco's *treatise*. Later in the sentence we find out that this treatise contains information on iconography, technique, and contemporary painters. Already this sounds like a broad and significant treatise. This is confirmed after the second blank, when we're told that the treatise is our *most comprehensive information* on these subjects. The word in the first blank will definitely be a positive one.

❷ It would be hard to prephrase this answer, but we know we're looking for a positive word in the first blank, and the second has to describe how we use the information now.

❸ Looking for a positive word in the first blank, we can narrow it down to choices (2), (5), and possibly (3). Choice (3) does not look very promising because *historical* is neither positive nor negative, and the second word, *lacks,* definitely rules this answer out. It's not logical that a treatise filled with so much information would now *lack* our most comprehensive information on these topics. Choice (2) looks good for both blanks. Let's see if we can rule out the others. Even though *important* is a good selection for the first blank in choice (5), the second word, *excludes,* does not make sense. An important treatise, filled with so much information, would not *exclude* our most comprehensive information. Choices (1) and (4) can be eliminated—the first word in both is negative. They both are contradicted by the text.

❹ *First published in 1649, Pacheco's* invaluable *treatise contains not only chapters outlining iconography and technique, but also commentary on contemporary painters that now* constitutes *our most comprehensive information on these artists, as well as the most thorough discussion available on Baroque aesthetics.*

2. Choice (1)

❶ Two important road signs help us in this sentence—the semicolon between the clauses and the word *however.* The semicolon indicates that the two clauses will contain similar thoughts; the second sentence goes on to explain or elaborate upon the first. The word *however* indicates that even though the second clause

will discuss the same topic as the first, something new or different has been brought in. In the first clause, we're told that not much is known about this writer. The second clause tells us that even though we don't know much about him, his writings are *eclectic,* which indicates something about him. Since the word *eclectic* means "drawn from various sources," we can get a sense of what should go in the second blank. Some way or another, Theophilus was exposed to a lot of different information.

❷ A prephrase for this one might be, "From his writings, we can presume him to be well traveled, well educated, or well versed."

❸ Choice (1) looks like a good match right away, although (4) seems to work as well. Both words in (1) are logical and sound correct in the sentence. In choice (4), *expect* is fine for the first blank, but *exposed* doesn't work in the second. It is idiomatically incorrect to say that he was *well exposed.* We would say that he was *exposed* to many or various things, but not that he was well exposed. Since we can eliminate (4), (1) looks like our answer. We'll check the others quickly just to be sure. Choices (2), (3), and (5) can be rejected because the second word in each is not consistent with the meaning of *eclectic.* It is from his eclectic writings that we can make an assumption about him. So, the second blank must be filled with a word that underscores the meaning of *eclectic.*

❹ *Very little is known of the writer Theophilus; however, from his eclectic writings, we can* assume *that he was well* educated*.*

3. Choice (5)

❶ The road sign *because* at the beginning of this sentence tells us that a reason is being given. The second part of the sentence tells us that it's surprising that he's known for a poem he wrote on painting, so he must not have been a writer, poet, or a painter. The first blank will describe a career that seems to be at odds with these art forms.

❷ A prephrase for this sentence would be difficult to formulate. We'll just evaluate the choices carefully, eliminating words that wouldn't fit in this context.

❸ Since we're looking for someone who was regarded as something other than an artist or writer, we can eliminate choices (1), (3), and (4). Of the remaining two, the first word in choice (2), *practitioner*, is not precise enough. We don't know what type of practitioner this might be, and we must have something in the first blank that clearly contrasts with the second. Choice (5) works well for both blanks.

❹ *Because he was highly regarded as a theoretical* mathematician *throughout his career, it is somewhat surprising that today he is remembered* exclusively *for a poem he wrote on painting.*

4. **Choice (4)**

❶ The first blank in this sentence describes the aspect of life that was rewarded by *her systematic approach.* From the context, it is likely that this aspect will be found in her work life as opposed to her home life, but we'll confirm that with the other information in the sentence. The word *but* after the comma is a "detour" road sign, indicating that there will be a contrast between the two clauses. So, her approach is helpful in one aspect of her life, but is detrimental in her personal life. We were right. The first blank will describe her life at work. The second blank will be filled with a word that describes her mind. We already know from the beginning of the sentence that she has a systematic approach to her research. The second missing word must be a descriptive word that is consistent with this systematic approach.

❷ A prephrase for this answer would be, "Her systematic approach was rewarded in her work life, but was disastrous when her analytical mind examined every flaw in her friends and family."

❸ Starting with the first blank, two choices fit perfectly, (1) and (4). Choice (3) might seem okay at first, but a *public* life does not necessarily mean "work." Since we have other selections that are more precise, we don't need one that is not a strong match. Of (1) and (4), choice (1) can be eliminated because the second word, *disorganized,* is contradictory to the sentence. We were told that she has a systematic approach, not a chaotic one. Choice (4) is perfect for both blanks. We'll quickly check the remaining two to confirm this. Choices (2) and (5) can be eliminated because the first word in each is the opposite of what we're looking for. The first blank describes her work life, not her "private" or "family" life.

❹ *Her systematic approach to scientific research was often rewarded in her* professional *life, but it proved disastrous when her methodical mind examined every*

flaw in her friends and family, preventing her from truly appreciating others.

5. **Choice (5)**

❶ The long descriptive clause at the beginning of this sentence sets the stage for figuring out the first blank. We're told that it's required that a determination, or decision, be made. So, what do judges have to do? The last clause answers this for us. It says *when in fact the evidence may not be* something, which suggests that the evidence may not always be conclusive. So, judges must be *forced* to act like the verdict is a good one, yet the end of the sentence implies that the evidence may not be quite so convincing.

❷ A prephrase of this answer might be, "A judge is forced to act as if a verdict is right, when in fact the evidence may not be compelling."

❸ Choice (5) immediately looks good, since both *self-evident* and *conclusive* match our predictions. We'll hold onto it, and check the others. Choice (1) can be eliminated because the first word, *negotiable,* is contrary to the sentence. We're told that the law requires that a *definite determination* be made—not a negotiable one. The second word in choices (2) and (4) does not work, since it's not logical that the evidence may not be *accessible* or *admissible.* It would have had to be both *accessible* and *admissible* in order for a decision to be reached based upon it. Choice (3) is out because evidence that is not *insubstantial* would be substantial, which is contrary to the meaning of this sentence. We want a word that implies that the evidence was not good enough.

❹ *Because law and custom require that a definite determination be made, a judge is forced to behave as if a verdict is* self-evident, *when in fact the evidence may not be* conclusive.

6. **Choice (1)**

❶ The first blank will be filled with a word that describes a characteristic of businessmen. The second part of this sentence tells us what type of word we're looking for in the first blank as well as the second. We're told that *whatever qualities they may lack,* they are *paragons,* or excellent models, of something. Normally the word paragon is used in a positive light. So, we don't know exactly what quality will fill these blanks, but most likely it will be positive. In any case, both words will reflect the same quality, so they will be similar in meaning.

❷ It would be hard to predict the words for these blanks, so we'll just evaluate each choice carefully, looking for a pair of words that are positive and have similar meanings.

❸ Choice (2) can be eliminated because it is negative. Choices (3), (4), and (5) can be eliminated because the words in each are contradictory or have no real link between them. *Virtuous* and *deceit* are opposites of each other, and being successful and having great ambition might be related, but do not have to be. Similarly, it's difficult to see how being *cautious* and having *achievement(s)* are necessarily linked.

❹ *The author presumably believes that all businessmen are* clever, *for her main characters, whatever qualities they may lack, are* virtual paragons *of* ingenuity.

7. Choice (5)

❶ The semicolon is a road sign that tells us that this is a "straight-ahead" sentence. The second half must agree with the first. If *personal correspondence* reflects the *spirit of the age,* then Swift's epistles, or letters, must reflect the spirit of this. That is, whatever quality that is represented by the first blank must also agree with the quality represented in the second blank.

❷ It would be hard to predict the words for these blanks, so we'll evaluate each choice carefully, looking for a pair of words that have similar meanings.

❸ Choice (5) works the best: *vitriol* is abuse, so this would mirror his society's love of *elegant disparagement.* Choice (1) can be eliminated because there is no link between *profundities* and *ditties* (songs). Choices (2), (3), and (4) can also be eliminated because the words in each are not necessarily linked.

❹ *Personal correspondence is often a marvelous reflection of the spirit of an age; the subtle* vitriol *of Swift's epistles mirrored the eighteenth-century delight in* elegant *disparagement.*

8. Choice (4)

❶ The road sign *and* directs us to the correct answer for this sentence. Both blanks occur in the second half of the sentence, so the first half will provide most of the information. We learn that Ginnie expects to be published every time she submits something. The words *and this*

time are a "straight-ahead" road sign that indicates the second half will support this notion. This time, Ginnie will probably be right.

❷ A good prephrase here would be, "This time, her expectation is likely to be realized."

❸ Choices (2), (3), and (4) all meet our prediction for the first blank, so we'll check the second word to eliminate the wrong ones. Looking at the selections for the second blank, choice (4), *vindicated,* is the only one that allows for her expectations to be fulfilled this time. We'll hold on to this answer, and check the others. Choice (2) does not work because *piqued* means aroused or excited. Since she always expects to be published, using the word *piqued* here would indicate that this time would be no different than all the other times. But the sentence indicates that *this time* her expectations will be fulfilled, which implies that this may not be true of all the times she submits. Choice (3) is out because *dampened* is the opposite of what we want. Likewise, choices (1) and (5) can be eliminated because the second word in each has a negative connotation. Each suggests that Ginnie will be disappointed. We want something that says her expectations will be fulfilled.

❹ *Ginnie expects her every submission to be published or selected for performance, and this time her* optimism *is likely to be* vindicated.

9. Choice (2)

❶ If the opponent was *frustrated* that the governor's support was not *eroded* by something, that thing must be negative. You wouldn't expect support to be eroded because of something positive about the candidate. We know from the phrase after the blank that this negative thing has something to do with *significant issues.* So, we're looking for a word that would indicate something negative about the governor and significant issues.

❷ There are many predictions that would work here, but some of the most obvious would be his "lack of interest in" or "lack of concern for" or "lack of knowledge of significant issues."

❸ We don't have a strong prediction here, so we'll have to evaluate each choice carefully. We need to also keep in mind that the word *of* follows the blank, so the correct choice will sound idiomatically correct with *of.* Choice (2) looks good right away, since *misapprehension* means "misunderstanding." We'll hold onto it and check the others. Choice (1) won't work, because you wouldn't expect the public to be unhappy about the *exaggeration* of issues that were important. They would be glad that those issues were getting attention. Choices (3), (4), and (5) are not negative in quality. There would be nothing wrong with the governor's *discussion, selection,* or *acknowledgment* of significant issues. If the governor did any of these things, the opponent would have no reason to believe that the public should be negatively impacted by them.

❹ *His opponent found it extremely frustrating that the governor's solid support from the voting public was not eroded by his misapprehension of significant issues.*

10. Choice (3)

❶ The road sign *but* before the blank indicates that a "detour" or shift in direction is coming. The spokesperson seems unsure of a victory, but feels something about facing the alternative. After the comma, we get an idea of what that something is. Apparently, the spokesperson doesn't want to admit it, due to a superstition that just saying it would make it happen.

❷ A good prephrase here would be, "The spokesperson is afraid to face the alternative, as if admitting the possibility would make it happen."

❸ Choice (3) is a perfect match. We'll check the others just to be sure. For (1) to work, the road sign before the blank would have to be *and,* indicating that the two things are closely linked. The spokesperson is unsure of the victory and unsure of facing the alternative. Even that doesn't make great sense, but *unsure of* will definitely not work with the "detour" road sign *but* before the blank. Choice (2) is acceptable, since *complacent* means "indifferent." Choices (4) and (5) are contradicted in the sentence. If the spokesperson is *uncertain* of the victory, he couldn't be *certain of* facing the future. And if the spokesperson is fearful of something, as we're told at the end of the sentence, then it's unlikely that he'd feel *helped by* it.

❹ *Our spokesperson seems to be uncertain of our eventual victory but is fearful of facing the alternative, as if merely admitting the possibility of defeat would lead to the dreaded thing itself.*

Chapter 3: **GRE Analogies**

The first step towards testing your best on GRE analogies is to get familiar with the format. Analogies test your vocabulary and your ability to figure out the relationships between pairs of words. You're given a pair of capitalized words (for example, POTATO : VEGETABLE), and you're asked to determine their relationship, then identify the answer choice that has the same relationship.

The directions for this question type look like this:

> **Directions:** In this question, a related pair of words is followed by five lettered pairs of words. Choose the one pair that best expresses a relationship similar to that expressed in the original pair.

On the GRE, the more questions you get right, the more difficult the analogies you encounter will become. If you perform well on GRE Verbal, you can expect to see analogies towards the end of the test that feature quite difficult, esoteric vocabulary.

THE FOUR FUNDAMENTALS

To improve your skill in answering GRE analogy questions, you'll need to familiarize yourself with the basic principles for approaching them—and you'll need some practice. The Four Fundamentals below will help you to increase your skills and confidence as you approach the day of the test. And with skills and confidence, you'll be able to earn points on Test Day!

GRE Analogy Questions Consist of Two Words

The two words, called the **stem pair**, are followed by five answer choices, each consisting of two words that are also separated by colons. Analogy questions on the GRE CAT look like this:

1. LITER : VOLUME ::

    ① bottle : can
    ② knob : radio
    ③ scale : height
    ④ gram : weight
    ⑤ juice : vitamin

 WHAT'S A STEM PAIR?

Analogy questions consist of two words–the stem pair–that are separated by a colon. Stem pairs look like this:

> PREPARATION : SUCCESS ::

 WHAT'S A BRIDGE?

A bridge is a short sentence that connects the two words in the stem pair. You should always build a bridge before you look at the answer choices.

There Will Always Be a Direct and Necessary Relationship between the Words in the Stem Pair

You can express the relationship between the two stem words by making a short sentence that we call a *bridge*. Your goals when you build an analogy bridge should be to keep it as short and as clear as possible.

For the analogy above, a strong bridge would be:

A LITER is by definition a measure of VOLUME.

Try to Build a "Bridge" before Looking at the Answer Choices

Because the GRE CAT is a standardized test, you'll find that certain kinds of bridges appear on the test over and over again. At Kaplan, we call these frequently appearing bridges Classic Bridges. Getting familiar with Classic Bridges now will help you quickly recognize these relationships when you encounter them on the GRE CAT.

The Five Classic Bridges

1. *Definition* ("is always" or "is never")
2. *Function or Purpose*
3. *Lack*
4. *Characteristic Actions or Items*
5. *Degree* (sometimes to the point of excess)

Each of the five classic bridges are illustrated below:

1. *The Definition Bridge*
   CYGNET : SWAN   A CYGNET is a young SWAN.

2. *The Function or Purpose Bridge*
   TRUSS : SUPPORT   A TRUSS is used as a SUPPORT.

3. *The Lack Bridge*

    LOUT : GRACE   A LOUT lacks GRACE.

4. *The Characteristic Actions or Items Bridge*

    SKUNK : SCENT   A SKUNK defends itself with its SCENT.

5. *The Degree Bridge (sometimes to the point of excess)*

    INTEREST : ENTHRALL   To INTEREST greatly is to ENTHRALL.

Remember the five classic bridges and keep them in mind as you practice for the GRE.

Watch Out for Common Wrong Answer Types

Because the bridges on GRE Analogies are predictable, wrong answer types to these questions are also predictable. If you get stumped on any GRE analogy, you can earn points by ruling out as many wrong answer choices as you can and then picking from the remaining choices. Here are some of the typical wrong answer choices that appear on GRE Analogies:

Unrelated Words

A pair of words with no strong relationship is a common wrong answer.

Same Subject Trap

The words in the answer choice are in the same fields (or have the same subject) as the words in the stem pair, but don't have the same bridge.

"Both Are" Bridges

This involves words that aren't related to each other, but are both related to a third word. For instance, the words *bracelet : necklace* refer to pieces of jewelry. Yet a *bracelet* has no necessary connection to a *necklace.*

Context Traps

These are words that often appear together in context, but don't have any relationship; for instance, *mitigating : circumstance.*

Reverse Analogy

The bridge would be right if the order of the words were reversed.

 **WHAT MAKES A STRONG BRIDGE?**

You might think that the words *apple* and *pie* have a strong bridge. Don't be fooled. You can make many things other than pies out of apples, such as apple juice and apple sauce. And there are many different types of pies. *Apple* and *fruit*, on the other hand, do have a strong bridge. An apple is a type of fruit. This is always true: It's a strong, definite relationship.

Au Contraire or Opposite Bridge

The bridge is the exact opposite of the bridge between the words in the stem pair.

Irrelevant Bridge

The bridge is strong, but it doesn't have anything to do with the bridge in the stem pair.

Drill

Identify the Classic Bridges in the following stem pairs.

1. MISER : CHEAP — *Definition*
2. BOOR : TACT — *Lack*
3. RULER : MEASURE — *Function*
4. ELATED : HAPPY — *Degree*
5. BEAK : BIRD — *Characteristic*

Now build a bridge for each of the following stem pairs.

1. CHICKEN : POULTRY — *Character* — Chicken is a type of poultry
2. FEAR : TERROR — *Degree*
3. LOOM : WEAVE — *Function* — A loom is to weave
4. RECLUSE : SOLITARY — *Defined*
5. LANGUID : ENERGY — *Lack* — Languid lacks

THE KAPLAN FOUR-STEP METHOD FOR ANALOGIES

Now that you have learned the basics for tackling Analogies questions, you're ready for Kaplan's strategic approach to Analogies on the GRE. Approaching Analogies in a systematic manner is the best way to avoid common pitfalls and improve your score.

❶ **Find a strong bridge between the stem words.**

- In most cases, the more precisely you can express the connection between the two words, the better. A precise formulation is more likely to help you find the right answer.

❷ **Plug the answer choices into the bridge.**

- Look for the answer choice pair that has the same relationship as the stem pair.
- Immediately eliminate answer choices that don't fit the bridge.
- Always try all the answer choices; you might find that more than one answer choice works with the bridge that you built.
- If only one answer choice works with the bridge you built, select that answer choice.

❸ **Adjust the bridge, if necessary.**

- If more than one answer choice works, you'll have to narrow your bridge (make it more precise).
- If none of the answer choices work, you probably need to expand it (make it more general).
- Consider alternate definitions for the stem words. Perhaps your bridge uses the wrong definition of a word.

❹ **If stuck, build bridges between answer choice pairs and work backwards.**

- Eliminate all answer choices that have no strong bridge.
- Eliminate all answer choices that have an identical bridge to another answer choice.
- Beware of answer choices that reverse the bridge.

Try It Out

Let's apply the Kaplan Four-Step Method for Analogies to an example.

2.　HANGAR : AIRCRAFT : :

　　① orchestra : music
　　② vault : money
　　③ hand : fingers
　　④ farm : trees
　　⑤ ecosystem : insect

❶ Begin by building a bridge: A HANGAR is a place built to keep AIRCRAFT.

❷ Now plug each of your answer choices into your bridge "a BLANK is a place to keep BLANK."

Is an *orchestra* a place built to keep *music*? No. Eliminate choice (1).

Is a *vault* a place built to keep *money*? Yes, so keep choice (2).

Is a *hand* a place built to keep a *fingers*? No, so eliminate this choice as well.

Is a *farm* a place built to keep a *trees*? Maybe, maybe not. Eliminate choice (4).

Is an *ecosystem* a place built to keep *insects*? No. Eliminate choice (5).

❸ There is no need to adjust the bridge, since only answer choice (2) worked.

❹ If we needed to work backwards, we could have eliminated choices (4) and (5), since there is no strong bridge between the words in these pairs.

PRACTICE SET

Now try the following Analogy questions on your own, using the Kaplan Four-Step Method. Give yourself a maximum of 30–45 seconds to do each example.

1. LUCID : OBSCURITY ::

   ① ambiguous : doubt
   ② provident : planning
   ③ furtive : legality
   ④ economical : extravagance
   ⑤ secure : violence

2. ATTENTIVE : RAPT ::

   ① loyal : unscrupulous
   ② critical : derisive
   ③ inventive : innovative
   ④ jealous : envious
   ⑤ kind : considerate

3. CLEAVER : BUTCHER ::

   ① palette : artist
   ② stage : dancer
   ③ dictionary : poet
   ④ lock : burglar
   ⑤ chisel : sculptor

Think about how you solved these Analogies questions. To maximize your score, it's important to start practicing these skills now. On the pages that follow, you'll find sets of GRE Analogies practice questions that will help you to hone your skills with this question type. Try these practice sets under timed conditions, moving from one question to the next at a rapid pace. Complete, strategic explanations to all of these questions follow so that you can check your answers and learn the most efficient means for completing each question correctly.

The answers to this section appear on the next page.

ANSWER KEY

Testlike Questions

1. (4)
2. (2)

Drill

1. Definition
2. Lack
3. Function
4. Degree
5. Characteristic Items/Actions

1. A CHICKEN is by definition a type of POULTRY.
2. To experience extreme FEAR is by definition to experience TERROR.
3. The purpose of a LOOM is by definition to WEAVE.
4. A RECLUSE is by definition SOLITARY.
5. Someone who's LANGUID is by definition lacking in ENERGY.

Practice Set

1. (4)
2. (2)
3. (5)

ANALOGIES: TEST 1

Time: 10 Questions/10 Minutes

Directions: In each question below, a related pair of words is followed by five lettered pairs of words. Choose the one pair that best expresses a relationship similar to that expressed in the original pair.

1. CYGNET : SWAN ::

   ① ring : jewel
   ② kid : goat
   ③ gander : goose
   ④ stamp : seal
   ⑤ message : pigeon

2. LEGIBLE : DECIPHER ::

   ① intelligible : understand
   ② cautious : tread
   ③ laudable : expect
   ④ nefarious : construe
   ⑤ written : write

3. DEHYDRATION : SATURATED ::

   ① antagonism : irksome
   ② restitution : paid
   ③ bankruptcy : wealthy
   ④ modernization : destructive
   ⑤ colonization : new

4. CASTIGATE : WRONGDOING ::

   ① congratulate : success
   ② amputate : crime
   ③ annotate : consultation
   ④ deface : falsehood
   ⑤ fulminate : habit

5. CUR : BASE ::

   ① victor : defeated
   ② octogenarian : wise
   ③ genius : twisted
   ④ villain : evil
   ⑤ athlete : heavy

6. SUBSTANTIAL : AMOUNT ::

   ① sufficient : effort
   ② compulsory : importance
   ③ imperative : desperation
   ④ extensive : size
   ⑤ simplistic : intelligence

7. PARTY : POLICY ::

   ① libation : law
   ② faith : doctrine
   ③ state : petition
   ④ clan : opposition
   ⑤ public : outcry

8. PATHETIC : RUTH ::

   ① cryptic : puzzlement
   ② lowly : suffering
   ③ wrong : punishment
   ④ beautiful : sorrow
   ⑤ crippled : loathing

9. SKUNK : SCENT ::

   ① tiger : stripes
   ② elephant : trunk
   ③ fawn : camouflage
   ④ porcupine : quills
   ⑤ shark : fins

10. LOUT : GRACE ::

    ① pedant : knowledge
    ② poltroon : courage
    ③ elder : wisdom
    ④ aristocrat : manner
    ⑤ impostor : identity

ANSWERS

1. Choice (2)

❶ A CYGNET is a young SWAN.

❷ Is a *ring* a young *jewel*? No. Eliminate.

Is a *kid* a young *goat*? Yes. Keep this one.

Is a *gander* a young *goose*? No, so eliminate.

Is a *stamp* a young *seal*? No. Eliminate.

Is a *message* a young *pigeon*? Nope. Eliminate.

❸ There's no need to adjust the bridge, since only one answer choice worked.

❹ Working backwards, a *ring* can contain jewels, but doesn't have to. A *kid* is a young *goat*, and a *gander* is a male *goose*. A *stamp* can be used as a *seal*, but not necessarily. And a *message* can be carried by a *pigeon*, but doesn't need to be. Only choices (2) and (3) work, and (3) is a "same subject" temptation—beware.

2. Choice (1)

❶ Something LEGIBLE is easy to DECIPHER.

❷ Is something *intelligible* easy to *understand*? Yes. Keep this one.

Is something *cautious* easy to *tread*? No. Eliminate.

Is something *laudable* easy to *expect*? No. Eliminate.

Is something *nefarious* easy to *construe*? No. Eliminate.

Is something *written* easy to *write*? No. Eliminate.

❸ There's no need to adjust the bridge, since only one answer choice worked.

❹ Working backwards, there is no strong bridge between *cautious* and *tread* or between *laudable* and *expect*. It's rare that the GRE would have the right answer contain two forms of the same word, such as in answer choice (5). So even if you don't recognize *nefarious*, which means "evil," you can eliminate several choices.

3. Choice (3)

❶ Something characterized by DEHYDRATION is not SATURATED.

❷ Is something characterized by *antagonism* not *irksome*? No. Eliminate.

Is something characterized by *restitution* not *paid*? No. Eliminate.

Is something characterized by *bankruptcy* not *wealthy*? Yes, so keep this one.

Is something characterized by *modernization* not *destructive*? No. Eliminate.

Is something characterized by *colonization* not *new*? No. Eliminate.

❸ There's no need to adjust the bridge, since only one answer choice worked.

❹ Working backwards, there is no strong bridge for answer choices (4) or (5). *Antagonism* and *irksome* are similar, as an antagonist is often irksome to others. Likewise, *restitution* is compensation, or payment.

4. Choice (1)

❶ People CASTIGATE others for their WRONGDOINGs.

❷ Do people *congratulate* others for their *success*? Yes. Keep this one.

Do people *amputate* others for their *crimes*? No. Eliminate.

Do people *annotate* others for their *consultations*? No. Eliminate.

Do people *deface* others for their *falsehoods*? No. Eliminate.

Do people *fulminate* others for their *habits*? No. Eliminate.

❸ There's no need to adjust the bridge, since only one answer choice worked.

❹ Working backwards, there is no strong bridge between *amputate* and *crime* or between *annotate* and *consultation*. *Deface* means "to disfigure," which doesn't have a strong bridge to *falsehood*. *Fulminate* means "to explode," which doesn't have anything to do with *habits*.

5. Choice (4)

❶ A CUR is characterized by being BASE.

❷ Is a *victor* characterized by being *defeated*? Nope.

Is an *octogenarian* characterized by being *wise*? Not necessarily.

Is a *genius* characterized by being *twisted*? No. Eliminate.

Is a *villain* characterized as being *evil*? Yep. Keep this choice.

Is an *athlete* characterized as being *heavy*? Not necessarily.

❸ There's no need to adjust the bridge, since only one answer choice worked.

❹ Working backwards, there is no strong bridge between *athlete* and *heavy,* nor is there a strong bridge between *twisted* and *genius.*

6. Choice (4)

❶ SUBSTANTIAL is large in AMOUNT.

❷ Is *sufficient* large in *effort*? No, sufficient is enough effort. Eliminate.

Is *compulsory* large in *importance*? No, it's a required performance. Eliminate.

Is *imperative* large in *desperation*? No. Eliminate.

Is *extensive* large in *size*? That's pretty good. Keep this choice.

Is *simplistic* large in *intelligence*? No. Eliminate.

❸ There's no need to adjust the bridge, since only one answer choice worked.

❹ Working backwards, there is no strong bridge between *imperative* and *desperation.*

7. Choice (2)

❶ Members of a PARTY share a common POLICY.

❷ Do members of a *libation* share a common *law*? Makes no sense, as a libation is a drink. Eliminate.

Do members of a *faith* share a common *doctrine*? This one works.

Do members of a *state* share a common *petition*? No. Eliminate.

Do members of a *clan* share a common *opposition*? No. Eliminate.

Do members of a *public* share a common *outcry*? Possibly, but a public can also be divided. Eliminate.

❸ There's no need to adjust the bridge, since only one answer choice worked.

❹ Working backward, there is no strong bridge between *state* and *petition* or *clan* and *opposition*. Eliminate these choices right away.

8. Choice (1)

❶ Something PATHETIC causes others to feel RUTH (which means "mercy" or "sympathy." Perhaps you know the word *ruthless*).

❷ Does something *cryptic* cause others to feel *puzzlement*? Yes. Keep this one.

Does something *lowly* cause others to feel *suffering*? No, usually the lowly individual feels suffering.

Does something *wrong* cause others to feel *punishment*? No. Eliminate.

Does something *beautiful* cause others to feel *sorrow*? No. Usually, beauty has the opposite effect. Eliminate.

Does something *crippled* cause others to feel *loathing*? No. Eliminate.

❸ There's no need to adjust the bridge, since only one answer choice worked.

❹ Working backwards, there is no strong bridge between *wrong* and *punishment* or between *crippled* and *loathing.* Eliminate these two choices.

9. Choice (4)

❶ A SKUNK defends itself with its SCENT.

❷ Does a *tiger* does not defend itself with its *stripes*? No, it uses its stripes to hide itself while it stalks prey.

An *elephant* does not use its *trunk* specifically for defense. Eliminate.

A *fawn* does not defend itself with its *camouflage*; the camouflage simply helps it hide. A fawn does not physically defend itself using the camouflage.

A *porcupine* does indeed defend itself with its *quills*. Keep this one.

Does a *shark* defend itself with its *fins*? No. Eliminate.

❸ There's no need to adjust the bridge, since only one answer choice worked.

❹ You can eliminate choice (5), because a *shark* swims with its *fins*, and a *skunk* doesn't use its *scent* for any sort of locomotion.

10. **Choice (2)**

   ❶ A LOUT lacks GRACE.

   ❷ Does a *pedant* lack *knowledge*? No, he is annoying because of the way he spouts his knowledge.

   Does a *poltroon* (whimpering coward) lack *courage*? Yes. Keep this choice.

   Does a *elder* lack *wisdom*? No, in fact, in most cultures elders are considered the wisest. Eliminate.

   Does an *aristocrat* lack *manner*? Depends what type of manner you're talking about. Eliminate.

   Does an *impostor* lack *identity*? No, an impostor takes over someone else's identity. Eliminate.

   ❸ There's no need to adjust the bridge, since only one answer choice worked.

   ❹ Choice (4) can be eliminated right away because there's no real bridge between *aristocrat* and *manner*. *Manner* is a general term for fashion or style. People don't lack manner, they just have different manners.

ANALOGIES: TEST 2

Time: 10 Questions/10 Minutes

Directions: In each question below, a related pair of words is followed by five lettered pairs of words. Choose the one pair that best expresses a relationship similar to that expressed in the original pair.

1. RECANTATION : BELIEF ::
   1. repetition : catechism
   2. reincarnation : soul
   3. untruth : axiom
   4. vacillation : vow
   5. repeal : law

2. CEPHALIC : SKULL ::
   1. notable : achievement
   2. cylindrical : vertebrae
   3. neural : nerves
   4. angular : scapula
   5. audible : apparition

3. PLUMMET : DESCEND ::
   1. kick : boot
   2. whirl : turn
   3. indicate : show
   4. decorate : nullify
   5. begin : conclude

4. RIG : TEAM ::
   1. train : locomotive
   2. steamer : piston
   3. sled : rail
   4. car : truck
   5. windjammer : crew

5. INTEREST : ENTHRALL ::
   1. corrupt : tempt
   2. squeeze : crush
   3. buoy : undergird
   4. abstain : surrender
   5. reproach : scold

6. ENLISTMENT : CONSCRIPTION ::
   1. rapprochement : arbitration
   2. surrender : bombardment
   3. resignation : dismissal
   4. contemplation : instruction
   5. acceptance : rejection

7. COBBLER : LEATHER ::
   1. chandler : wax
   2. executrix : paper
   3. actor : words
   4. cartwright : wheels
   5. prosthetist : limbs

8. ELECTRICITY : WIRE ::
   1. fluid : pipe
   2. car : highway
   3. river : bank
   4. light : bulb
   5. music : instrument

9. INFLAMMABLE : IGNITED ::
   1. fragile : shattered
   2. flexible : broken
   3. somber : mourned
   4. famous : plagiarized
   5. small : magnified

10. SCOLD : BERATE ::
    1. predict : foresee
    2. threaten : impend
    3. counsel : advise
    4. retreat : retire
    5. respect : venerate

4/10

KAPLAN

ANSWERS

1. Choice (5)

❶ A RECANTATION is the withdrawal of a BELIEF.

❷ Is a *repetition* the withdrawal of a *catechism*? No, there's no bridge between these words. Eliminate.

Is a *reincarnation* the withdrawal of a *soul*? No. Eliminate.

Is an *untruth* the withdrawal of an *axiom*? No. Eliminate.

Is a *vacillation* the withdrawal of a *vow*? No. Eliminate.

Is a *repeal* the withdrawal of a *law*? Yes. Since no other choice works with this bridge, this is your answer.

❸ There's no need to adjust the bridge, since only one answer choice worked.

❹ None of the other choices have strong bridges.

2. Choice (3)

❶ CEPHALIC means having to do with the SKULL.

❷ Does *notable* mean having to do with *achievement*? No, although this is a common phrase. Eliminate.

Does *cylindrical* mean having to do with *vertebrae*? No. Eliminate.

Does *neural* mean having to do with *nerves*? Yes. Keep this alternative.

Does *angular* mean having to do with the *scapula*? No. Eliminate.

Does *audible* mean having to do with an *apparition*? No. Eliminate.

❸ There's no need to adjust the bridge, since only one answer choice worked.

❹ None of the other choices has a strong bridge.

3. Choice (2)

❶ To PLUMMET is to DESCEND furiously or with great speed.

❷ *Kick* and *boot* are synonymous; they aren't degrees of one another. Eliminate.

To *whirl* is to turn *furiously*. Keep this choice.

Indicate is synonymous with *show*. Eliminate.

Decorate and *nullify* have no strong bridge. Eliminate.

Begin and *conclude* are antonyms. They don't match our bridge, so eliminate.

❸ There's no need to adjust the bridge, since only one answer choice worked.

❹ Eliminate choice (4) because there's no strong bridge. Eliminate (1) and (3) because the answer choices have the same bridge.

4. Choice (1)

❶ A RIG is pulled by a TEAM.

❷ Is a *train* pulled by a *locomotive*? Yep. Keep it.

Is a *steamer* pulled by a *piston*? No. Eliminate.

Is a *sled* pulled by a *rail*? No. Eliminate.

Is a *car* pulled by a *truck*? No. Eliminate.

Is a *windjammer* pulled by a *crew*? No. Eliminate.

❸ There's no need to adjust the bridge, since only one answer choice worked.

❹ Answer choices (2) and (3) don't have strong bridges.

5. Choice (2)

❶ To INTEREST greatly is to ENTHRALL.

❷ Is to *corrupt* greatly to *tempt*? While these words are used together, they don't share this bridge.

Is to *squeeze* greatly to *crush*? Yes. Keep this choice.

Is to *buoy* greatly to *undergird*? No. Eliminate.

Is to *abstain* greatly to *surrender*? No. If you surrender, you fail to abstain from something. Eliminate.

Is to *reproach* greatly to *scold*? No, these words are synonyms. Eliminate.

❸ There's no need to adjust the bridge, since only one answer choice worked.

❹ Choices (1) and (3) do not have strong bridges, so eliminate them.

6. Choice (3)

❶ ENLISTMENT is voluntary, while CONSCRIPTION is forced.

❷ Is *rapprochement* voluntary while *arbitration* is forced? No, neither is usually voluntary. Eliminate.

Is *surrender* voluntary while *bombardment* is forced? No. Surrender is not a voluntary form of bombardment. Eliminate.

Is *resignation* voluntary while *dismissal* is forced? Yes. Keep it.

Is *contemplation* voluntary while *instruction* is forced? No. Eliminate.

Is *acceptance* voluntary while *rejection* is forced? No, these words are antonyms. Eliminate.

❸ There's no need to adjust the bridge, since only one answer choice worked.

❹ Choices (1), (2), and (4) have no strong bridges, so eliminate.

7. Choice (1)

❶ A COBBLER's raw material is LEATHER.

❷ Is a *chandler's* raw material *wax*? Yes, a chandler makes candles. Keep this choice.

Is an *executrix's* raw material *paper*? No, an executrix is a female executor. Eliminate.

Is an *actor's* raw material *words*? Not really.

Is a *cartwright's* raw material *wheels*? No; although *cartwright* is the name for someone who makes wheels, wheels aren't a raw material. Eliminate.

Is a *prosthetist's* raw material *limbs*? No. Eliminate.

❸ There's no need to adjust the bridge, since only one answer choice worked.

❹ Choices (2) and (3) don't have strong bridges, so eliminate them.

8. Choice (1)

❶ ELECTRICITY runs through a man-made conduit called a WIRE.

❷ Do *fluids* run through a man-made conduit called a *pipe*? Yes. Keep this one.

Do *cars* run through a man-made conduit called a *highway*? No, they run on a highway. Eliminate.

Does a *river* run through a man-made conduit called a *bank*? No, a bank is the side of the river, not a conduit.

Does *light* run through a *bulb*? No, it is emitted by a bulb. Eliminate.

Does *music* run through an *instrument*? No, it is created by an instrument. Eliminate.

❸ There's no need to adjust the bridge, since only one answer choice worked.

❹ Eliminate (4) and (5) because they have the same bridge.

9. Choice (1)

❶ INFLAMMABLE means easily IGNITED. Be careful—in this case *IN* doesn't mean "not."

❷ Does *fragile* mean easily *shattered*? Yes. Keep it.

Does *flexible* mean easily *broken*? No, flexible things are usually harder to break. Eliminate.

Is something *somber* easily *mourned*? No. Someone who's somber may be in mourning. Eliminate.

Is something *famous* easily *plagiarized*? There's no strong bridge here. Eliminate.

Is something *small* easily *magnified*? No. Eliminate.

❸ There's no need to adjust the bridge, since only one answer choice worked.

❹ Choices (3), (4), and (5) all lack strong bridges.

10. Choice (5)

❶ To SCOLD greatly is to BERATE.

❷ Is to *predict* greatly to *foresee*? No, these words are synonyms. Eliminate.

Is to *threaten* greatly to *impend*? No. Eliminate.

Is to *counsel* greatly to *advise*? No, these are synonyms. Eliminate.

Is to *retreat* greatly to *retire*? No. Eliminate.

Is to *respect* greatly to *venerate*? Yes. Since this is the only choice that works, it's the answer.

❸ There's no need to adjust the bridge, since only one answer choice worked.

❹ You can eliminate (1) and (3) because they have the same bridge.

ANALOGIES: TEST 3

Time: 10 Questions/10 Minutes

Directions: In each question below, a related pair of words is followed by five lettered pairs of words. Choose the one pair that best expresses a relationship similar to that expressed in the original pair.

1. TRUSS : SUPPORT ::

   ① calcium : bone
   ② fence : barrier
   ③ tile : patio
   ④ wood : burn
   ⑤ tobacco : cigarette

2. REEL : TAPE ::

   ① ball : string
   ② turntable : record
   ③ tire : wheel
   ④ skein : yarn
   ⑤ spool : thread

3. SHINGLE : ROOF ::

   ① rind : melon
   ② armor : knight
   ③ feather : wing
   ④ patch : cloth
   ⑤ canopy : bed

4. LEGERDEMAIN : MAGICIAN ::

   ① rhetoric : orator
   ② baggage : immigrant
   ③ justice : lawyer
   ④ map : cartographer
   ⑤ tractor : farmer

5. INDISPUTABLE : QUESTION ::

   ① unlikely : know
   ② amoral : perform
   ③ incredible : prove
   ④ immutable : change
   ⑤ insoluble : submerge

6. UNSCATHED : DAMAGE ::

   ① ameliorated : improvement
   ② obliterated : invisibility
   ③ rolled : flatness
   ④ shaken : homogeneity
   ⑤ arid : dampness

7. PROTRACTION : DURATION ::

   ① extension : length
   ② retraction : instant
   ③ corruption : truth
   ④ taxation : wealth
   ⑤ altercation : shape

8. CHARACTERIZATION : PARODY ::

   ① serialization : novel
   ② drama : musical
   ③ theater : vaudeville
   ④ saga : epic
   ⑤ portrait : caricature

9. STARS : GALAXY ::

   ① cells : prison
   ② sand : dune
   ③ nuclei : atom
   ④ eggs : nest
   ⑤ hair : head

10. ATROPHY : INACTIVITY ::

    ① resistance : timidity
    ② frown : anger
    ③ growth : youth
    ④ rot : refrigeration
    ⑤ debt : overspending

KAPLAN

ANSWERS

1. Choice (2)

❶ A TRUSS is used as a SUPPORT.

❷ Is a *calcium* used as a *bone*? No. Calcium is one of the elements that make up bones. Eliminate.

  Is a *fence* used as a *barrier*? Yes, keep this choice.

  Is a *tile* used as a *patio*? No, sometimes tiles are coverings on patios. Eliminate.

  Is *wood* used to *burn*? It could be, but wood is also used for other things. Eliminate.

  Is *tobacco* used to *cigarette*? No, tobacco is part of a cigarette. Eliminate.

❸ There's no need to adjust the bridge, since only one answer choice worked.

❹ You can eliminate (3) and (4) because they lack strong bridges.

2. Choice (5)

❶ A REEL is an object that TAPE winds around.

❷ Is a *ball* an object that *string* winds around? No, string forms a ball when wound. Eliminate.

  Is a *turntable* an object that a *record* winds around? No. Eliminate.

  Is a *tire* an object that a *wheel* winds around? No, a tire sits on a wheel. Eliminate.

  Is a *skein* an object that *yarn* winds around? No, a bunch of yarn is called a skein. Eliminate.

  Is a *spool* an object that *thread* winds around? Yes. Here's your answer.

❸ There's no need to adjust the bridge, since only one answer choice worked.

❹ You can eliminate (1) and (4) because they have the same bridge.

3. Choice (3)

❶ Many SHINGLEs make up the outer covering of a ROOF.

❷ A *melon* only has one *rind*. Eliminate.

  Many *armors* do not make up the outer covering of a *knight*. Eliminate.

  Many *feathers* make up the outer covering of a *wing*. Keep it.

A *patch* is a small piece of *cloth*. Eliminate.

A *canopy* is a cloth that sits above a *bed,* but can be used in many other places as well. Eliminate.

❸ There's no need to adjust the bridge, since only one answer choice worked.

❹ You can eliminate (5) because it lacks a strong bridge.

4. Choice (1)

❶ LEGERDEMAIN is a skill used by a MAGICIAN.

❷ *Rhetoric* is a skill used by an *orator.* Keep this one.

  Baggage is not a skill used by an *immigrant.* Eliminate.

  Justice is not a skill used by a *lawyer.* Eliminate.

  A *map* is a product of a *cartographer,* not a skill used by one. Eliminate.

  A *tractor* is machinery used by a *farmer,* but isn't a skill as legerdemain is. Eliminate.

❸ There's no need to adjust the bridge, since only one answer choice worked.

❹ You can eliminate (3) because it lacks a strong bridge.

5. Choice (4)

❶ Something that's INDISPUTABLE cannot be QUESTIONed.

❷ The statement "something *unlikely* cannot be *known*" doesn't make sense. Eliminate.

  There's no bridge between *amoral* and *perform.* Eliminate.

  Can something that's *incredible* not be *proved*? No, it's just hard to believe. Eliminate.

  Can something that's *immutable* not be *changed*? True. Keep this choice.

  Can something *insoluble* be *submerged*? Yes, but it can't be dissolved. Eliminate this choice.

❸ There's no need to adjust the bridge, since only one answer choice worked.

❹ (1), (2), and (5) lack a strong bridge.

6. Choice (5)

❶ Something UNSCATHED lacks DAMAGE.

❷ Does something *ameliorated* lack *improvement*? No. Eliminate.

  Does something *obliterated* lack *invisibility*? No. Eliminate.

Does something *rolled* lack *flatness*? No, things are usually rolled to make them flat. Eliminate.

Does something *shaken* lack *homogeneity*? No, shaking usually increases homogeneity. Eliminate.

Does something *arid* lack *dampness*? Yes. Since this is the only choice that works, it's the answer.

❸ There's no need to adjust the bridge, since only one answer choice worked.

❹ You can eliminate (1) and (2) because they lack a strong bridge.

7. Choice (1)

❶ A PROTRACTION is an increase in DURATION.

❷ An *extension* is an increase in *length*. Keep this one.

A *retraction* isn't an increase of anything. Eliminate.

Corruption is not an increase in *truth*. Eliminate.

Taxation is not an increase in *wealth*. At least not if you're the one being taxed. Eliminate.

An *altercation* is not an increase in *shape*. Eliminate.

❸ There's no need to adjust the bridge, since only one answer choice worked.

❹ None of the wrong answer choices has a strong bridge.

8. Choice (5)

❶ A CHARACTERIZATION that is exaggerated is a PARODY.

❷ A *serialization* is a *novel* that appears in several parts. Eliminate.

A *drama* may or may not be a *musical*. Eliminate.

A *theater* may feature *vaudeville*, but there's no necessary link. Eliminate.

A *saga* and an *epic* are both literary works. Eliminate.

A *portrait* that is exaggerated is a *caricature.* Since this is the only choice that works, it's the answer.

❸ There's no need to adjust the bridge, since only one answer choice worked.

❹ You can eliminate (2) and (3) because they lack a strong bridge.

9. Choice (2)

❶ STARS make up a GALAXY.

❷ Do *cells* make up a *prison*? Not exclusively—there are also offices, cafeterias, etc. Eliminate.

Does *sand* make up a *dune*? Yes. Keep it.

Do *nuclei* make up an *atom*? No, one nucleus and other particles (electrons) make up an atom. Eliminate.

Do *eggs* make up a *nest*? No, they rest in one. Eliminate.

Does *hair* make up a *head*? No. Eliminate.

❸ There's no need to adjust the bridge, since only one answer choice worked.

❹ You can eliminate (1) and (3) because they lack a strong bridge.

10. Choice (5)

❶ ATROPHY is caused by INACTIVITY.

❷ *Resistance* is not be caused by *timidity,* but rather by boldness. Eliminate.

A *frown* may be caused by *anger,* but it may also be caused by other emotions. Eliminate.

Growth and *youth* have no strong bridge. Eliminate.

Rot is usually caused by a lack of *refrigeration.* Eliminate.

Debt is caused by *overspending.* Since this is the only choice that works, it's the answer.

❸ There's no need to adjust the bridge, since only one answer choice worked.

❹ You can eliminate (1), (2), and (3) because they lack a strong bridge.

ANALOGIES: TEST 4

Time: 10 Questions/10 Minutes

Directions: In each question below, a related pair of words is followed by five lettered pairs of words. Choose the one pair that best expresses a relationship similar to that expressed in the original pair.

1. PROPONENT : THEORY ::

   1. nonbeliever : sin
   2. traitor : country
   3. adherent : belief
   4. attorney : law
   5. scientist : hypothesis

2. DISCHARGED : SOLDIER ::

   1. fired : cannon
   2. graduated : student
   3. appointed : judge
   4. transferred : employee
   5. docked : salary

3. OUTFOX : STRATEGY ::

   1. outdo : trickery
   2. defeat : stamina
   3. outlast : force
   4. victimize : terror
   5. outrun : speed

4. COAX : BLANDISHMENTS ::

   1. amuse : platitudes
   2. compel : threats
   3. deter : tidings
   4. batter : insults
   5. exercise : antics

5. TITLED : NOBLE ::

   1. elected : president
   2. acclaimed : artist
   3. commissioned : officer
   4. deposed : ruler
   5. initiated : argument

6. NOD : ASSENT ::

   1. glance : beneficence
   2. shudder : rudeness
   3. wink : mystification
   4. shrug : indifference
   5. frown : capriciousness

7. EPIC : VERSE ::

   1. story : odyssey
   2. symphony : song
   3. saga : prose
   4. freeway : asphalt
   5. musical : play

8. NOMADIC : SEDENTARY ::

   1. transitory : temporary
   2. excessive : sumptuary
   3. loquacious : taciturn
   4. expressive : elegant
   5. garrulous : bombastic

9. IRK : SOOTHING ::

   1. inspire : elevating
   2. support : undermining
   3. provoke : irritating
   4. denounce : vilifying
   5. laud : conciliating

10. FERVID : EMOTIONAL ::

    1. zealous : talkative
    2. ravenous : hungry
    3. torpid : energetic
    4. angry : outrageous
    5. eager : hopeful

KAPLAN

ANSWERS

1. Choice (3)

❶ A PROPONENT is one who agrees with a THEORY.

❷ A *nonbeliever* doesn't agree with *sin*. Eliminate.

A *traitor* betrays a *country*, he doesn't agree with it. Eliminate.

An *adherent* agrees with a *belief*. Keep this.

Attorneys don't necessarily agree with a *law*. Eliminate.

A *scientist* doesn't necessarily agree with a *hypothesis*. Eliminate.

❸ There's no need to adjust the bridge, since only one answer choice worked.

❹ Choices (1) and (4) don't have strong bridges.

2. Choice (2)

❶ A DISCHARGED SOLDIER is one whose term has ended.

❷ A *fired cannon* can be reloaded. Eliminate.

A *graduated student* is one whose term has ended. That works, so keep it.

A *judge* is often *appointed*, but can be elected, so there's no strong bridge.

An *employee* may or may not be *transferred*. Again, no strong bridge. Eliminate.

Some people have their *salary docked*, but the words don't have anything to do with the end of a term.

❸ There's no need to adjust the bridge, since only one answer choice worked.

❹ Choices (3) and (4) lack strong bridges.

3. Choice (5)

❶ To OUTFOX is to use superior STRATEGY.

❷ To *outdo* means to defeat, not necessarily to use superior *trickery*. Eliminate.

Defeat does not necessarily involve *stamina*, so there's no strong bridge here.

Outlasting something involves stamina, not *force*. Eliminate.

Victimizing someone may or may not include *terror*. Eliminate.

To *outrun* is to use superior *speed*. This works, so keep it.

❸ There's no need to adjust the bridge, since only one answer choice worked.

❹ None of the wrong answer choices has a strong bridge.

4. Choice (2)

❶ You COAX someone by using BLANDISHMENTS (flattering remarks).

❷ *Platitudes* are trite statements, and aren't usually *amusing*. Eliminate.

You *compel* someone by using *threats*. Keep this choice.

You don't *deter* someone by using *tidings*. Eliminate.

You don't *batter* someone with *insults*. Battering is a physical process. Eliminate.

You can't *exercise* someone with *antics*? No, there's no bridge here. Eliminate.

❸ There's no need to adjust the bridge, since only one answer choice worked.

❹ None of the wrong answer choices has strong bridges.

5. Choice (3)

❶ When one is TITLED, one is a NOBLE.

❷ When one is *elected*, one may be *president*, but may also hold a variety of other offices.

When one is *acclaimed*, one may or may not be an *artist*. There's no strong bridge here.

When one is *commissioned*, one becomes an *officer*. Keep this one.

When one is *deposed*, one is no longer a *ruler*. Eliminate.

There's no bridge between *initiated* and *argument*. Eliminate.

❸ There's no need to adjust the bridge, since only one answer choice worked.

❹ Choices (2) and (5) lack a strong bridge.

6. Choice (4)

❶ A NOD is a gesture of ASSENT.

❷ A *glance* is simply a look, not necessarily a gesture of *beneficence*. Eliminate.

A *shudder* is usually a gesture of fear, not of *rudeness*. Eliminate.

A *wink* is not a gesture of *mystification.*

A *shrug* is a gesture of *indifference,* so keep this choice.

A *frown* is not a gesture of *capriciousness* (whimsy). Eliminate.

❸ There's no need to adjust the bridge, since only one answer choice worked.

❹ None of the wrong answer choices has a strong bridge.

7. **Choice (3)**

❶ An EPIC is a narrative written in VERSE.

❷ A *story* is not a narrative written in *odyssey.* Eliminate.

Symphony and *song* have no strong bridge, although they both deal with music. Eliminate.

A *saga* is a *narrative* written in prose. Keep this choice.

A *freeway* is not written in anything, although it's covered by *asphalt.* Eliminate.

A *musical* is a type of *play,* but isn't written in play. Eliminate.

❸ There's no need to adjust the bridge, since only one answer choice worked.

8. **Choice (3)**

❶ Someone NOMADIC is not SEDENTARY.

❷ Something *transitory* is *temporary*. Eliminate.

If anything, something *excessive* may be characterized as *sumptuous*. Eliminate.

Someone *loquacious* (very talkative) is not *taciturn* (quiet). This makes sense, so keep it.

Someone *expressive* may or may not be *elegant*. There's no strong bridge here. Eliminate.

Someone *garrulous* is very talkative. Someone *bombastic* is pompous. These things don't necessarily relate to each other. Eliminate.

❸ There's no need to adjust the bridge, since only one answer choice worked.

❹ Eliminate (4) and (5) because they lack a strong bridge.

9. **Choice (2)**

❶ Something that IRKs is not SOOTHING.

❷ Something that *inspires* is *elevating*. Eliminate.

Something that *supports* is not *undermining*. Keep this one.

Something that *provokes* can be *irritating,* although it doesn't have to be. Eliminate.

Something that *denounces* can *vilify.* Eliminate.

Something that *lauds* (praises) may well be *conciliating* (pleasing). Eliminate.

❸ There's no need to adjust the bridge, since only one answer choice worked.

❹ Choices (3) and (5) lack strong bridges.

10. **Choice (2)**

❶ FERVID is extremely EMOTIONAL.

❷ Someone *zealous* is not very *talkative*, but rather is very committed to a goal. Eliminate.

Ravenous is indeed extremely *hungry*. Keep this one, but check the others.

Torpid means lacking *energy,* so this bridge is the reverse of ours. Eliminate.

Angry and *outrageous* lack a strong bridge. Eliminate.

Eager means "having great interest," *hopeful* has no connection here. Eliminate.

❸ There's no need to adjust the bridge, since only one answer choice worked.

❹ You can eliminate (1), (4), and (5) because they lack strong bridges.

ANALOGIES: TEST 5

Time: 10 Questions/10 Minutes

Directions: In each question below, a related pair of words is followed by five lettered pairs of words. Choose the one pair that best expresses a relationship similar to that expressed in the original pair.

1. DAMPEN : RESTRAIN ::

    ① stagnate : flow
    ② purify : liquefy
    ③ dilate : expand
    ④ melt : disband
    ⑤ stabilize : instill

2. COUNTERFEIT : AUTHENTICITY ::

    ① wayward : mutability
    ② refined : unpredictability
    ③ methodical : fallibility
    ④ elaborate : simplicity
    ⑤ natural : affinity

3. DROSS : METAL ::

    ① sawdust : wood
    ② coke : steel
    ③ sludge : wine
    ④ ozone : atmosphere
    ⑤ fossil : dinosaur

4. PANDEMONIUM : AGITATION ::

    ① inception : knowledge
    ② greisen : quartz
    ③ bliss : joy
    ④ lethargy : activity
    ⑤ dereliction : poverty

5. FICKLE : STEADFAST ::

    ① theocentric : complacent
    ② disloyal : traitorous
    ③ ingenuous : naive
    ④ fatuous : wise
    ⑤ relenting : idiosyncratic

6. COMPENDIOUS : BRIEF ::

    ① tacit : silent
    ② colossal : small
    ③ dilated : constricted
    ④ explosive : emotional
    ⑤ recalcitrant : deferent

7. LAVISH : SPARTAN ::

    ① perforated : punctured
    ② perfidious : artless
    ③ decorous : tinted
    ④ unadorned : bare
    ⑤ extravagant : lively

8. MENDACIOUS : VERACITY ::

    ① nosy : inquisitiveness
    ② irreproachable : isolation
    ③ amoral : fidelity
    ④ tardy : punctuality
    ⑤ dubious : question

9. ARCANUM : SECRECY ::

    ① quest : confidentiality
    ② guffaw : anger
    ③ grudge : generosity
    ④ slumber : arousal
    ⑤ genius : intelligence

10. ARCHIVE : RECORDS ::

    ① box : shoes
    ② locker : uniform
    ③ arsenal: arms
    ④ pantry : bread
    ⑤ arsenide : death

KAPLAN

ANSWERS

1. Choice (3)

❶ When you DAMPEN something, you RESTRAIN it (such as when you dampen emotions).

❷ When something *stagnates,* it stops *flowing.* Eliminate.

You don't have to *liquefy* something to *purify* it, so there's no bridge here. Eliminate.

When you *dilate* something, you *expand* it. Keep this.

When you *melt* something, you don't *disband* it. Again, no strong bridge. Eliminate.

When you *stabilize* something, you make it steadier. *Instill* means "to plant." Eliminate.

❸ There's no need to adjust the bridge, since only one answer choice worked.

❹ Choices (2), (4), and (5) don't have strong bridges.

2. Choice (4)

❶ Something that is COUNTERFEIT lacks AUTHENTICITY.

❷ Something that is *wayward* (that has gone astray) has nothing to do with *mutability* (the ability to be changed). Eliminate.

Something *refined* may or may not lack *unpredictability.* Eliminate.

Something *methodical* can still be *fallible.* Eliminate.

Something *elaborate* lacks *simplicity.* Keep this choice.

Natural and *affinity* don't have a strong bridge, as *affinity* means "liking" or "attraction." These two words are often used together, but that doesn't give them a strong GRE Analogy bridge. Eliminate.

❸ There's no need to adjust the bridge, since only one answer choice worked.

❹ Choices (1), (2), and (3) lack strong bridges.

3. Choice (1)

❶ DROSS is a waste product from working with METAL.

❷ *Sawdust* is a waste product from working with *wood.* Keep this choice.

Coke is a residue of *coal,* not *steel.* Eliminate.

Sludge has nothing to do with *wine.* Eliminate.

Ozone is part of the *atmosphere,* not a waste product. Eliminate.

A *fossil* can be the remains of a *dinosaur,* but it can be the remains of other organisms as well. Eliminate.

❸ There's no need to adjust the bridge, since only one answer choice worked.

❹ Choices (2) and (3) lack strong bridges.

4. Choice (3)

❶ PANDEMONIUM is a state of extreme AGITATION.

❷ *Inception* means "beginning," and has no definitive connection with *knowledge.* Eliminate.

Greisen is a rock made up partially of *quartz.* Eliminate.

Bliss is a state of extreme *joy.* Keep this one.

Lethargy is a lack of *activity.* Eliminate.

Dereliction: poverty may be tempting, since *derelicts* are often poor, but *dereliction* means neglect, not *poverty.* Eliminate.

❸ There's no need to adjust the bridge, since only one answer choice worked.

❹ Choices (1) and (2) lack strong bridges.

5. Choice (4)

❶ One who's FICKLE is not STEADFAST.

❷ There is no strong bridge between *theocentric* (centered around a god) and *complacent,* so eliminate.

Someone who is extremely *disloyal* is *traitorous,* but this is the reverse of our bridge. Eliminate.

Someone who is *ingenuous* is often *naive.* Again, this is the reverse of our bridge.

Someone *fatuous* (silly, foolish) is not *wise,* so keep this choice.

Relenting and *idiosyncratic* (quirky) have no strong bridge. Eliminate.

❸ There's no need to adjust the bridge, since only one answer choice worked.

❹ Choices (1) and (5) lack strong bridges.

6. Choice (1)

❶ Something COMPENDIOUS is BRIEF.

❷ Something *tacit* is *silent.* Keep this choice.

Something *colossal* is definitely not *small.* Eliminate.

Something *dilated* is expanded, not *constricted.* Eliminate.

Something *explosive* could be *emotional* (such as an explosive personality), but not necessarily (an explosive compound). Eliminate.

Something *recalcitrant* (resistant) is anything but *deferent* (submissive). Eliminate.

❸ There's no need to adjust the bridge, since only one answer choice worked.

❹ Choice (4) lacks a strong bridge, and the other three wrong answer choices have "are not" as a bridge.

7. Choice (2)

❶ Something LAVISH (extravagant) is not SPARTAN (bare or unadorned).

❷ *Perforated* means *punctured*, so these words are synonyms. Eliminate.

Something *perfidious* (treacherous) is not *artless* (without deceit). Keep this choice

There's no link between *decorous* and *tinted*. Eliminate.

Something *unadorned* is *bare,* so these are synonyms. Eliminate.

Extravagant and *lively* have no bridge. Eliminate.

❸ There's no need to adjust the bridge, since only one answer choice worked.

❹ Choices (1) and (4) have the same bridge, while choices (3) and (5) lack strong bridges.

8. Choice (4)

❶ Someone who is MENDACIOUS (apt to lie) is not characterized by VERACITY.

❷ Someone who is *nosy* is characterized by *inquisitiveness,* but we're looking for "NOT characterized." Eliminate.

Someone *irreproachable* is beyond criticism. *Isolation* means "alone." There's no bridge here. Eliminate.

Someone *amoral* (lacking morals) may or may not be characterized by a lack of *fidelity* (faithfulness). To lack morals, to be amoral, is a general failing that may or may not include faithlessness. Eliminate.

Someone who's *tardy* is not characterized by *punctuality.* Keep this choice.

Something *dubious* deserves to be *questioned*. Eliminate.

❸ There's no need to adjust the bridge, since only one answer choice worked.

❹ Eliminate (2) and (3) because they lack strong bridges.

9. Choice (5)

❶ An ARCANUM is characterized by SECRECY.

❷ A *quest* has nothing to do with *confidentiality.* Eliminate.

A *guffaw* is a laugh, so it is never caused by *anger.* Eliminate.

A *grudge* is a feeling of resentment and doesn't have anything to do with *generosity.* Eliminate.

A *slumber* is not characterized by *arousal.* Eliminate.

A *genius* is characterized by *intelligence.* It's the only choice that matches our bridge, so it must be right.

❸ There's no need to adjust the bridge, since only one answer choice worked.

❹ Choices (1) and (3) lack strong bridges.

10. Choice (3)

❶ An ARCHIVE is a place designed for storing RECORDS.

❷ Is a *box* designed for storing *shoes*? Some are, but not all boxes. Eliminate.

Is a *locker* designed for storing a *uniform*? It's designed for storing clothes, not necessarily uniforms.

Is an *arsenal* designed to store *arms*? Yep. Keep this choice.

Is a *pantry* designed to store *bread*? It's designed to store food, but not necessarily bread. Eliminate.

Arsenide (a compound of arsenic) is not designed to store *death,* since death can't really be stored. Eliminate.

❸ There's no need to adjust the bridge, since only one answer choice worked.

❹ You can eliminate (5) because it lacks a strong bridge.

Chapter 4: **GRE Antonyms**

Antonyms make up about one fourth of the GRE Verbal Section. They are also the Verbal question type that many students find the most difficult to improve their performance on. Antonym questions are designed to test your vocabulary, so your first step in preparing for this question type is to start building your knowledge by using the GRE Vocabulary Builder section of this book. In this chapter, we'll give you some vocabulary skill-building pointers and show you how to answer Antonym questions strategically. If you approach antonyms strategically, you'll find that you'll get many questions right even if you don't know the exact definitions of the tested words.

The directions for these questions look like this:

Directions: This question consists of a capitalized word that is followed by five words or phrases. Choose the lettered word or phrase whose meaning is most nearly opposite to the meaning of the capitalized word. Because some questions require you to distinguish fine shades of meaning, it is advisable to consider all the choices before deciding on the best choice.

On the GRE, the more questions you get right, the harder the Antonym questions you'll see. If you perform well on GRE Verbal, you'll find that using Kaplan's vocabulary strategies becomes increasingly important on later antonyms.

THE FOUR FUNDAMENTALS

To improve your skills in answering GRE antonyms, you'll need to familiarize yourself with the basic principles for approaching them—and you'll need some practice. The Four Fundamentals below will help you to increase your skills and confidence as you approach the day of the test. And with the skills and confidence, you'll be able to earn points on Test Day!

Use Kaplan's Strategies for Decoding Difficult Vocabulary Words

On hard Antonyms, it might seem at first glance as if you don't know anything about the stem word. However, you need only a little bit of information to guess at a word's meaning. The following techniques can give you enough of an idea about what the stem word means to solve the question.

Think of a Context in which You've Heard the Word Before

You might be able to figure out the meaning of a word from a familiar context; for example, "crimes and *misdemeanors*," "*mitigating* circumstances," or "*abject* poverty."

Look at Word Roots, Stems, and Suffixes

If you don't know what a particular word means, you might be able to guess its meaning based on your knowledge of one or more of the word's parts. If you don't know the meaning of *benediction*, for example, its prefix (*bene,* which means good) tells you that its opposite is likely to be something bad. Perhaps the answer will begin with *mal,* as in *malefaction.*

Use Your Knowledge of a Romance Language

You might be able to guess a word's meaning because it sounds like a word you might have learned in foreign language class. You might guess at the word *credulous,* for instance, because you know the Italian word *credere;* or you might notice that *moratorium* sounds like the French word *morte* or that the word *mundane* sounds like the Spanish word *mundo.*

Use the Positive or Negative "Charges" of Words to Help You to Guess an Answer

When all other vocabulary decoding strategies fail, use your ear. If you know a stem word sounds positive, for example, you know that its antonym must be negatively charged—and vice versa! This strategy can work wonders on harder questions. Here's a sample tough antonym question.

1. SCABROUS:

    ① thorny
    ② unblemished
    ③ perplexing
    ④ blank
    ⑤ examined

 BE STRATEGIC

Antonyms are designed to test your vocabulary, but if you attack these questions strategically, you'll get many questions right even if you don't know the exact definition.

Notice that SCABROUS sounds harsh—it has a negative (–) charge. Now let's check out the charges of the answer choices. Both *thorny* and *perplexing* are negatively charged, so choices (1) and (3) cannot be antonyms of the stem word. The words *blank* and *examined* are neutral, they are neither positive or negative. The only positively charged word here is choice (2), *unblemished.* This is our answer; SCABROUS means rough or covered with unwholesome patches

Watch Out for Common Wrong-Answer Types

Even if you have no idea what the word in the stem means, don't panic! Eliminating answer choices that you know are wrong will give you a good chance of guessing the right answer. Typical wrong answer types on GRE Antonyms follow.

Words That Have No Clear Opposites

Such words as birthright and priority, and deserve, for example, can't be antonyms for any stem word!

Any Answer Choices That Have the Same Opposites as Each Other

If two or more of the answer choices have the same antonym, that choice can't be an antonym for the stem word because then there would be more than one correct answer to the question!

Au Contraire, or Opposite, Answers

These answers mean exactly the opposite of the word you're looking for. In other words, they are synonyms, rather than antonyms, for the stem word.

Drill

Each of the word lists below relates to two concepts that are opposite in meaning. Practice categorizing words relating to these opposites as a means for preparing for GRE Antonyms. If you are unfamiliar with the meaning of any word, use the strategies for decoding tough vocabulary to decipher its meaning.

Write "harsh" next to those words that are harsh sounding; write "pleasant" next to those words that are pleasant sounding.

CACOPHONOUS   harsh

DISCORDANT   harsh

DULCET   pleasant

FRACAS   harsh

RAUCOUS   harsh

SONOROUS   pleasant

STRIDENT   pleasant

Label each word according to its general meaning. Write either "caring" or "indifferent" in the lines provided.

APATHETIC   _Indifferent_

CONCERN   _Caring_

DESULTORY   _ndif_

DISINTEREST   _indiff_

REGARD   _caring_

IMPASSIVITY   _indiff_

INQUISITIVE   _curing_

INTRIGUE   _Caring_

LASSITUDE   _indiff_

THE KAPLAN FOUR-STEP METHOD FOR ANTONYMS

Now that you have learned the basics, you're ready to learn Kaplan's strategic approach to Antonyms on the GRE CAT. Approaching antonyms in a systematic manner is the best way to avoid common traps on the test and improve your score.

❶ Define the stem word.

- Even if you don't know the precise definition of the word, a general knowledge of the word is usually sufficient.

- Use Kaplan vocabulary strategies, such as looking for familiar roots, to try to get a rough definition of the word.

❷ Define its opposite and prephrase an answer.

- Whenever possible, you should have an idea of what you're looking for before checking any answer choices.

- Consciously prephrasing an answer will reduce the chance that you'll select a choice that's a synonym.

❸ Find the answer choice that best matches your prephrase.

- Sometimes one or more answer choices will be close to your prephrase. Check all the answer choices for the best fit.

- Consider alternate definitions for the stem words. Perhaps you're using the wrong definition of a word.

❹ **Use guessing strategies, if necessary.**

- Eliminate any answer choices that have no clear opposite.

- Eliminate answer choices that are synonyms of one another.

- Use word charge and answer choice patterns to avoid other probable wrong answers.

Try It Out

Let's apply the Kaplan Four-Step Method for Antonyms to an example:

2. TRAIL:

   ① age
   ② depress
   ③ rule
   ④ wander
   ⑤ precede

❶ Begin by defining our stem word, TRAIL. What does TRAIL mean? You will notice in this context that trail is a verb. It has to be, because choices (2), (3), and (4) can only be verbs, and the answer choices and the stem word must be the same part of speech. As a verb, TRAIL means "to follow".

❷ Since TRAIL means "to follow", we need a word that means "to lead" or "come before."

❸ Choice (5), precede, means "to come before" so it is the best answer.

❹ If you had to guess, you could have eliminated *age* and *rule*, since they have no clear opposite.

PRACTICE SET

Now try the following Antonym questions on your own, using the Kaplan Four-Step Method. Time yourself: Give yourself a maximum of 30–45 seconds to do each example.

1. AMIABLE:

   ① faithful
   ② insulted
   ③ distasteful
   ④ indecent
   ⑤ unfriendly

2. ACUTE:

   ① conspicuous
   ② relevant
   ③ aloof
   ④ dull
   ⑤ distant

3. RECANT:

   ① affirm
   ② rectify
   ③ offend
   ④ ignore
   ⑤ withdraw

Think about how you attacked these antonym questions. To maximize your score, it's important to start practicing the techniques we covered in this chapter. On the pages that follow, you'll find sets of GRE Antonym practice questions that will help you to hone your skills with this question type. Try these practice sets under testlike conditions, moving from one question to the next at a rapid pace. Complete, strategic explanations to all of these questions follow so that you can check your answers and learn the most efficient means for completing each question correctly.

ANSWER KEY

Testlike Questions

1. (2)
2. (5)

Drill

CACOPHONOUS	harsh
DISCORDANT	harsh
DULCET	pleasant
FRACAS	harsh
RAUCOUS	harsh
SONOROUS	pleasant
STRIDENT	harsh
APATHETIC	indifferent
CONCERN	caring
DESULTORY	indifferent
DISINTEREST	indifferent
REGARD	caring
IMPASSIVITY	indifferent
INQUISITIVE	caring
INTRIGUE	caring
LASSITUDE	indifferent

Practice Set

1. (5)
2. (4)
3. (1)

ANTONYMS: TEST 1

Time: 10 Questions/10 Minutes

Directions: Each question below consists of a capitalized word that is followed by five words or phrases. Choose the lettered word or phrase whose meaning is most nearly opposite to the meaning of the capitalized word. Because some questions require you to distinguish fine shades of meaning, it is advisable to consider all the choices before deciding on the best choice.

1. IMPURE:
   1. harmonious
   2. integral
   3. unalloyed ✓
   4. assiduous
   5. simple

2. SCALE:
   1. enlarge
   2. collapse
   3. moderate ✓
   4. weigh
   5. descend

3. LEVITY:
   1. inequality
   2. gravity ✗
   3. laxity
   4. excitability
   5. credulity

4. INTERMINABLE:
   1. brief
   2. constant
   3. external
   4. physical
   5. separate

5. TRADITIONAL:
   1. improvident
   2. unconscionable
   3. uninhabitable ✓
   4. anachronistic
   5. iconoclastic

6. ABANDON:
   1. arrival
   2. presence
   3. security
   4. restraint
   5. deficiency

7. PROBITY:
   1. lack of talent
   2. dishonesty
   3. disinterest
   4. lack of simplicity
   5. impossibility

8. LOGY:
   1. irrational
   2. upset
   3. alert
   4. patient
   5. chagrined

9. CEDE:
   1. make sense of
   2. fail
   3. get ahead of
   4. flow out of
   5. retain

10. PROSCRIBE:
    1. risk
    2. deny
    3. support
    4. permit
    5. agree

3/10

KAPLAN

ANSWERS

1. Choice (3)

❶ Since the *IM* prefix means "not," then something IMPURE is not pure.

❷ The correct answer choice will be a synonym for "pure."

❸ *Harmonious* means "acting in harmony"; usually, it is used to describe pleasing music. Eliminate.

Integral means "essential" or "necessary." Eliminate.

Unalloyed means "not alloyed," or "pure." Hold onto this one. (If you had trouble working out what *unalloyed* means, you could have used word roots: *UN* means "not," and an *alloy* is a mixture of two or more metals. So *unalloyed* means "not a mixture," which is pretty close to "pure" in meaning.)

Assiduous means hardworking and attentive. Eliminate.

Simple is not a synonym for "pure." Eliminate.

2. Choice (5)

❶ The answer choices tell you that SCALE is being used as a verb. To SCALE is to climb up, as in "scale a mountain."

❷ The correct answer choice will mean "climb down."

❸ *Enlarge* means "make larger." Eliminate.

Collapse means "to fall down." Eliminate.

Moderate, as a verb, means "to make less harsh." Eliminate.

Weigh means "to determine the weight of," or "to decide between two things." Eliminate.

Descend means "to climb down." This is the correct answer.

❹ If you needed to guess, you could eliminate *collapse* and *weigh,* since they have no clear opposites.

3. Choice (2)

❶ LEVITY means "lightness" and "humor."

❷ The correct answer choice will be a word that means "seriousness" or "lack of humor."

❸ *Inequality* may be a serious issue, but it does not itself mean "seriousness." Eliminate.

Gravity is not only the force that holds us to Earth, but it also means "seriousness." This is the correct answer.

Laxity means "slackness" and "lack of rigor." Eliminate.

Excitability is the measure of how excitable something is. Eliminate.

Credulity means "willingness to believe." Someone who is credulous believes things easily. Eliminate.

❹ If you needed to guess, note that *excitability* is a neutral word. Unlike excitable, which means "easily excited," *excitability* has no clear opposite, and cannot be the answer in this case.

4. Choice (1)

❶ The prefix *IN* usually means "not," so something that is INTERMINABLE is not terminable, that is, never ending.

❷ The correct answer choice will be a word that means "short-lived."

❸ *Brief* means "short-lived." This is the correct answer.

Constant means "never changing." Eliminate.

External means "on the outside." Eliminate.

Physical relates to material, as opposed to spiritual, things. Eliminate.

Separate does not mean "short-lived." Eliminate.

5. Choice (5)

❶ Something TRADITIONAL is well established, such as a custom.

❷ The correct answer choice will be a word that means "not well established."

❸ *Improvident* means "incautious" or "lacking in foresight." Eliminate.

Unconscionable means "not restrained by a conscience," that is, ruthless. Eliminate.

Uninhabitable means "not able to be lived in." Eliminate.

Anachronistic means "chronologically out of place" (to see a wristwatch in a movie about ancient Rome would be anachronistic). Eliminate.

Iconoclastic means "against tradition," that is, tending to overthrow any kind of established ideals, beliefs, or custom. This is the correct answer.

❹ If you needed to guess, remember that the prefixes *IM, UN,* and *AN* mean "not." You could use this to eliminate answer choices.

6. Choice (4)

❶ The verb ABANDON means to desert or forsake, to leave behind. However, the answer choices tell you that here, it is being used as a noun; that is, it refers to a complete surrender of inhibitions.

❷ The correct answer choice will be a word that means "restraint."

❸ Choice (4) is exactly what you are looking for.

7. Choice (2)

❶ PROBITY is not related to "probing"—it has to do with high moral character, rectitude, integrity, or honesty.

❷ The correct answer choice will be a word that means "lacking honesty."

❸ *Dishonesty* is the only choice that works.

Disinterest is the quality of being free of bias. (Don't confuse it with *uninterested,* which means "bored.")

8. Choice (3)

❶ LOGY means "lethargic" or "lacking in energy or vitality." It usually refers to a combination of mental and physical slowness.

❷ The correct answer choice will be a word that means "wakeful" and "fresh."

❸ *Alert* fits the bill here. Of the other choices, the only unfamiliar word is *chagrined,* which means "ashamed."

❹ If you had to guess, note that because there is only one difficult vocabulary word, *chagrined,* in the answer choices, it is unlikely to be right.

9. Choice (5)

❶ To CEDE is to yield, give up, or transfer title to someone else—one country cedes land to another, for instance.

❷ If you don't give something up, you hang onto it, so a synonym for "keep" will be the correct answer.

❸ *Retain* is the answer choice you are looking for.

❹ There is no precise antonym for *make sense of,* so you could have eliminated this choice if you needed to guess.

10. Choice (4)

❶ To PROSCRIBE is to forbid or to prohibit as harmful. (It shouldn't be confused with *prescribe,* which means "to set down as a rule," such as when you order someone to take medicine.)

❷ The correct answer choice will be a word that means "allow."

❸ Choice (4) fits well here.

❹ You could easily establish that *risk* has no clear opposite, except, maybe, *play it safe.* All the answer choices here are single words. Therefore, *risk* is not the answer here.

ANTONYMS: TEST 2

Time: 10 Questions/10 Minutes

Directions: Each question below consists of a capitalized word that is followed by five words or phrases. Choose the lettered word or phrase whose meaning is most nearly opposite to the meaning of the capitalized word. Because some questions require you to distinguish fine shades of meaning, it is advisable to consider all the choices before deciding on the best choice.

1. ESCHEW:
   1. relax
   2. restrain
   3. indulge in ✓
   4. reunite
   5. swallow whole

2. MENDICANT:
   1. disembodied
   2. deteriorated
   3. self-sufficient ✓
   4. self-satisfied
   5. nondenominational

3. CONVOKE: assemble
   1. pacify
   2. disperse
   3. arc
   4. forswear
   5. outfox

4. COLLAR:
   1. misstate
   2. untwist
   3. free ✓
   4. abscond
   5. deceive

5. IOTA:
   1. molecule
   2. plethora ✓
   3. dispatch
   4. scrap
   5. falsehood

6. AMBULATORY:
   1. surefooted
   2. fast moving
   3. fixed ✓
   4. healthy
   5. wheeled

7. PURBLIND:
   1. obtuse
   2. visible
   3. negotiable
   4. perceptive
   5. analogical

8. PREVARICATION:
   1. capacity
   2. ostentation ✓
   3. function
   4. donation
   5. verity

9. LEVELING:
   1. darkening
   2. illuminating
   3. expanding
   4. canting
   6. reviewing

10. LULL:
    1. upset
    2. dislike
    3. fool
    4. mull over
    5. account for

ANSWERS

1. Choice (3)

❶ ESCHEW has nothing to do with either sneezing or chewing. To eschew something is to shun, abstain from, or avoid it.

❷ The correct answer choice will be a word that means "embrace" or "indulge in."

❸ Choice (3) works perfectly. Be careful here: If you had misinterpreted the stem word to mean "chew," you might have chosen *swallow whole.* But *chew* and *swallow whole* aren't really opposites anyway.

❹ If you had to guess, you could eliminate *swallow whole;* it has no clear opposite.

2. Choice (3)

❶ To be MENDICANT is to depend on charity to live. (A MENDICANT is a beggar.)

❷ The correct answer choice will be a word that means "not needing charity," like "self-supporting."

❸ *Self-sufficient* is the only answer that comes close.

❹ Eliminate *self-satisfied* as it has has no clear antonym.

3. Choice (2)

❶ To CONVOKE is to assemble in a group. (You may have heard the term *convoke a meeting,* which means to call a meeting.)

❷ The correct answer choice will be a word that means to separate.

❸ Answer choice (2) works best here. Of the remaining words, to *pacify* is to calm down, *arc* means "to move in a curve," to *forswear* is to renounce, and to *outfox* is to outthink or to fool.

❹ If guessing proved to be necessary, note that *arc* and *outfox* have no good antonyms, and could be taken out of the running.

4. Choice (3)

❶ Aside from what you might wear around your neck, to COLLAR is to grab or seize. (You may have heard the phrase *police collared the criminal,* meaning that they caught the criminal.)

❷ The correct answer choice will be a word that means "let go."

❸ Choice (3) is the closest match. Choice (4), *abscond,* means "to leave quickly and secretly."

5. Choice (2)

❶ An IOTA is a tiny amount or a minuscule portion.

❷ The correct answer choice will be a word that means "a lot."

❸ A *molecule* is a group of atoms, which is tiny. Eliminate.

A *plethora* is a great amount. This is the correct answer here.

A *dispatch* is a message. Eliminate.

A *scrap* is also small. Eliminate.

A *falsehood* is a lie. Eliminate.

❹ If you needed to guess, you could note that a *molecule* and a *dispatch* are physical things. As such, they have no antonyms, and must be incorrect.

6. Choice (3)

❶ To be AMBULATORY is to be able to move. (To amble is to walk slowly.)

❷ The correct answer choice will be a word that means "unable to move."

❸ *Fixed* means "immobile" or "stationary." This is the correct answer.

❹ Eliminate *wheeled* when guessing. It has no clear opposite. Also, all the other answer choices have to do with motion, so it is unlikely that *healthy* is the correct answer here.

7. Choice (4)

❶ As you might guess from the word *blind,* to be PURBLIND is to be unable to see.

❷ The correct answer choice will be a word that means "able to have sight."

❸ *Obtuse* means "stupid." Eliminate.

To be *visible* is to be capable of being seen. Be careful—this is not the same as being able to see! Eliminate.

Negotiable means "open to compromise." Eliminate.

Those who are *perceptive* are able to perceive, that is, able to discern things. This is the correct answer.

Analogical means "based on analogy." Get rid of this choice.

❹ It's hard to think of any precise and specific antonym for *analogical*. For this reason, it could be removed from the list of possible answers if you had to guess.

8. Choice (5)

❶ PREVARICATION is lying.

❷ The correct answer choice will be a word that means "truthfulness."

❸ *Capacity* is a measure of how much something can hold. Eliminate.

Ostentation means "pretentious display" or "boasting." Eliminate.

Function means "purpose." Eliminate.

A *donation* is something given to a cause or charity. Eliminate.

Verity means "truthfulness." This is the correct answer.

❹ It's hard to think of precise and specific antonyms for *capacity, function,* or *donation*. These choices can be disregarded.

9. Choice (4)

❶ LEVELING is the act of making something level or flat.

❷ The correct answer choice will be a word that means "to make uneven."

❸ *Illuminating* means "lighting up." Eliminate.

Canting is setting something at an angle, that is, stopping it from being level. This is the correct answer.

❹ There is no good antonym for *reviewing*. If you had to guess, you could eliminate this one.

10. Choice (1)

❶ To LULL is to soothe. You may have thought of the word *lullaby,* a song that is meant to soothe a child to sleep.

❷ The correct answer choice will be a word that means "to cause distress."

❸ *Upset* is the correct answer.

To "mull over" is to think carefully about something.

❹ Since there is no good antonym for *account for*, it can be disregarded.

ANTONYMS: TEST 3

Time: 10 Questions/10 Minutes

Directions: Each question below consists of a capitalized word that is followed by five words or phrases. Choose the lettered word or phrase whose meaning is most nearly *opposite* to the meaning of the capitalized word. Because some questions require you to distinguish fine shades of meaning, it is advisable to consider all the choices before deciding on the *best* choice.

1. LICENSE:
    1. curb
    2. tie
    3. rule
    4. impress
    5. age

2. FEBRILE:
    1. lacking fever
    2. unable to climb
    3. unable to grasp
    4. sturdy
    5. coarse

3. INSIDIOUS:
    1. comparable
    2. direct
    3. external
    4. moral
    5. fearless

4. VIRTUOSO:
    1. malefactor
    2. gnome
    3. incompetent
    4. lackey
    5. sinner

5. POLARIZE:
    1. delay
    2. welcome
    3. cancel
    4. insulate
    5. unite

6. UNGUENT:
    1. irritant
    2. depressant
    3. solvent
    4. penitent
    5. emolument

7. WHIMSICAL:
    1. grave
    2. dull
    3. proud
    4. thought-provoking
    5. hardworking

8. DANDY:
    1. rogue
    2. fatalist
    3. careless dresser
    4. dull conversationalist
    5. stern disciplinarian

9. MAR:

   ① deaden

   ② flatter

   ③ praise

   ④ soothe

   ⑤ enhance

10. STANCH:

   ① cause to flow

   ② allow to disintegrate

   ③ feel uncertain

   ④ attempt to conceal

   ⑤ provoke disrespect

ANSWERS

1. Choice (1)

❶ In this question, LICENSE is a verb. It must be, because choice (4), *impress,* can't be a noun, so all the choices in this question must be verbs. As a verb, license means "to allow."

❷ The correct answer choice will be a synonym for "prohibit."

❸ To *curb* is to restrain. Hold on to this one.

Tie means "to knot." Eliminate.

Rule means "to make a decision or to command." Eliminate.

To *impress* is to create a vivid imprint or image. Eliminate.

Age means "to get older." Eliminate.

❹ If you needed to guess, you could eliminate *rule* and *impress* because they have no clear opposites.

2. Choice (1)

❶ *Febrile* means feverish.

❷ The correct answer choice will be a synonym for "not feverish."

❸ *Lacking fever* looks good. Hold on to this one.

Unable to climb doesn't have anything to do with fever. Eliminate.

Unable to grasp has nothing to do with fever. Eliminate.

Sturdy means "strong" or "robust." Eliminate.

Coarse means "rough." Eliminate.

❹ If you needed to guess, you could eliminate *unable to climb* because it has no clear opposite.

3. Choice (2)

❶ *Insidious* describes something that spreads harmfully in a subtle or stealthy manner.

❷ The correct answer choice will be a synonym for "overt" or "direct."

❸ *Comparable* has nothing to do with directness. Eliminate.

Direct is exactly what we're looking for. Hold on to this one.

External means "outward," and while this is a tempting choice, something that's insidious does not have to be internal. Eliminate.

Moral may be tempting, since someone that's *insidious* is likely to be immoral. However, insidious can refer to things other than people ("insidious disease," for instance). Eliminate.

Fearless has nothing to do with directness. Eliminate.

4. Choice (3)

❶ A VIRTUOSO has great skill.

❷ The correct answer choice will be a synonym for "one who lacks ability."

❸ *Malefactor* probably looks good if you mistake *virtuoso* for someone who's virtuous. Eliminate.

A *gnome* is a mythical creature, or a small, wise person. Eliminate.

An *incompetent* describes one who can't do something adequately. Hold onto this one.

Lackey means "servant." Eliminate.

A *sinner* is one who does wrong. Eliminate.

❹ If you needed to guess, you could eliminate *gnome,* because it has no clear opposite.

5. Choice (5)

❶ To *polarize* is to cause to concentrate around two conflicting positions. For instance, the Vietnam War polarized the American people into two camps—those for the war and those protesting it.

❷ The correct answer choice will be a synonym for "bring together."

❸ *Delay* means "to draw out" or "lengthen." This one's out.

To *welcome* is to greet. Eliminate.

Cancel means "to annul" or "invalidate." Eliminate.

To *insulate* is to isolate or to prevent the passage of heat or cold through into or out of something. Eliminate.

Unite means "bring together as one." Here's our winner.

❹ If you needed to guess, you could eliminate *cancel* and *welcome,* which have no clear opposites.

6. Choice (1)

❶ An UNGUENT is an ointment used to soothe or heal.

❷ The correct answer choice will be a synonym for something that irritates or aggravates.

❸ *Irritant* looks good. Hold on to this one.

A *depressant* is something that depresses. Eliminate.

A *solvent* is something that dissolves another substance. Eliminate.

Penitent describes one who feels sorry for his or her misdeeds or sins. Eliminate.

Emolument means "compensation" or "payment for employment." Eliminate.

❹ If you needed to guess, you could eliminate *emolument* and *solvent* because they have no clear opposites.

7. Choice (1)

❶ WHIMSICAL means "playful."

❷ The correct answer choice will be a synonym for "not playful" or "serious."

❸ *Grave* means "very serious," so it looks good. Hold on to this one.

Dull is boring or not sharp. Eliminate.

Proud has nothing to do with playfulness. Eliminate.

Thought-provoking may seem tempting, but something that's playful can still be thought-provoking. Eliminate.

Hardworking is also tempting, but one's sense of whimsy does not address one's work ethic. Eliminate.

❹ If you needed to guess, you could avoid *thought-provoking* because it has no clear opposite.

8. Choice (3)

❶ A DANDY is one who is very elegant in dress or manners.

❷ The correct answer choice will be a synonym for "one who is not elegant in dress or manners."

❸ A *rogue* is a scoundrel or unprincipled person. This term doesn't have anything to do with dress, so eliminate it.

A *fatalist* is one who thinks things can't be changed by human effort. Eliminate.

Careless dresser matches our prephrase pretty well. Keep this one.

Dull conversationalist has nothing to do with dress or manners. Eliminate.

Stern disciplinarian deals with one's management style, not dress habits. Eliminate.

❹ Avoid *fatalist* if you find that you have to guess, because it has no clear opposite.

9. Choice (5)

❶ To MAR is to damage in a way that makes something less attractive or perfect.

❷ The correct answer choice will be a synonym for "beautify."

❸ *Deaden* means "to make less energetic" or to "lessen." Eliminate.

Flatter means "to compliment." Eliminate.

Praise is a synonym of flatter, so it doesn't work, either. Eliminate.

To *soothe* is to calm or to relieve the pain of something. It has nothing to do with damage, so eliminate.

Enhance means "to increase the value or beauty" of something. It matches our prephrase, so we have a winner.

❹ If you needed to guess, you could eliminate *flatter* and *praise* because they're synonyms.

10. Choice (1)

❶ STANCH means "to stop the flow" of something.

❷ The correct answer choice will be a synonym for "cause the flow of."

❸ *Cause to flow* is just what we're looking for. Hold on to this one.

Allow to disintegrate has nothing to do with the flow of anything. Eliminate.

Feel uncertain would have an antonym—"feel certain." Eliminate.

Attempt to conceal would be the opposite of "display openly," which doesn't work here. Eliminate.

Provoke disrespect has nothing to do with the flow of any fluid. Eliminate.

❹ *Allow to disintegrate* has no clear opposite, and it can be disregarded.

ANTONYMS: TEST 4

Time: 10 Questions/10 Minutes

Directions: Each question below consists of a capitalized word that is followed by five words or phrases. Choose the lettered word or phrase whose meaning is most nearly opposite to the meaning of the capitalized word. Because some questions require you to distinguish fine shades of meaning, it is advisable to consider all the choices before deciding on the best choice.

1. ABSTEMIOUS:
   1. festive
   2. boisterous
   3. frigid
   4. hedonistic
   5. pure

2. ADMONISH:
   1. reduce
   2. commend
   3. discourage
   4. scan
   5. obey

3. IMPASSE:
   1. resolution
   2. priority
   3. victory
   4. birthright
   5. easement

4. QUIET:
   1. militate
   2. agitate
   3. exalt
   4. confront
   5. elicit

5. FANTASTIC:
   1. disappointing
   2. certified
   3. parochial
   4. intangible
   5. prosaic

6. COUNTENANCE:
   1. denude
   2. turn around
   3. forbid
   4. move away
   5. imply

7. FAMILIAR:
   1. frightening
   2. motley
   3. inhuman
   4. alien
   5. malformed

8. INSENSIBLE:
   1. cognizant
   2. pragmatic
   3. pompous
   4. patrician
   5. judicial

9. WARRANT:
    - ① behave rashly
    - ② seep slowly
    - ③ allow to escape
    - ④ not justify
    - ⑤ not worry

10. DILUTION:
    - ① obsequiousness
    - ② clarity
    - ③ concentration
    - ④ cloudlessness
    - ⑤ alloy

ANSWERS

1. Choice (4)

❶ One who is ABSTEMIOUS abstains from certain pleasures.

❷ The correct answer choice will be a synonym for *indulgent*.

❸ *Festive* means "celebratory" or "joyful." Eliminate.

Boisterous is rowdy, unrestrained. Eliminate.

Frigid is very cold. Eliminate.

Hedonistic means "indulgent in pleasure and enjoyment." Keep this.

Pure doesn't fit here. Eliminate.

2. Choice (2)

❶ To ADMONISH is to reprove mildly or warn against something.

❷ The correct answer choice will be a synonym for "approve of."

❸ *Reduce* means "to make smaller." Eliminate.

To *commend* is to approve of one's actions. It matches our prephrase, so keep this one.

Discourage is basically a synonym for *admonish*. Eliminate.

Scan is to look quickly over an area. Eliminate.

Obey doesn't match our prephrase. Eliminate.

❹ If you needed to guess, you could eliminate *discourage*, because it's a synonym of the stem word, and *scan*, because it has no good opposite.

3. Choice (1)

❶ An IMPASSE is a deadlock.

❷ The correct answer choice will be a synonym for "solution" or "agreement."

❸ *Resolution* looks good. Hold on to this one.

Priority has to do with precedence or urgency. Eliminate.

Victory doesn't work here. Eliminate.

Birthright has nothing to do with a solution. Eliminate.

Easement is something that provides comfort, which doesn't match our prephrase. Eliminate.

❹ If you needed to guess, you could eliminate *birthright* and *priority* because they have no clear opposites.

4. Choice (2)

❶ Notice that the answer choices are verbs, so the stem word must be a verb. To QUIET a situation is to calm it down.

❷ The correct answer choice will be a synonym for "irritate" or "aggravate."

❸ *Militate* may sound good because going to battle sounds like the opposite of quieting a situation, but it actually means "to have influence." Eliminate.

Agitate means "to stir up," which works with our prephrase. Hold onto this one.

To *exalt* is to raise in status. It has nothing to do with calming or irritating a situation. Eliminate.

Confront may be tempting, since confrontation gives an impression of making a situation escalate. However, confrontation may lead to a solution, and thus a quieting, of the situation. Eliminate.

Elicit means "to draw out of," such as in eliciting answers to question. Eliminate.

❹ If you needed to guess, you could eliminate *elicit* because it has no clear opposite.

5. Choice (5)

❶ Something that's FANTASTIC is out of the ordinary. Be careful here, because this word is commonly taken to mean "outstanding" or "wonderful."

❷ The correct answer choice will be a synonym for "everyday" or "ordinary."

❸ *Disappointing* looks good if you use the "wonderful" definition of the stem word. However, even if you use this definition, there's no reason to assume that something not fantastic was disappointing. If you don't have any expectations going in, then you won't feel disappointment coming out. Eliminate.

Certified has nothing to do with how everyday something is. Eliminate.

Parochial means "pertaining to a parish." Eliminate.

Intangible means "untouchable." Eliminate.

Prosaic means "ordinary," which matches our prephrase. It's the winner.

6. **Choice (3)**

❶ As a verb, COUNTENANCE means "to approve of" something.

❷ The correct answer choice will be a synonym for "disapprove."

❸ *Denude* means "to expose," which doesn't match our prephrase. Eliminate.

Turn around doesn't work here. Eliminate.

Forbid is a pretty good match of our prephrase. Hang on to this one.

Move away doesn't match our prephrase. Eliminate.

Imply means "to hint at indirectly," which doesn't fit in with our expectations. Eliminate.

❹ If you needed to guess, you could eliminate Turn *Around* because it has no clear opposite.

7. **Choice (4)**

❶ Something that's FAMILIAR is well known.

❷ The correct answer choice will be a synonym for "unknown" or "strange."

❸ *Frightening* may be tempting, since strange things are often frightening, but it doesn't match our prephrase. Eliminate.

Motley means "diverse." Eliminate.

Inhuman means "brutal." Eliminate.

Alien is another word for foreign or strange. We've got a match, so keep this one.

Malformed means "imperfectly formed." Eliminate.

8. **Choice (1)**

❶ *Insensible* does not mean "senseless," but rather "unaware" or "unable to feel."

❷ The correct answer choice will be a synonym for "able to feel."

❸ *Cognizant* means "aware." This is a perfect match with our prephrase, so keep it.

Pragmatic means "sensible" or "practical." If you use the wrong definition of the stem word, you may pick this choice. However, it doesn't match our prephrase, so eliminate it.

Pompous means "self-important." Eliminate.

Patrician means "aristocratic." Eliminate.

Judicial pertains to the court system. Eliminate.

❹ If you needed to guess, you could eliminate Judicial because it has no clear opposite.

9. **Choice (4)**

❶ To WARRANT is to justify or merit some sort of treatment.

❷ The correct answer choice will be a synonym for "not justify" or "not merit."

❸ *Behave rashly* does not match our prephrase. Eliminate.

Seep slowly has nothing to do with merit or justification, so eliminate it.

Allow to escape has nothing to do with warrant, so eliminate.

Not justify matches our prephrase perfectly. This is probably our winner.

Not worry doesn't work. Eliminate.

❹ If you needed to guess, you could eliminate *Allow to escape* because it has no clear opposite.

10. **Choice (3)**

❶ *Dilution* means "weakening" or "making less concentrated."

❷ The correct answer choice will be a synonym for "strengthening."

❸ *Obsequiousness* refers to excessive compliance. Eliminate.

Clarity has nothing to do with strength, so eliminate.

Concentration means "strengthening" or "making more concentrated." Keep this one.

Cloudlessness doesn't work. Eliminate.

Alloy is a mixture of different metals. Eliminate.

❹ If you needed to guess, you could eliminate *Alloy* because it has no clear opposite.

ANTONYMS: TEST 5

Time: 10 Questions/10 Minutes

Directions: Each question below consists of a capitalized word that is followed by five words or phrases. Choose the lettered word or phrase whose meaning is most nearly opposite to the meaning of the capitalized word. Because some questions require you to distinguish fine shades of meaning, it is advisable to consider all the choices before deciding on the best choice.

1. LARGESS:
   1. emaciation
   2. potability
   3. poverty
   4. economy
   5. admiration

2. MERCURIAL:
   1. dull
   2. secular
   3. nontoxic
   4. stable
   5. gaseous

3. DISPERSE:
   1. account for
   2. gather up
   3. apply to
   4. concentrate on
   5. take apart

4. SEDULITY:
   1. nonchalance
   2. loyalty
   3. hurriedness
   4. willingness
   5. majesty

5. INNATE:
   1. exterior
   2. acquired
   3. false
   4. gaudy
   5. proud

6. VENERATE:
   1. detest
   2. disrespect
   3. renew
   4. uncover
   5. deserve

7. GAUNT:
   1. plump
   2. lenient
   3. secular
   4. embellished
   5. needy

8. CULPABILITY:
   1. vulnerability
   2. flexibility
   3. irreproachability
   4. covertness
   5. ineptitude

9. OBLIVIOUS:

    ① visible
    ② subtle
    ③ active
    ④ intelligent
    ⑤ mindful

10. TRUNCATE:

    ① wrap around
    ② add on
    ③ darken
    ④ handle carelessly
    ⑤ retain

ANSWERS

1. Choice (4)

❶ LARGESS is generosity, or willingness to spend money in bunches.

❷ The correct answer choice will be a synonym for "thriftiness."

❸ *Emaciation* is extreme thinness. Eliminate.

Potability means "drinkability." Eliminate.

Poverty may be tempting, since it has to do with money, but lack of money is not the opposite of "willing to spend money." Eliminate.

Economy means "thriftiness," which matches our prephrase. Keep it.

Admiration means "respect." Eliminate.

2. Choice (4)

❶ In this question, MERCURIAL means "erratic" or "fickle."

❷ The correct answer choice will be a synonym for "constant" or "steady."

❸ *Dull* means "blunt" or "boring." Eliminate.

Secular is defined as not religious. Eliminate.

Nontoxic describes something that is not poisonous. This may be tempting, since mercury is a poisonous metal, but the stem word does not mean poisonous, so you have to eliminate this choice.

Stable matches our prephrase. Keep it.

Gaseous may be tempting because mercury is a liquid metal, but the stem word has nothing to do with states of matter. Eliminate.

❹ If you needed to guess, you could eliminate *gaseous* because it has no clear opposite.

3. Choice (2)

❶ When you DISPERSE something, you scatter it.

❷ The correct answer choice will be a synonym for "bring together."

❸ *Account for* doesn't work. Eliminate.

Gather up matches our prephrase pretty closely. Keep this one.

Apply to doesn't match our expectation, so eliminate this choice.

Concentrate on means "to focus attention on" something, which doesn't work. Eliminate.

Take apart doesn't work, either. Eliminate.

❹ If you needed to guess, you could eliminate *account for* because it has no clear opposite.

4. Choice (1)

❶ SEDULITY is defined as blatant attentiveness or concentration.

❷ The correct answer choice will be a synonym for "not attentive" or "lack of concern."

❸ *Nonchalance* refers to a lack of concern or a lack of attention. That matches our prephrase, so keep it.

Loyalty is a feeling of attachment or devotion. Eliminate.

Hurriedness has nothing to do with attentiveness, so get rid of it.

Willingness has nothing to do with the stem, so eliminate it.

Majesty means "greatness" and "dignity." Eliminate.

5. Choice (2)

❶ Something that's INNATE is something that you're born with.

❷ The correct answer choice will be a synonym for "learned."

❸ *Exterior* means "outer" or "outside." Just because the stem word begins with *IN* and this choice starts with *EX*, which means "out" or "from," you may be tempted here. Don't be. Eliminate.

Acquired matches our prephrase. If you have to acquire something, it can't be something you're born with. Keep this choice.

False doesn't have anything to do with the stem. Eliminate.

Gaudy describes something tasteless or showy. Eliminate.

Proud doesn't match our prephrase. Eliminate.

6. Choice (2)

❶ To VENERATE is to treat with respect.

❷ The correct answer choice will be a synonym for "treat with disrespect."

❸ *Detest* means "hate." While it may seem close to disrespect, detest deals with feelings, not actual treatment. You can detest someone without being disrespectful. Eliminate.

Disrespect matches our prephrase almost word for word. Keep it.

Renew doesn't match our prephrase, so you have to eliminate this choice.

Uncover has nothing to do with respect or disrespect. Eliminate.

Deserve fails to match our expectation. Eliminate.

❹ If you needed to guess, you could eliminate *deserve* because it has no clear opposite.

7. Choice (1)

❶ GAUNT is thin or emaciated.

❷ The correct answer choice will be a synonym for "thick."

❸ *Plump* works well, since it's a close match to our prephrase. Keep it.

Lenient means "bending" or "yielding." Eliminate.

Secular means "not religious." Eliminate.

Embellished means "made beautiful." Eliminate.

Needy doesn't match our prephrase. Eliminate.

8. Choice (3)

❶ CULPABILITY is responsibility for blame.

❷ The correct answer choice will be a synonym for "not responsible for blame."

❸ *Vulnerability* is the state of being defenseless. Eliminate.

Flexibility is the ability to bend or stretch. Eliminate.

Irreproachability refers to the quality of being free of reproach or criticism. This is the word we're looking for in this question.

Covertness means "secrecy," and has nothing to do with respect or disrespect. Eliminate.

Ineptitude fails to match our expectation. Eliminate.

9. Choice (5)

❶ OBLIVIOUS means "unaware."

❷ The correct answer choice will be a synonym for "aware."

❸ *Visible* means "able to be seen." Eliminate.

Subtle is a good opposite for "obvious," but the stem word is *oblivious,* and so this choice doesn't fit. Eliminate.

Active has nothing to do with awareness. Eliminate.

Intelligent doesn't match our prephrase. Eliminate.

Mindful means "aware" or "conscious of." This matches our prephrase, so keep it.

10. Choice (2)

❶ TRUNCATE means "to shorten," usually by cutting something off.

❷ The correct answer choice will be a synonym for "add more to something."

❸ *Wrap around* has nothing to do with adding on. Eliminate.

Add on matches our prephrase perfectly. Keep it.

Darken has nothing to do with adding or shortening something. Eliminate.

Handle carelessly doesn't work with our prephrase. Eliminate.

Retain doesn't work either, as its opposite would mean "give away," not "shorten." Eliminate.

❹ If you needed to guess, you could eliminate *wrap around* because it has no clear opposite.

Chapter 5: **GRE Reading Comprehension**

Reading Comprehension is the only question type that appears on all major standardized tests, and the reason for this isn't too surprising. No matter what academic area you pursue, you'll have to make sense of some dense, unfamiliar material. The topics for GRE Reading Comp passages are taken from three areas: social sciences, natural sciences, and humanities. So in a way, Reading Comp is the most realistic of all the question types on the test. And right now is a good time to start shoring up your critical reading skills, both for the test and for future study in your field.

The directions for this question type look like this:

> **Directions:** This passage in this test is accompanied by questions based on its content. After reading a selection, choose the best response to each question. Your replies are to be based on what is actually stated or implied in the passage.

On the GRE CAT you will see two to four Reading Comp passages, each with two to four questions. You will have to tackle the passage and questions as they are given to you.

THE FOUR FUNDAMENTALS

To improve your Reading Comprehension skills, you'll need a lot of practice—and patience. You may not see dramatic improvement after only one drill. But with ongoing practice, the basic principles below will help you to increase your skill and confidence on this section by the day of the test.

 ZOOM IN!

As you read the first third of the passage, try to zoom in on the main idea of the passage, first by getting a sense of the general topic, and then by pinning down the scope of the passage. Finally, zero in on the author's purpose in writing the passage.

Read Actively: Don't Just "Read" the Passage

To do well on this section of the test, you'll need to do more than just read the words on the page. You'll need to read actively. Active reading involves keeping your mind working at all times, while trying to anticipate where the author's points are leading. It means thinking about what you're reading as you read it. It means paraphrasing complicated-sounding ideas and jargon. Here are some pointers on reading a GRE passage actively:

DON'T WASTE YOUR TIME!

You don't have to memorize or understand every little thing as you read the passage. Remember, you can always refer back to the passage to clarify the meaning of any specific detail.

- Identify the topic.
- Narrow it down to the precise scope that the author includes.
- Make a hypothesis about why the author is writing and where he or she is going with it.
- As you're reading, ask yourself: "Why did the author include this paragraph?" "What shift did the author have in mind when moving on to this paragraph?" "What bearing does this paragraph have on the author's main idea?" "What's the author's main point here?" "What's the purpose of this paragraph? Of this sentence?"

Read for Structure: Your Goal Is Not to Memorize Every Detail!

In their efforts to understand what the author says, test takers often ignore the less glamorous but important structural side of the passage—namely, how the author says it. One of the keys to success with Reading Comprehension is to understand not only the passage's purpose but also the structure of each passage. Why? Because the questions at the end of the passage ask both what the author says and how he or she says it. To ensure that you read for structure, remember to do the following:

ATTACK THE PASSAGE!

You can be an active reader by:

- **Thinking about what you're reading.**
- **Paraphrasing the complicated parts.**
- **Asking yourself questions about the passage.**
- **Jotting down notes.**

- Always look for Keywords, the structural signals that authors use to indicate logical connections between sentences.
- Don't try to memorize details! Skim them until the questions demand them.
- Look for topic sentences to help you to determine the function of each paragraph.
- Be alert for comparisons and contrasts between:
  - Two thinkers or theories.
  - Different points in time.
  - The author's view and other views.
  - What's known and what's unknown.
- Remember, GRE Reading Comp passages usually do one of the following:
  - Argue a position
  - Discuss a specific subject
  - Explain new findings or research

Recognize the Most Common Question Types

GRE Reading Comprehension questions are predictable. The test writers put the same types of questions on the test year after year. Practicing identifying and answering the following question types will help you get ready for them on test day:

Global: Ask you to identify the central idea or primary purpose of the passage.

Explicit Detail/Text: Ask you to find what is true "according to the passage" or what the passage states.

Inference: Ask you to determine what the passage suggests, what it implies, what conclusion it supports, or a statement the author would be most likely to agree with.

Logic: Ask you why the author includes a particular example sentence or phrase, or ask you to determine the function of a paragraph.

Vocabulary-in-Context: Ask you to define a word or phrase as it is used in the passage.

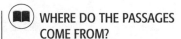 **WHERE DO THE PASSAGES COME FROM?**

Topics for Reading Comp passages come from:

- The social sciences
- The natural sciences
- The humanities

Watch Out for Wrong Answer Types

Because the GRE Reading Comprehension question types are predictable, wrong answer types to these questions are also predictable. If you get stumped on any GRE Reading Comp question, you should rule out as many wrong answer choices as you can and then pick from the remaining choices. Typical wrong answers to look for on GRE Reading Comp are:

Au Contraire: Sounds very similar to the correct answer but directly contradicts the passage.

Outside the Scope: Raises a topic that's never mentioned in the passage.

Distortion: Distorts or twists the facts or the main idea; sounds superficially plausible because it incorporates words or phrases from the passage, but actually confuses the author's intended meaning.

Faulty Use of Detail: Mentions true points not relevant to the question (often from the wrong paragraph).

Extreme: Sounds too positive or too negative; uses exaggerated-sounding language, such as *only, never,* or *always.*

Half-Right, Half-Wrong: Present some information that is correct and some that is incorrect.

MORE STRATEGIES FOR SENTENCE COMPLETION QUESTIONS

Global: In general, any answer choice that zeroes in on the content of only one sentence or paragraph will be wrong. Often, scanning the verbs in the global answer choices is a good way to take a first cut at the question. Common wrong answer choices associated with this question type are those that are too broad or narrow in scope, as well as those that are inconsistent with the author's tone. The beginning of a passage is often a good place to start when looking for the correct answer choice.

Explicit Detail/Text: Explicit Detail/Text questions are usually related to the passage's main idea (the author's purpose in writing the passage), and correct choices tend to be related to major points. In addition, the question and the correct answer choice can repeat a word or phrase from the passage. When you match a key word in the question with one in the passage, go right to that spot and reread the sentence.

Inference: Don't expect to find the answer to an Inference question quoted in the passage. Instead, go through the answer choices and ask yourself if you could come to that conclusion based on what you just read. The right answer to an Inference question, if denied, will contradict or significantly weaken the passage.

Logic: As you look at the answer choices, keep in mind the author's main idea. What role does the paragraph play with regard to that idea and the evidence to support or refute it? Predict the answer in your head, then review the remaining answer choices.

Vocabulary-in-Context: If you don't know the meaning of the word outright, its context can give you a clue here, just as the context helps in Sentence Completion questions. Look to a sentence's charge, keywords, and structural road signs. (In addition, you can quickly brush up on your vocabulary by reviewing the word groups, root lists, and top GRE words in the back of this book.)

Drill

The correct answers to GRE Reading Comp questions must be irrefutable. For this reason, answer choices that are extreme or too emotional tend to be wrong. Decide whether each of the following sentences sounds Extreme or Moderate:

1. Reporters tend to focus on news stories that they believe will improve ratings.   Extreme / Moderate

2. It is impossible that one person could have authored all of the plays we currently consider to have been written by Shakespeare.   Extreme / Moderate

3. Scientists who refrain from making bold statements to their peers about the significance of their experiments often employ far less technical language in news releases.   Extreme / Moderate

4. The melting of Antarctic ice sheets is one of several potential threats to the stability of the Earth's climate.   Extreme / Moderate

5. Though Copernicus is generally associated with the discovery of the sun-centered universe, Aristarchus may have conceived of the idea in 200 B.C.   Extreme / Moderate

Now, read the following GRE-like sentence:

Marathon running has become increasingly popular as people have become more and more concerned about their health.

Remember that on GRE Reading Comp, some answer choices will sound like they fit the passage, but will actually distort the author's point. Decide which of the three statements below agrees with the GRE-like sentence above:

1. Marathon running has become an international event that promotes friendship between cultures.
2. The fact that more people are running in marathons highlights the public's increasing interest in pursuing healthy activities.
3. The majority of people who take up marathon running do so because they are concerned about their health.

THE KAPLAN FOUR-STEP METHOD FOR READING COMPREHENSION

Now that you have the basics for tackling Reading Comprehension questions, you're ready to learn Kaplan's strategic approach to Reading Comp on the GRE CAT. As is the case with all other GRE question types, approaching Reading Comp in a systematic manner is the best way to avoid common pitfalls and improve your score.

❶ Read the first third.

Identify topic and scope, zero in on the purpose of the passage, and predict where the passage will go.

Topic: The broad concept or idea addressed in the passage

Scope: The more narrow and specific area of the topic that is being discussed

Purpose: A hypothesis about why the author is writing and where he or she is going with the passage

Here's a hypothetical example. Suppose you encounter a reading passage about the Battle of Gettysburg on the GRE. The broad topic of "The Battle of Gettysburg, " for example, would be a lot to cover in a Reading Comp passage. So if you encountered such a passage, you would also need to ask yourself, "What is the scope of this author's passage?" or, in this case, "What specific aspect of the battle does the author address?" Whatever that chunk is—the prebattle scouting, how the battle was fought—is the passage's scope. Finally, you should also consider why the author is writing. For example, is the author writing to refute an established point of view (a common format on the GRE), or to contrast two interpretations of why the battle occurred? Being able to answer this question will tell you how the passage is organized.

❷ Read the remaining two thirds.

Create a brief "road map"—jot down some brief notes—as you read.

❸ Review your "road map."

Confirm topic, scope and purpose.

❹ **Attack the questions.**
- Use the stem to plan your attack!
- Reread any relevant text.
- Predict an answer.
- Choose an answer.

PRACTICE SET

Now that you've got the fundamentals of GRE Reading Comp under your belt and you've had some practice in identifying Reading Comp wrong answer types, let's put your knowledge to use on the following testlike passage and questions.

> *Tsunamis* are huge, fast-moving waves that are capable of causing enormous destruction and loss of life if they broach the shoreline on a populated coast. To communities that have been devastated by such an event, the tsunami often seems to come out of nowhere, and survivors are mystified as to why such a huge wave could appear with so little warning. The terrifying suddenness of a tsunami's arrival is a consequence of where and how they are created.
>
> When submarine tectonic activity distorts the sea floor, it vertically displaces the overlying sea water. As the displaced water seeks equilibrium under the influence of gravity, waves form, and when the distortion is of sufficient magnitude, a tsunami can result. If the earthquake occurs near the shore, the tsunami may take only minutes to reach a populated coast.
>
> Tsunamis attain their enormous heights through a process of decreasing speed and increasing height. The energy flux of a tsunami is constant, which leads to an inversely proportional relationship between the wave's speed and its height. Since speed is directly proportional to water depth, as the wave approaches shallower water, its speed decreases, causing its height to increase to compensate for the loss and thus maintain the wave's energy flux. Through this process, a barely perceptible deep ocean wave formed by an earthquake far from shore can rapidly transform into a tsunami that can exceed 30 meters at its final runup height, which it attains onshore above sea level.

1. The author is primarily concerned with

   ① establishing that tsunamis are formed by submarine tectonic activity.

   ② explaining why tsunamis can appear so suddenly and with so little warning.

   ③ arguing that a tsunami's energy flux results in its great height and destructive capacity.

   ④ demonstrating that devastating tsunamis must be formed by earthquakes close to shore.

   ⑤ challenging long-held beliefs about the formation of deep ocean waves.

2. It may be inferred from the passage that a tsunami that entered deeper water would experience an increase in

   ① destructive power
   ② speed
   ③ energy flux
   ④ visibility
   ⑤ height

Think about how you attacked these Reading Comprehension questions. To maximize your score, it's important to start practicing the techniques we've covered in this chapter now. On the pages that follow, you'll find sets of GRE Reading Comp passages and practice questions that will help you to hone your skills with this question type. Try these practice sets under testlike conditions, moving from one question to the next at a rapid pace. Complete, strategic explanations to all of these questions follow so that you can check your answers and learn the most efficient means for completing each question correctly.

ANSWER KEY

Drill

1.   Moderate
2.   Extreme
3.   Moderate
4.   Moderate
5.   Moderate

Distortion Exercise

1.   Distortion
2.   Inference
3.   Distortion

Practice Set

1.   (2)
2.   (2)

READING COMPREHENSION: TEST 1

Time: 10 Questions/12 Minutes

Directions: Each passage in this test is followed by questions based on its content. After reading a selection, choose the best response to each question. Your replies are to be based on what is actually stated or implied in the passage.

While many different influences determine local air movements, the large-scale motion of winds over the earth's surface depends on two factors. The first is differential heating. Equatorial air absorbs more solar energy than air at higher latitudes. Thus it rises, and cool air from higher latitudes flows under it, while the equatorial air flows toward the poles. Eventually it cools and sinks, continuing as surface wind. Hence, surface winds move toward the equator at low latitudes and toward the poles at higher latitudes.

Global wind motions are also affected by the Coriolis effect, which influences objects moving within a rotating system such as the earth. Objects on the earth's surface move eastward at the same speed as the earth's rotation—about 1,000 miles per hour at the equator, basically zero at the poles. An air mass that has moved north or south from the equator retains this inertial velocity, but the earth it passes over is moving more slowly. Hence, the air is deflected to the east. Winds from the poles toward the equator, on the other hand, have a low velocity compared to the areas they pass over; they are deflected toward the west.

1.   The author is primarily concerned with

   ① summarizing evidence
   ② explaining phenomena
   ③ outlining opposing views
   ④ offering hypotheses
   ⑤ recording scientific observations

2.   According to the passage, winds near the equator usually do which of the following?

   I.   Absorb solar energy at an unvarying rate
   II. Flow toward the equator near the earth's Surface and away from it at higher altitudes
   III. Rush toward the east faster than the earth's rotation

   ① I only
   ② II only
   ③ I and II only
   ④ II and III only
   ⑤ I, II, and III

3.   The passage suggests that if the Coriolis effect did not exist, high-altitude wind near the equator would do which of the following?

   ① It would not appear to move, because it would flow east at the same speed as the earth.
   ② It would flow west faster than the earth's rotation.
   ③ It would flow directly north or south from the equator.
   ④ It would remain stationary and mix with the warmer air from higher latitudes.
   ⑤ It would be deflected more toward the east than air near the poles.

4.   The author would describe global air movements, in comparison with local winds, as

   ① less regular
   ② less well understood
   ③ less interesting
   ④ more predictable
   ⑤ basically similar

The two essays in which Virginia Woolf pursues women's role in art and politics have traditionally been seen as a problematical adjunct to her novels. While *A Room of One's Own*, with its acerbic wit, has been given grudging respect, the outspokenly programmatic *Three Guineas* has been dismissed as a pacifist-feminist tract. No doubt these essays lack the subtlety and superb control of the novels, but to a recent generation of critics they remain significant because of their anticipation of many of the concerns of contemporary feminism.

A Room of One's Own (1929) is written in the form of a lecture "delivered" at a fictitious women's college. Woolf begins by contrasting the paltry luncheon given at the college with the luxurious fare offered at a nearby men's university. The difference symbolizes more profound disparities that—Woolf now comes to her main point—bear directly on the fortunes of women artists. For the woman author, financial independence, opportunities for education, tranquillity, and privacy are necessary preconditions, without which women are unlikely to produce works of genius. Great art can never be expected from "labouring, servile, or uneducated people." (Among modern feminists, Tillie Olsen makes a similar point in *Silences*, though without Woolf's undertone of class condescension.) When a woman obtains a room of her own, in all its senses, she may, according to Woolf, develop what Coleridge termed "the androgynous mind," one which, having united its "male" and "female" sides, "transcends and comprehends the feelings of both sexes."

In *Three Guineas* (1938), Woolf's central argument, again foreshadowing a key contention of later feminism, is that the process of changing gender restrictions in the public world and in the private individual are interdependent. Such issues as childrearing (which she felt should be a shared responsibility) and professional equality between the sexes are not separate considerations, but rather different aspects of the same problem. Woolf also attempts to define women's responsibilities in the larger political world. Discussing the probability of another world war, she argues that women with jobs in manufacturing should refuse to produce arms for use in a male-instigated debacle. Both at the time and since, many readers have found this argument naive. One working-class reader, Agnes Smith, wrote Woolf that the book was decidedly class bound; working women could hardly afford to jeopardize their employment for a pacifist idea. Current feminist critics accept the validity of

Smith's point—indeed, they acknowledge that it exposes a limitation of Woolf's feminism generally—but they also note that the mild derision that greeted *Three Guineas* from the male establishment was typical of the reception often given a woman thinker's ideas.

5. As used by Woolf, the phrase "a room of one's own" apparently refers to all of the following *EXCEPT*

  ① freedom from economic insecurity

  ② separation of the "male" and "female" sides of consciousness

  ③ educational opportunities for women equal to those available to men

  ④ personal autonomy

  ⑤ the ability to work without distractions

6. Judging from the second paragraph, which of the following assumptions did Woolf make in the discussion of women writers?

  ① The mind can be characterized as having masculine and feminine aspects.

  ② All great authors have come from economically privileged backgrounds.

  ③ There have been no truly great women writers in the past.

  ④ Artistic development is independent of formal education.

  ⑤ Investigation of feelings and emotions is the most important goal of literature.

7. The passage provides information to answer which of the following questions?

  ① Why did Woolf write *A Room of One's Own* as a lecture when in fact it was not?

  ② Why did Woolf's tone shift in *Three Guineas* as compared to *A Room of One's Own*?

  ③ How did Woolf struggle against male prejudice in her writing career?

  ④ What conditions foster the development of the "androgynous mind"?

  ⑤ What were readers' responses to the ideas in *A Room of One's Own*?

8. The author would state that, in comparison to her novels, Woolf's essays on feminist themes could be regarded as more

   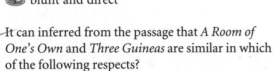

   ① original
   ② familiar to the public
   ③ accepted by critics
   ④ artistically disciplined
   ⑤ blunt and direct

9. It can inferred from the passage that *A Room of One's Own* and *Three Guineas* are similar in which of the following respects?

   I.   Both discuss social issues in terms of artistic development.

   II. Neither presents specific ways in which women can fight a male-dominated society.

   III. Both deal implicitly with the concerns of economically advantaged women.

   ① I only
   ② III only
   ③ I and II only
   ④ II and III only
   ⑤ I, II, and III

10. Which of the following provides the most appropriate title for the passage?

    ① Virginia Woolf: Pacifist Pioneer
    ② The Genesis of Virginia Woolf's Feminism
    ③ A Precursor of Modern Feminism
    ④ Virginia Woolf's Marriage of Art and Politics: A Critical Evaluation
    ⑤ The Myth of Virginia Woolf's Feminism

ANSWERS

Global Winds Passage

Topic and Scope: Wind; specifically, why winds move the way they do on a large scale.

Purpose and Main Idea: The author wants to explain the mechanisms that control large-scale wind motion.

Paragraph Structure: Paragraph 1 hinges on the key word *while*, which indicates that there is going to be a contrast: Local air movements are complicated, and large-scale movements depend on only two factors. He then describes the first factor, differential heating. Paragraph 2 describes the second factor, the Coriolis effect.

1.   Choice (2)

This is a "global" question. Choice (2) fits our outline best; the author is describing and explaining observable phenomena. Choice (1) would require some statement that the facts the author mentions are proof or support for some theory. Only one view is presented (choice (3)), and it is presented, implicitly, as the accepted scientific consensus, not as a hypothesis (choice (4)). Choice (5) is incorrect; no observations are recorded, and the subject is talked about without much reference to actual readings.

2.   Choice (2)

Here we have a straight, "Explicit Detail" question. Go to the points in the passage at which the behavior of winds near the equator is described (namely, at the end of each paragraph).

Statement II is easy to verify; it rephrases material in the fourth and sixth sentences of paragraph 1. Statements I and III are easy to rule out because they contain exaggerated or absurd ideas. Watch for these—the GRE will often make a potentially tricky choice clearly wrong by using one plainly foolish word. In statement I, the word is *unvarying*—why would the rate be unvarying? It should at least vary between night and day, and perhaps at different times of the year; in any case, the idea of "unvarying" never appears in the passage. In III, "rush" should stand out; whatever the winds do, it isn't this.

3.   Choice (3)

Here's a difficult inference question, because the Coriolis effect itself is hard to understand if you're not familiar with it.

Reread the passage that describes the Coriolis effect, that is, the second paragraph.

In paragraph 2, we're told that the Coriolis effect *deflects* the winds. So, if there were no Coriolis effect, they would simply rise and flow away from the equator—either north or south, since the equator has two sides (choice (3)).

The other answer choices can be eliminated. Choice (1) is tricky; the wind's speed *would* match that of the earth, initially, but it leaves out differential heating, which causes the wind to move away from the equator. Choices (2) and (4) are clearly contrary to the passage: Winds flowing away from the equator are deflected east, not west, and the wind would not remain stationary, because of differential heating. Choice (5) is again a little confusing, but nothing in the passage *supports* it; if you think about it, the air's eastward motion would diverge *least* from the earth's at the equator, so this choice is false.

4.   Choice (4)

This is an inference question. The first sentence specifies that "many" influences determine local winds, while only two determine global air movements. Logically, the interaction of "many" factors would be harder to predict.

Choice (1) is wrong—the drift of the whole passage is that global air movements are highly regular.

Choice (2) is beyond the scope of the passage; global winds seem to be quite well understood, and we have no basis for a comparison with local winds on this point.

Choice (3) would depend on what one is interested in, wouldn't it? There is no basis for this choice.

Choice (5) is false: We're not told about local air movements, but the first sentence (and common sense) suggests that they're quite different from the big, regular movements of the global winds.

Virginia Woolf Passage

Topic and Scope: The first paragraph gives you these. The topic is Virginia Woolf, more specifically two of her essays that deal with feminist issues.

Purpose and Main Idea: The author is evaluating these essays, giving a synopsis of the ideas contained in each and the critical reaction to these ideas.

Paragraph Structure: Paragraph 1 introduces the essays. There is a key word here: *because*. This is going to tell you why the works were significant. Paragraph 2 describes *A Room of One's Own*, and its arguments. Paragraph 3 describes *Three Guineas*, and also provides some criticism of this work.

5. Choice (2)

For this detail question, go to paragraph 2, in which the preconditions needed for women to produce works of genius, which are then figuratively summed up as "a room of [one's] own, in all its senses," are described. These preconditions provide our wrong answers. Choices (1) and (3) are virtual paraphrases of "financial independence" and "opportunities for education," respectively. If a writer is no longer "labouring and servile," she is then relatively autonomous (choice (4)). Choice (5) refers to the need for "tranquility and privacy." That leaves choice (2), the correct choice. It is something to be overcome after one obtains a "room of one's own."

6. Choice (1)

This is an inference question. According to paragraph 2, one goal of a woman writer is to develop an "androgynous mind," one that has united "male" and "female" characteristics. Thus Woolf's assumption is that there is a division of mental processes according to gender, one that is "transcended" by genius. The assumption in choice (1) is required for Woolf's discussion to make sense.

Choice (2) makes an all-inclusive generalization that distorts Woolf's emphasis on financial security; it implies that no great artists have come from lower-class backgrounds—a distortion of the idea that women writers must gain financial security.

Choice (3) is beyond the scope of the passage. That Woolf would think there has never been a great woman writer is implausible; paragraph (2) merely says that without financial independence, women are *unlikely* (not unable) to produce great art.

Choice (4) is contrary to Woolf's argument; she is saying that education is needed for women to become great writers.

Choice (5) mistakes *one* goal of the "androgynous" mind (comprehending the feelings of both sexes) for the *main* goal of all literature.

7. Choice (4)

A detail question is being asked here. The conditions for the development mentioned in choice (4) are discussed in paragraph 3. If a woman author obtains a room of her own in all its meanings (education, financial independence, etc.), she may then go on to develop an "androgynous" mind.

Choice (1) goes too far, since no information is given on why Woolf used the "lecture" format in *A Room of One's Own*.

Choice (2) is also unmentioned; although a tone shift between *A Room of One's Own* and *Three Guineas* is implied by the terms used to describe them (paragraph 1), the cause of the change is not specified.

Choice (3) is out since the passage gives only one example of apparent male prejudice against Woolf—the response to *Three Guineas*—and we don't learn what Woolf's reaction to this was.

Choice (5) is tricky. We are told how the public reacted to *Three Guineas*, but not to *A Room of One's Own*.

8. Choice (5)

This is another detail question. The novels are mentioned only in the first paragraph, where the author concedes that the essays "no doubt . . . lack the subtlety" of the novels. The essays, then are "unsubtle," and this idea is expressed in choice (5).

9. Choice (2)

Question (9) is a lengthy inference question that requires you to skip between the last two paragraphs.

Taking the statements one at a time, you can see Statement I is not true; only *A Room of One's Own* discusses artistic development. Statement II is also incorrect; specific ways of fighting against male domination are brought up only in *Three Guineas* (pacifist action against a "male-instigated" war). Statement III is correct. As paragraph 2 makes clear, *A Room of One's Own* discusses the achievement of financial independence by women who already possess some education and freedom from poverty; the fictitious setting of the college underlines this point. *Three Guineas*, as demonstrated by the criticism of Agnes Smith, was "class-bound"—relevant mainly to non-working-class women. The author refers to this as a "limitation of Woolf's feminism generally," further strengthening III.

10. Choice (3)

This is a special type of global question. A "best title" question asks you to identify the main theme of the passage, which is what a good title will focus on. Here, the last sentence of paragraph 1 states the theme: The essays are valuable because of their "anticipation . . . of contemporary feminism." This idea is directly paraphrased in correct choice (3). Don't worry that this choice doesn't mention Woolf; it focuses squarely on what the author says about Woolf. The remainder of the passage surveys two aspects of Woolf's feminism, both of which foreshadow present-day feminism, as paragraph 3 states directly and as the reference to Tillie Olsen in paragraph 2 suggests.

Choice (1) focuses on supporting detail—pacifism—a relatively minor issue in the passage.

Choice (2) is outside the scope of this passage. The genesis of Woolf's ideas (in other words, how they originated) is not discussed.

Choice (4) is half right, half wrong. Although Virginia Woolf's politics are evaluated, her novels, that is her art, are not discussed.

Choice (5) is too critical. Woolf's feminism is taken seriously and is not criticized as a myth.

READING COMPREHENSION: TEST 2

Time: 10 Questions/12 Minutes

Directions: Each passage in this test is followed by questions based on its content. After reading a selection, choose the best response to each question. Your replies are to be based on what is actually stated or implied in the passage.

Satire attained a dominating position between 1660 and 1730 that it had not had before. As an oblique expression of the writer's wish to reform society, or as the somewhat baser tool of his scorn and ridicule, Restoration satire had diverse outlets. Political parties, religious sects, and fashionable philosophies were as much the delights of satirists as were topical gossip and assorted fops, pedants, and bigots.

Pope's mock heroic epic, *The Rape of the Lock*, probes the excesses of romantic etiquette: Lady Belinda's tresses are cropped by a suitor while she lingers over her coffee. According to Samuel Johnson, such an incident was a questionable topic for poetic treatment: "The subject of the poem is an event below the common incidents of common life." Yet the frivolous subject matter provides the ideal setting for a gentle lambasting of traditional epic machinery and a delicate exposure of the romantic conventions of the day.

1. The passage supports which of the following statements concerning satire?

    I.   Satirists may focus both on the foibles of individuals and on larger, societal ills.

    II. Satire could be used to mock poetic conventions.

    III. Satire often served as a formidable weapon for personal revilement.

    1. I only
    2. III only
    3. I and III only
    4. II and III only
    5. I, II, and III

2. According to the description in the passage, which of the following would be a satiric work?

    1. A polemic decrying Calvinism
    2. A vigorous denial of Lockean ethics
    3. An exposé of patronage at the court of Charles II
    4. A fanciful description of a mythical land
    5. A cleverly disguised attack on an academic

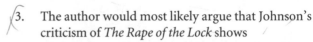

3. The author would most likely argue that Johnson's criticism of *The Rape of the Lock* shows

    1. a narrow conception of the appropriate content of poetry
    2. an obsession with minor stylistic flaws at the expense of an appreciation of the work as a whole
    3. a failure to realize that the work is intentionally humorous
    4. a belief that the work mocks the dignity of everyday life
    5. an outdated code of values

4. The passage implies which of the following about the period before 1660?

    1. Satire dealt only with subjects of political and religious importance.
    2. Readers objected to satirists' mocking of conventional values.
    3. The conventions of heroic poetry were considered above criticism.
    4. Satire was seen as only one among several important literary genres.
    5. Because there was greater political freedom, writers could express political ideas directly rather than through satire.

KAPLAN

Before the recent encroachments of tourism and commercialization, the culture of the Gullah communities on the Sea Islands off the southeast coast of the United States retained a unique identity derived partially from the Islands' history as an area reserved for freed slaves after the Civil War. As an almost exclusively black community, the Gullah preserved African traditions concerning family structure and religious practices. At the same time, as a community of ex-slaves, the residents retained several facets of the Southern life they had left behind. This mixture provided a heritage that until recently was strong enough to sustain a vital culture.

As Patricia Jones-Jackson has pointed out, the basic unit of social life on the Sea Islands, as in West Africa, is the extended family. Since many islands are sectioned off into family communities, kinship ties are important to one's acceptance into the social structure. Membership in the extended family also affects property rights. In the traditional Gullah system, family members do not normally buy land from one another, but acquire it by an unwritten contract known as "heir's land." Rules pertaining to marriage seem to be at least as broad in scope. Common-law marriages are considered as legitimate as marriages recorded by contract under law. Indeed, the infrequent occurrence of divorce and separation within the Sea Island communities demonstrates the strong cohesion of Gullah marital and familial institutions.

Unlike the laws and customs relating to family structure, the religious practices of the Sea Islanders, on the surface at least, bespeak a U.S. heritage. Depending on the village, a Baptist or Methodist church acts as an essential social institution. Yet, in contrast to the dualistic body-soul approach to the individual found in Christian teaching, the Gullah believe that a person has an earthly body, a soul that returns upon death to the Divine Kingdom, and a separate spiritual entity that can remain on Earth and influence the lives of those still living. This belief in a "body spirit" is prevalent among West African peoples, according to Jones-Jackson. She also notes the African influences on the interaction between the minister and the congregation: The prayers and sermons "embody a classical, Ciceronian rhetorical style and employ sophistic ornaments capable of divinely inspiring and passionately persuading a congregation to respond with raucous and joyous replies."

5. Which of the following provides the most appropriate title for the passage?

   ① Religious Beliefs of the Sea Islanders
   ② "Heir's Land"—Key to the Gullah Culture
   ③ African and U.S. Influences on Gullah Life
   ④ Family Structure and Property Rights and the Gullah
   ⑤ How Commercialization Has Brought Change to the Sea Islands

6. According to the passage, all of the following aspects of the culture of the Sea Islanders show the influence of African traditions *EXCEPT* the

   ① family structure
   ② conception of the afterlife
   ③ method of acquiring land
   ④ style used in prayers and sermons
   ⑤ importance of the churches as social institutions

7. It can be inferred that the institution of "heir's land" allows the transfer of property under the terms of

   ① a formal grant by the government
   ② a marriage settlement between families
   ③ an oral agreement among family members
   ④ a written deed of ownership
   ⑤ an alteration of communal rights

8. On the basis of information supplied by the passage, which of the following would most likely resemble a social experience of a Sea Islander?

   ① Dividing property in a divorce settlement under court supervision
   ② Being required to sell one's home because it lies in the path of a new highway
   ③ Growing up in a communal household composed of unrelated adults
   ④ Learning how to play a traditional song on a centuries-old instrument
   ⑤ Being given employment by a relative on the basis of one's standing in the family

9. The author's attitude towards the Gullah can best be described as

    1. sympathetic and receptive
    2. ambivalent and uncertain
    3. detached and quizzical
    4. morally outraged
    5. quietly scornful

10. According to the passage, Patricia Jones-Jackson believes which of the following reveals an African influence on Gullah religious services?

    1. The role of music in Gullah services
    2. The number of Gullah sermons on African topics
    3. The infrequency of divorce among Gullah families
    4. The type of vocal participation by the Gullah congregation
    5. The Gullah belief in the African origins of their institutions

4/6

7/10

ANSWERS

Restoration Satire Passage

Topic and Scope: Satire between 1660 and 1730, particularly Pope's *The Rape of the Lock.*

Purpose and Main Idea: Satire achieved a dominating position basically because it provided a new means of lambasting society.

Paragraph Structure: Paragraph 1 is an introduction to Restoration satire and what it allowed writers to do. Paragraph 2 is a criticism of *The Rape of the Lock* and a defense of the poem. The key word *yet* indicates that a rebuttal to Johnson's criticism is coming up.

1. Choice (5)

Because this is a detail question, take the statements one at a time.

Statement I summarizes the diverse targets of satire, as detailed in the second and third sentences of paragraph 1.

Statement II is supported by the example of *The Rape of the Lock*, in paragraph 2.

Statement III goes back to paragraph 1. Satire was used as a tool for scorn and ridicule, and "fops, pedants, and bigots" were among its targets.

2. Choice (5)

Here we find an application question. The correct answer will fit into the definition of satire given in the passage. The description referred to in the question stem has two main points: Satire is both an "oblique"—or indirect—way of suggesting the need for social change, and a "baser" method of personal attack and vilification. Choice (5) satisfies the latter part of this definition, as its target is a person. It also brings in the notion of using an indirect method, although this does not seem to be requisite in a work satirizing a person. The last sentence of paragraph 1 also supports this choice; a list of "pedants" (scholars or teachers) might well have included an academic. All the other choices fail to make the proper distinctions. Choices (1), (2), and (3) emphasize the idea of social reform, without the equally important qualification of making their points indirectly. They are earnest, direct approaches and hence not satirical. Choice (5) is a genre that could be used for satire, but is not necessarily satirical in nature.

3. Choice (1)

You need to infer what the author believes about Johnson's criticism, so reread the author's rebuttal to it in the final paragraph. Johnson's statement criticizes the subject matter of Pope's mock epic: He thinks it too "common." The sentence following the quote introduces the author's disagreement with this assessment (with *yet*). The author claims that Pope used both the triviality of his subject and his mock serious treatment of it to make a social comment on the "excesses of romantic etiquette." The implication is that Johnson ignored the uses Pope made of his subject matter in poetry. Alternatively, one can write poetry about common life. Either way, choice (1) correctly makes the point that Johnson presupposes a narrow definition of the medium.

Choice (2) is untrue, as the author does not admit any stylistic flaw in the poem, calling heroic couplets a "perfect vehicle" for Pope's purposes.

Choices (3) and (5) are beyond the scope of the passage. Nowhere does the author suggest that Johnson misunderstood Pope's intention, or suggest that Johnson's views were particularly old-fashioned.

Choice (4) distorts Johnson's meaning. If anything, his criticism reveals a contempt for ordinary life, not an idea of its "dignity."

4. Choice (4)

This is another inference question. If, as the first sentence says, satire had a "dominating position between 1660 and 1730 that it had not had before," then before 1660 it did not have a dominant position; choice (4) states this idea in different words.

The other choices pick up on details about post-1660 satire scattered throughout the passage—its use of topical and personal as well as political and religious topics (choice (1)), Pope's satire of romantic conventions and the conventions of epic or heroic poetry (choices (2) and (3)), and satire as an oblique weapon of reform (choice (5)). But the passage gives us no basis for a pre- versus post-1660 comparison on any of these points. Choice (5) is worth noting as a slightly cumbersome, plausible-sounding statement that has no basis at all; the GRE uses this type of answer choice often. The opening generalization in choice (5) is questionable, and it's never suggested that writers used satire for political expression because more open expression was forbidden.

Gullah Society Passage

Topic and Scope: The society of the Gullah, especially their customs.

Purpose and Main Idea: The author wishes to show that the Gullah heritage is a mixture of African and U. S. cultures.

Paragraph Structure: Paragraph 1 is an introduction to the Gullah and why their identity is unique. Paragraph 2 covers aspects of Gullah culture that are obviously of African origin. Paragraph 3 describes how religious customs of the Gullah seem to be of U.S. origin, but actually also reveal their African heritage. The key word is *yet*.

5. Choice (3)

This is a global question, so look to your scope and purpose. The second and third sentences of paragraph 1 indicate that the unique identity of the Gullah cult is attributable to the combined influences of African and U.S. elements. Paragraphs 2 and 3 go on to consider both African and U.S. aspects of beliefs and practices.

Choice (1) focuses on a detail, a topic discussed only in paragraph 3.

Choice (2) is beyond the scope of the passage. The author never claims that "heir's land" is the key to Gullah culture.

Choice (4) hits on another detail.

Choice (5) raises a subject alluded to in the passage, but never discussed specifically.

6. Choice (5)

For this detail question, go through each answer choice one at a time, looking for the place in the passage that supports the relevant detail.

Paragraph 3 is built on a contrast between elements of Gullah religion that "bespeak a U.S. heritage" and those that are African in origin. Immediately following the statement that Gullah religious practices at least superficially reflect a U.S. heritage, the author cites the role of Baptist and Methodist churches as "essential social institutions." Inferably, then, the social role of the churches is an American, not an African, element of the culture.

All the other choices are African elements in Gullah culture. The first sentence of paragraph 2 offers the extended family (choice (1)) as an example of West African influence on Gullah social life. In paragraph 3, we're told that the Gullah conception of the "body spirit" is similar to a West African belief (choice (2)). As for choice (3), we're told in paragraph 2 that membership in the extended family—itself an African element—"affects property rights;" the system of "heir's land" is cited as an example. While it's not clear that "heir's land" existed in Africa, the method of acquiring land was indirectly influenced by the African institution of the extended family. Finally, choice (4) is mentioned an African influence by Jones-Jackson in the first paragraph.

7. Choice (3)

Here's another inference question. The author states that "heir's land" is a way for family members to acquire land through an "unwritten contract," without paying for it. Any contract is by its nature an agreement, and since this kind of agreement is not on paper, it follows that it is orally communicated.

Choice (1) is way beyond the scope of this passage. The only government grant referred to is the original grant of the Sea Islands, after the Civil War. It's not implied that this said anything about land tenure or individual acquisition of land.

Choice (2) distorts the passage by linking "heir's land," which operates within families, to marriage agreements between families. It's never suggested that "heir's land" has anything to do with marriage.

The fact that "heir's land" is defined as an unwritten contract eliminates choice (4).

No alterations in communal rights are mentioned, disposing of choice (5).

8. Choice (5)

In this application question, look for a social experience that parallels one described, probably in more general terms, in the passage. The second paragraph states the importance of family ties and illustrates this by discussing how family members can acquire land through these ties. This is similar to acquiring a job, or any other benefit, through family connections. (Note that you don't need to find evidence that the Sea Islanders get jobs in this way—the point is that choice (5) is logically similar to an experience of the Sea Islanders, not that they might have this exact experience.)

Choice (1) is out, primarily because of its reference to court supervision. The only reference to property (the third and fourth sentences of paragraph 2) emphasizes exchanges within the family with no such supervision. More generally, courts and other government institutions are not mentioned anywhere in the passage.

Choice (2) is certainly not like anything in traditional Gullah life; it might be like an experience that has occurred since the "encroachments of tourism and commercialization," except that we're never told what these encroachments have been.

Choice (3) relates to the importance of family units, but it is the extended family that is important to the Gullah, whereas choice (3) involves unrelated adults.

Choice (4) comes out of left field (the GRE does occasionally throw in such farfetched choices). It has two problems. First, we're not told whether or not Gullah culture contains artistic or other intellectual elements handed down from time immemorial as traditions. Second, choice (4) could refer to relearning a moribund tradition as well as to learning to perform in a living tradition; the passage, however, makes it clear that Gullah traditions as a whole are still very much alive.

9.   Choice (1)

This is a tone question. The author is relatively objective, but still favorable to Gullah culture, calling it "unique" and "vital," and its heritage "strong." This makes the positive, but restrained, terms in choice (1) accurate.

Choice (2) describes a hesitant, wavering approach, one that would be characterized by mixed feelings or conflicting ideas—this simply doesn't fit the author's approach. Given the relative objectivity just mentioned, "detached" in choice (3) is not too far off, but "quizzical" (puzzled, bemused) is totally out. Choices (4) and (5) are the opposite of what you are looking for and show an un-GRE-like emotionality.

10. Choice (4)

Another detail question. Jones-Jackson's views on the African influences on Gullah religious services appear in quotes in the final paragraph. The "classical, Ciceronian rhetorical style" and "sophistic ornaments"—elements of the style of Gullah prayers and sermons—inspire the congregation to make "raucous and joyous replies." Choice (4) focuses on this latter aspect.

Choice (1) misinterprets the mention of "classical . . . style," which refers to stylistic elements of the prayers and sermons, not to any type of music, which is never mentioned.

Choice (2) mistakes Africa as an influence on Gullah services for Africa as a topic of the sermons; sermon topics are never mentioned.

Choice (3) refers to a detail mentioned in paragraph 2; it is not clear what, if anything, this has to do with religious services. Choice (5) is never mentioned at all. We do not know what the Gullah people believe about their institutions.

READING COMPREHENSION: TEST 3

Time: 10 Questions/12 Minutes

Directions: Each passage in this test is followed by questions based on its content. After reading a selection, choose the best response to each question. Your replies are to be based on what is actually stated or implied in the passage.

In some circles, Mendelssohn's reputation diminished rapidly after his death in 1847. By 1852, he was already regarded by many as "the object of pitying disparagement." European musical audiences, newly enamored with the expansiveness of Wagner's *Tristan and Isolde*, soon found Mendelssohn's music too restrained and academic.

As time progressed, post-Wagnerian anti-Romanticism did little to salvage the composer's standing. Proponents of Schoenberg and his twelve-tone serialism regarded Mendelssohn as a quaint, conservative composer who crafted superficial, "tenderly sentimental" music.

Such "arbiters" as these have moved far too illiberally to certain conclusions. The atmospheric melodic beauty of the *Overture to a Midsummer Night's Dream* shows the imprint of an original mind, anticipating the orchestral achievement of Rimsky-Korsakov. At the time of its composition, the Octet displayed unexampled lightness and rhythmic effect; the impressionistic *Hebrides Overture* inspired the painting of Turner. And Mendelssohn's greatest pictorial works, the Scottish and Italian symphonies, constantly reveal new vistas. The work of one of the first, great nineteenth-century Nature composers, Mendelssohn's music simply endures; critics would do well to ask why.

1. It can be inferred that the author apparently regards certain critics of Mendelssohn as
   1. ignorant and ill bred
   2. shortsighted and ungenerous
   3. brilliantly perceptive
   4. cowardly and overcautious
   5. ambitious and insincere

2. The author refers to the proponents of Wagner and Schoenberg in the first two paragraphs primarily in order to do which of the following?
   1. Explain the differences between their musical tastes
   2. Make the point that the critics of Mendelssohn have also failed to appreciate the work of other great composers
   3. Introduce the idea that the music critics of a given period usually lack sensitivity towards earlier composers
   4. Illustrate how some people have unjustly neglected the musical achievement of Mendelssohn
   5. Contrast the musical ideas of Wagner and Schoenberg to those of Mendelssohn

3. On the basis of the passage, the author would be likely to say that Mendelssohn's music
   I. was constrained by traditional forms and styles
   II. was innovative and influential
   III. should be judged on its own terms, not according to the standards of later taste
   1. I only
   2. II only
   3. III only
   4. I and II only
   5. II and III only

4. The author's argument in favor of Mendelssohn is primarily developed by
   1. appealing to the authority of post-Wagnerian and anti-Romantic critics
   2. citing examples that demonstrate Medelssohn's originality and skill
   3. pleading that Mendelssohn has been unfairly measured against far greater composers
   4. pointing out that Mendelssohn's critics have focused on unrepresentative aspects of his work
   5. favorably comparing Mendelssohn's achievements to those of admired composers like Rimsky-Korsakov and Wagner

KAPLAN

Until the 1970s, the pattern of early marine animal evolution seemed to be well established. Most present-day animal phyla had appeared during the "Cambrian explosion," an extraordinary burgeoning of multicellular life in the warm seas of the Cambrian period, between 570 and 500 million years ago. It was assumed that, despite the very large number of species that appeared during the Cambrian explosion, nearly all fit into the same rather small number of phyla that exist today. Each phylum—a group of organisms with the same basic pattern of organization, such as the radial symmetry of jellyfish and other coelenterates or the segmented structure of worms and other annelids—was seen as evolutionarily stable. Innumerable individual species have arisen and died out, but development and extinction were assumed to take place within existing phyla; the elimination of entire phyla was thought to be extremely rare.

However, a diverse group of marine fossils, known collectively as the "Problematica," presented difficulties for this interpretation. The Problematica show patterns of organization so bizarre that it is hard to fit any of them into present-day phyla. They include the banana-shaped Tullimonstrum and the spiked, spiny Hallucigenia, creatures whose very names reflect the classifier's discomfort. The "Ediacaran fauna," which respired, absorbed nutrients, and eliminated wastes directly through their external surfaces, are also included among the Problematica. Theirs was an approach taken by only a few modern multicelled creatures (such as tapeworms) that are otherwise totally unlike them.

Recently, several theorists have argued that the Problematica are not just hard to classify—they are evidence that the conventional view of the Cambrian explosion is wrong. They contend that the Cambrian explosion represented the simultaneous appearance of a much larger number of animal phyla than exists today. Each was a separate "experiment" in basic body design, and the Cambrian seas teemed with many different phyla, or basic body plans, each represented by only a few species. Today, the number of phyla has fallen drastically, but each surviving phylum contains a much larger number of species. The Problematica, then, were not unsuccessful variants within present-day phyla; each represented a distinct phylum in its own right.

Revisionists and conventional theorists agree that modern marine species are products of natural selection. But the revisionists contend that the selection process eliminated

not only particular unfavorable traits, but entire body plans and approaches to survival. The Ediacaran fauna, for example, represented a particular structural solution to the basic problems of gas and fluid exchange with the environment. This approach to body engineering was discarded at the same time as the Ediacaran fauna themselves were wiped out; given the improbability of duplicating an entire body plan through chance mutation, it was unlikely that this particular approach would ever be tried again.

5. The author implies that revisionists would view efforts to classify the Problematica in present-day phyla
    ① enthusiastically
    ② optimistically
    ❸ skeptically
    ④ with indifference
    ⑤ with outrage

6. The description in the latter half of the second paragraph of how the Ediacaran fauna carried out respiration, absorption, and excretion tends to support the view that they
    ① were probably not members of any present-day phylum
    ❷ had physiologic processes different from those of any other known organisms
    ③ could not absorb or excrete fluids
    ④ were members of the same phylum as Tullimonstrum
    ⑤ were closely related to tapeworms

7. The passage implies that present-day phyla contain
    ① only a few species each
    ② species more dissimilar than many phyla in the Cambrian period
    ❸ many species showing basic structural similarities
    ④ species that undergo no evolutionary change
    ⑤ species that have existed continuously since the Cambrian period

8. The author mentions coelenterates and annelids in order to give examples of

① phyla that died out because their body plans were not viable

② the structural patterns characteristic of some modern phyla

③ phyla that are closely related to the Problematica

④ phyla that have evolved since the Cambrian period

⑤ groups of organisms that do not fit into conventional evolutionary models

9. The passage implies that conventional and revisionist theorists disagree about all of the following EXCEPT

① the accuracy of the conventional view of early marine evolution

② the probable number of marine animal phyla during the Cambrian period

③ the likelihood of entire phyla becoming extinct

④ the applicability of the theory of natural selection to the Cambrian period

⑤ whether or not the Problematica can be assigned to present-day phyla

10. According to the passage, the Problematica are difficult to classify because

I. some had unusual shapes

II. some of them functioned physiologically differently from modern organisms

III. they became extinct at the end of the Cambrian period

① I only

② II only

③ I and II only

④ I and III only

⑤ I, II, and III

5/10

9/10

ANSWERS

Mendelssohn Passage

Topic and Scope: Mendelssohn, especially Mendelssohn's reputation after his death.

Purpose and Main Idea: The author considers that Mendelssohn's reputation has been unfairly disparaged by critics, and rebuts their criticism using examples of Mendelssohn's talent.

Paragraph Structure: Paragraph 1 concerns what happened to Mendelssohn's reputation just after he died: People liked Wagner better. Paragraph 2 discusses how later schools of thought liked him even less. In paragraph 3, it is stated that these judgments are too harsh; examples are used to show that Mendelssohn's work has value.

1. Choice (2)

This is a tone question. In the first sentence of the last paragraph, the author says Mendelssohn's critics have "moved far too illiberally"; that is, they have gone too far in their criticism of Mendelssohn. This fits choice (2)'s "ungenerous" best.

You could easily eliminate the other choices. The author likes Mendelssohn, so it follows that he will dislike his critics. Eliminate choice (3). Choices (1) and (4) refer to critics as *ill-bred* and *cowardly*. These judgments are entirely too strong for the GRE. Finally, choice (5) makes claims about the critics the author never mentions. He may not agree with their judgment, but he never questions their sincerity or motives.

2. Choice (4)

This is a logic question; why is the author doing what he is doing? The first two paragraphs cover attitudes towards Mendelssohn by admirers of Wagner and Schoenberg and we are told that these admirers did not like Mendelssohn for a variety of reasons. He then goes on to say that they have "moved far too illiberally to certain conclusions"; that is, that they have overly disparaged Mendelssohn. This best fits with answer choice (4).

Choice (1) misrepresents the author's purpose. The passage is about Mendelssohn, and has nothing to do with comparing the tastes of Wagner's proponents with those of Schoenberg.

Choice (2) actually goes against what the author says: He states in the first paragraph that some who found Mendelssohn too restrained were enamored with Wagner.

Choice (3) goes too far. It is too general a statement for a tightly focused passage such as this.

Choice (5) is tricky, but although the author mentions the other composer's styles, he does not do so in order to contrast them directly with Mendelssohn.

3. Choice (5)

For this Roman numeral inference question, take the statements one at a time.

Statement I reflects the views of Mendelssohn's detractors, not of the author, who likes Mendelssohn. Discard this statement.

The views the author expresses in the third paragraph make it likely that he would agree with Statement II. If Mendelssohn's music "shows the imprint of an original mind," it should be innovative. If it inspired Turner to paint, it was influential.

Statement III pretty much agrees with the author's main idea; the author argues that the later critics of Mendelssohn have treated him too harshly.

4. Choice (2)

The author primarily defends Mendelssohn in paragraph 3. He does this by citing a number of examples that illustrate how good Mendelssohn actually is. This equates most closely with answer choice (2).

Choice (1) is out—the post-Wagnerian and anti-Romantic critics didn't like Mendelssohn (paragraph 2).

Choice (3) is also incorrect; the author does not seem to regard any of the other composers mentioned as greater than Mendelssohn.

Choice (4) is way off; this is never mentioned anywhere in the passage.

Choice (5) is also wrong; nowhere does the author compare Mendelssohn to Wagner in order to show Mendelssohn in a good light.

Early Marine Evolution Passage

Topic and Scope: The pattern of early marine evolution, particularly whether or not there were more phyla immediately after the Cambrian explosion than today.

Purpose and Main Idea: The author considers the argument between conventional theorists and revisionists. Conventional theorists thought they had early marine evolution figured out, assigning even odd-ball fossils like the Problematica to present-day phyla. The revisionists, in contrast, think the Problematica occupy phyla of their own, which arose during the Cambrian explosion and then died out.

Paragraph Structure: Paragraph 1 consists of a discussion of the appearance of the present day phyla during the Cambrian explosion and a few notes on what makes up a phylum. Paragraph 2 describes the Problematica and why they don't fit in present-day phyla. Paragraph 3 details the conclusions that revisionists draw from this—there were other phyla that appeared in the Cambrian and then died out. Paragraph 4 is a summing up of the difference between the conventional theorists' and the revisionists' views.

5. Choice (3)

This inference question is a good illustration of the value of a firm grip on the main idea and author's purpose. The revisionists think the Problematica occupy phyla of their own, which arose during the Cambrian explosion and then died out. Hence, they are critical of trying to classify them into present phyla. Choice (3) reflects this attitude.

Choices (1) and (2) misidentify the revisionists' point of view; since they see these efforts as wrong-headed, they won't react in either of these ways.

Choice (4) is wrong because they have a clear, sharp point of view on the question.

Choice (5) has exaggerated their negative response to the point of absurdity—its tone is not typical of the GRE.

6. Choice (1)

This looks like an explicit detail question, but is actually an logic question. Why is the author doing what he is doing? Paragraph 1 states the conventional view that the Cambrian species all (or nearly all) fit in present phyla; paragraph 2 challenges this idea, and then gives several examples. Obviously, the examples given will be creatures that don't fit neatly into present phyla, which is choice (1). Choice (1) is also specifically justified by the last sentence of paragraph 2: If the Ediacaran fauna approach to respiration was like that of only a few modern creatures that are totally different from them in other ways, then they would not fit comfortably into any known phylum.

Choice (2) is wrong. At least some of these physiological processes were similar to those of tapeworms; however, since they differed from tapeworms in nearly every other way, choice (5) is wrong too. They could and did absorb and excrete fluids (choice (3))—even though they did it in an unusual manner. And the fact that they didn't resemble modern creatures doesn't mean that they were closely related to Tullimonstrum. All we know about Tullimonstrum is that it was banana shaped.

7. Choice (3)

This is an inference question about present-day phyla, so look in the passage in which modern phyla are mentioned. A phylum (as stated in the middle of paragraph 1) is a group of organisms with "the same basic pattern of organization," that is, possessing similar structures; today, there is a small number of phyla, each containing a large number of species (fourth sentence of paragraph 3). Putting these two points together gives us choice (3).

Choice (1) is the situation that existed during the Cambrian, according to the revisionists. Choice (2) is also out; diversity within phyla is not mentioned.

Choices (4) and (5) are contradicted by the discussion of natural selection in paragraph 4: All species undergo evolutionary change, and few, if any, have existed continuously for 500 million years.

8. Choice (2)

This is another logic question. These organisms are mentioned in the middle of paragraph 1, when the author defines phylum as "a group of organisms with the same basic pattern of organization," such as the "radial symmetry of jellyfish and other coelenterates." The author is giving familiar examples to illustrate the concept of a pattern of organization, and jellyfish and worms are present-day creatures. Choice (2) captures this idea.

These phyla have not died out, so you can eliminate choice (1).

As they are present-day phyla, they are not closely related to the Problematica (choice (3)).

The passage never mentions when these organisms evolved (choice (4)).

Since they are mentioned in paragraph 1, which deals with the conventional view, they do fit conventional models (Choice (5)).

9. **Choice (4)**

This detail question asks what the conventional and revisionist theorists do not disagree about. They disagree on nearly everything, but they agree on choice (4), as stated explicitly at the beginning of paragraph 4. This is our answer. (That sentence doesn't mention the Cambrian period specifically, but the entire passage is about the Cambrian.)

Choice (1) is an *"au contraire"* choice: It actually identifies the scientists' overall disagreement.

Choices (2), (3), and (5) are also specific points of disagreement.

10. **Choice (3)**

This is a detail question, so go to paragraph 2 in which the Problematica are discussed.

Statement I is true; the Problematica had unusual "patterns of organization"—that is, unusual shapes—which make them difficult to fit into modern phyla.

Statement II is also true; the second half of paragraph 3 notes that the unusual physiology of the Ediacaran fauna place it within the Problematica.

Statement III is not mentioned in the passage; we don't know when these organisms became extinct.

READING COMPREHENSION: TEST 4

Time: 10 Questions/12 Minutes

Directions: Each passage in this test is followed by questions based on its content. After reading a selection, choose the best response to each question. Your replies are to be based on what is actually stated or implied in the passage.

The acquisition of vocabulary has been less intensively studied than the internalization of operational grammar, but it is an equally complex task. To learn a new word, a child must associate sound and meaning; surprisingly, the concept may take less time to master than the mechanics of recognizing and producing the word. It is also harder to learn distinctions within semantic categories than between them: A child may know that fuchsia refers to a color and not a smell, but be unsure of what color it is.

Vocabulary study through word lists and dictionaries, as practiced in school, poses new problems, primarily because of the mechanics of dictionary study as opposed to interaction with responsive adults. The most common error is that of substitution: A child looking up an unfamiliar word such as *meticulous*, and finding a familiar phrase such as *very careful* as part of the definition, will treat the new word as interchangeable with the familiar phrase, producing sentences such *as I was meticulous about falling off the cliff*. Hence, though the normal child masters some 80,000 words in sixteen years—about fourteen per day—little of this learning takes place in school.

1. The author is primarily concerned with

    ① encouraging more intensive study of vocabulary acquisition

    ② describing some aspects and problems of the process of vocabulary acquisition

    ③ criticizing the teaching of vocabulary in schools

    ④ comparing the processes of learning vocabulary and grammar

    ⑤ resolving contradictions in the theoretical understanding of vocabulary development

2. The passage implies that learning vocabulary from dictionaries may be difficult because

    ① the child cannot test the understanding of new words by interaction with another person

    ② dictionary definitions do not reveal all the shades of meaning of a word

    ③ the child is required to learn too many words each day

    ④ teachers disagree over the proper way to study from a dictionary

    ⑤ dictionaries do not indicate the rules of grammar that the child must master

3. The author suggests that a child studying with a dictionary may use a new word incorrectly in a sentence because he or she

    ① is not familiar with any of the words used in the definitions

    ② is able to understand the word's meaning but not to compose a sentence using the word

    ③ is unaware that the word may not have exactly the same meaning as a phrase used in defining it

    ④ does not know how to use the alphabetized entries in a dictionary

    ⑤ cannot understand the dictionary symbols used to indicate pronunciation

4. It can be inferred that a typical growing child learns most of his or her vocabulary

    ① before acquiring a knowledge of grammar

    ② from dictionaries and word lists

    ③ without being able to associate sound and meaning

    ④ through interaction with adults

    ⑤ by memorizing semantic categories

It is notorious that breakthroughs in science often come in tandem: The same, or almost the same, theoretical advance is made simultaneously by two or more investigators. Watson and Crick "raced" Linus Pauling to verify the helical structure of DNA; Darwin and Alfred Wallace announced the essentials of evolutionary theory simultaneously in 1858. Why should this occur? Why—to take another example— should Newton and Leibniz have worked out the differential calculus independently and in isolation from one another, when they were not even working on the same sorts of problems?

Newton's work on the calculus stemmed from his interest in the physical problem of the measurement of continuously changing quantities. Take, for example, the problem of determining the velocity of a freely falling body at a given instant. The body is constantly accelerating due to gravity. An approximate velocity at any time may be found by measuring the distance traveled over a very brief time interval, such as a hundredth of a second; if one reduces the time interval measured until it approaches zero, the approximate velocity over the interval approaches the actual velocity at any instant as a limit. Newton's genius was to grasp how to calculate such a change over an infinitesimal time period through a mathematical operation known as differentiation.

For various reasons, Newton delayed publishing a clear account of his calculus for nearly forty years. In the meantime, Leibniz approached the calculus from a completely different standpoint, that of the formal geometric problem of determining the tangent to a curve (later, for the integral calculus, the area under a curve). This geometric problem was mathematically equivalent to Newton's consideration of bodies in motion, however, since the changing position of such a body over time can be plotted graphically as a curve in which the tangent to the curve at any point represents the velocity of the body at a given instant. Thus, Leibniz's formal geometric approach duplicated Newton's results.

This phenomenon of simultaneous discovery is surprising only to a public that views such breakthroughs as solitary acts of genius. In reality, Newton and Leibniz's ground had been thoroughly prepared in advance. In the century before Newton's birth, Europe had seen an explosion of scientific inquiry. Copernicus, Kepler, and others had formulated the laws of planetary motion and celestial mechanics. More specifically, when he began his mathematical work, Newton was already familiar with Descarte's coordinate geometry, the mathematics of infinitesimal intervals recently developed by John Wallis, and the method of finding tangents through differentiation worked out by Isaac Barrow. Thus, both the scientific problems and the conceptual tools that stimulated and facilitated Newton's astonishingly rapid development of the differential calculus were already the common property of science. Given Newton's delay in publishing his work, an independent discovery of the calculus by some other genius became not only possible but likely.

5. The primary purpose of this passage is to

   ① present mathematical discoveries

   ② clarify a recurring phenomenon in scientific history

   ③ solve a long-standing puzzle in intellectual history

   ④ describe a period of rapid scientific change

   ⑤ recollect a scandalous incident

6   According to the author, Newton devised the differential calculus in an attempt to understand

   ① why falling bodies accelerate

   ② how to measure continuously varying quantities

   ③ how to measure the area under a curve

   ④ the relationship between average and actual speeds

   ⑤ how to find tangents by differentiation

7. It can be inferred that the author regards the development of the calculus as

   ① an outgrowth of previous intellectual developments

   ② a unique act of genius

   ③ an achievement whose significance has been overestimated

   ④ an unusual case of near-simultaneous discovery

   ⑤ a breakthrough that solved a classic scientific problem

8. The passage implies that Newton and Leibniz arrived at similar results because

    1. they used similar approaches
    2. they knew of each other's work
    3. no one had previously considered the problem of continuous motion
    4. the problems they considered were mathematically equivalent
    5. they were competing to win recognition for the discovery of the calculus

9. The author suggests that cases of simultaneous discovery

    1. cannot really be called breakthroughs, since the important work has been done by others
    2. are extremely rare in science
    3. are made by individuals unaware of the historical influences on their thought
    4. seem remarkable to a public influenced by an inaccurate notion of genius
    5. usually occur when one discoverer delays publication of his results

10. In the final paragraph the author draws connections between the work of Leibniz and Newton and the work of Copernicus and Kepler primarily in order to

    1. provide support for the "great man" view of scientific history
    2. argue that the work of most scientific geniuses reveals unusually coincidental patterns of discovery
    3. expose the myth of independent scientific discovery
    4. describe the evolutionary nature of scientific achievement
    5. compare the work of physicists to that of mathematicians

ANSWERS

Acquiring Vocabulary Passage

Topic and Scope: Acquiring vocabulary, especially why it can be difficult.

Purpose and Main Idea: This is a descriptive passage. The author is not concerned with attacking or defending a viewpoint; rather, she wants to detail a few difficulties in learning vocabulary.

Paragraph Structure: Paragraph 1 concerns how a child must associate a sound and a meaning to learn a word and cannot learn a detailed description right away. Paragraph 2 states that merely learning words from a dictionary leads to misunderstandings.

1. Choice (2)

This is a global question, and the answer should be summed up by the purpose and main idea of the passage. Choice (2) fits this nicely: The "aspects" (associating sound and meaning, learning distinctions between and within semantic categories) are the topic of paragraph 1, while the "problems" (the difficulty of learning through dictionary study) are the topic of paragraph 2.

Choice (1) is beyond the scope of the passage, since it is purely descriptive.

Choice (3) focuses on a detail, the topic of paragraph 2, only.

Choice (4) never happens; grammar is never mentioned after the first sentence.

Choice (5) is also beyond the scope of the passage; no theoretical contradictions are mentioned or implied.

2. Choice (1)

This is an inference question that refers to learning from a dictionary, so look at paragraph 2. The first sentence of paragraph 2 says that dictionary learning "poses new problems, primarily because of the mechanics of dictionary study as opposed to interaction with responsive adults." The paragraph then goes on to give an example of a misunderstanding. It is implied that feedback from a person is needed to clear up this type of error; this paraphrases choice (1).

Choice (2) is wrong because it refers only to the example of a misunderstanding (the definition of *meticulous*) without answering the question.

Choice (3) is probably referring to the information that the typical child successfully learns about fourteen words a day; there's no indication that the child is *required* to learn this many in school, or that that's why dictionary learning is unsuccessful.

Choice (4) is out; since there's no reference at all to any disagreements among teachers, it's beyond the scope.

Choice (5) is also incorrect; we're talking about learning vocabulary, not grammar.

3. Choice (3)

This is a detail question, covered by the example in the later part of paragraph 2. The example of the child trying to use *meticulous* in a sentence indicates that the child makes an error because he or she assumes that *meticulous* means exactly the same thing as *very careful*. That is, the child is unaware that the word may not have exactly the same meaning as a phrase used in defining it (choice (3)).

Eliminate choices (1) and (2); the example shows that the child *is* familiar with some words in the definition and can compose a syntactically correct sentence.

Choice (4) is out—the child must know how to use alphabetized entries, since he or she has looked up *meticulous*.

Choice (5) is irrelevant in this context.

4. Choice (4)

The last sentence of the passage tells us that a typical child learns 80,000 words over sixteen years, but that "little of this learning takes place in school." In paragraph 2 we learn that vocabulary study in school is relatively unsuccessful because of the lack of "interaction with responsive adults." We can infer that such interaction is how most successful learning takes place, and choice (4) is our answer.

Choice (1) picks up on the reference to grammar in the first sentence; from the passage, we don't know whether vocabulary is learned before, after, or at the same time as grammar.

Choice (2) is wrong because the author indicates that learning from dictionaries and word lists is *not* very successful.

Choice (3) is out, since the second sentence in paragraph 1 makes it clear that successful learning does involve associating sound and meaning.

Choice (5) distorts the last sentence of paragraph 1; the child does not necessarily *memorize* semantic categories, as opposed to learning to use them in practice, and must also learn much else besides.

Newton and Leibniz Passage

Topic and Scope: Why scientific discoveries come in pairs, especially the discovery of the differential calculus by Newton and Leibniz.

Purpose and Main Idea: The author wants to explain a phenomenon: why breakthroughs come in "tandem." Using the example of Newton and Leibniz, she posits that this occurs because the groundwork needed for breakthroughs is widely known, and only insight needs to be added to achieve the breakthrough.

Paragraph Structure: Paragraph 1 discusses why scientific discoveries come in tandem. Paragraph 2 describes how Newton discovered the differential calculus, and paragraph 3 how Leibniz discovered the differential calculus. Finally, paragraph 4 explains why they discovered the differential calculus at the same time—they were working from groundwork prepared in advance, and only insight was needed.

5. Choice (2)

Here we have a global question that asks for the primary purpose of the passage. This should be a paraphrase of the primary purpose you decided upon when you read the passage. The author wishes to explain why breakthroughs occur in tandem. This is closest to choice (2).

Choices (1) and (4) are too narrow. The author is interested in the calculus and the scientific advances of Newton's time only insofar as they illustrate the broader points about how great discoveries are made.

Choice (3) is out, since the author never implies that the "puzzle" of Newton and Leibniz's simultaneous discovery is "long-standing," or that she is going to "solve" this puzzle.

Choice (5) is also incorrect. The passage is not merely descriptive, and the incidents described in the passage could scarcely be called "scandalous."

6. Choice (2)

This is a detail question, so go back to the second paragraph in which the author talks about Newton's discovery of the

differential calculus. Choice (2) is stated explicitly in the first sentence of paragraph 2.

Choice (1) is wrong because the acceleration of falling bodies is mentioned by the author as an *example* of the problem of continuous motion; it is not clear that this was the specific problem Newton was working on, or that Newton didn't understand "why" falling bodies accelerate.

Choice (3) is mentioned as one of *Leibniz's* concerns.

Choice (4) is not mentioned at all.

Choice (5) is something Newton already knew—this problem had been worked out by Isaac Barrow (see the last paragraph).

7. Choice (1)

The main question raised by the passage is: Why do simultaneous discoveries occur? The answer, given in the last paragraph, is: because the groundwork is prepared in advance. This point is made specifically in relation to Newton and Leibniz in the second sentence of paragraph 4. This idea is paraphrased in choice (1).

Choice (2) is an *au contraire* answer. The fact that Newton and Leibniz discovered the calculus independently rules it out.

Choice (3) is way off. The author doesn't question the *significance* of the achievement—only the misconceived idea of "solitary acts of genius."

Choice (4) is another *au contraire* answer. The point of the passage is that such occurrences are *not* unusual. Choice (5) is out since we are not told that the problem of continuous motion was a "classic" one. On the contrary, it is implied that the problem had been posed by recent developments.

8. Choice (4)

Paragraph 3 states that although Leibniz's approach was "completely different" from Newton's (ruling out choice (1)), the geometric problem he considered was "mathematically equivalent" to Newton's and "thus . . . duplicated Newton's results." Choice (4) sums this up.

Leibniz and Newton worked independently, ruling out Choice (2).

Choice (3) is not stated, and wouldn't explain their similar results anyway.

Choice (5) is absurd, given their isolation and Newton's delay in publishing (first sentence of paragraph 4).

9.   Choice (4)

This choice paraphrases the first sentence of the last paragraph.

Choice (1) goes too far. The author does stress the preliminary work done by others, but doesn't suggest that the discovery of the calculus (or similar discoveries) was not a breakthrough.

Choice (2) is contradicted in the first paragraph.

Choice (3) is not implied—we don't know what influences Leibniz, Newton, Darwin, et al., may have been aware of.

Newton is the only example given of delayed publication, making choice (5) unlikely.

10. Choice (4)

This is a logic question—what is the author trying to do by drawing this connection? Copernicus and Kepler are mentioned in the fourth sentence of the last paragraph, in the context of the series of scientific and mathematical advances that "prepared the ground" for Newton and Leibniz. So the point is that science builds on earlier work; it is evolutionary even when making great advances.

The "great man" view in choice (1) probably refers to the misconception that breakthroughs are "solitary acts of genius" (first sentence of paragraph 4); this is *not* the author's view.

Choice (2) is a big overstatement; the passage says that simultaneous discoveries occur *often*, not all the time.

Choice (3) overstates the case. The author *doesn't* think independent discovery is a myth at all. Newton and Leibniz are examples of independent discovery. Neither one, of course, was wholly "independent" of previous developments, but their discoveries were made on their own.

Choice (5) never happens. Physicists, or at least astronomers, are mentioned, as are mathematicians, but they are not compared.

READING COMPREHENSION: TEST 5

Time: 10 Questions/12 Minutes

Directions: Each passage in this test is followed by questions based on its content. After reading a selection, choose the best response to each question. Your replies are to be based on what is actually stated or implied in the passage.

Desert plant populations have evolved sophisticated physiological and behavioral traits that aid survival in arid conditions. Some send out long, unusually deep taproots; others utilize shallow but widespread roots, which allow them to absorb large, intermittent flows of water. Certain plants protect their access to water. The creosote bush produces a potent root toxin that inhibits the growth of competing root systems. Daytime closure of stomata exemplifies a further genetic adaptation; guard cells work to minimize daytime water loss, later allowing the stomata to open when conditions are more favorable to gas exchange with the environment.

Certain adaptations reflect the principle that a large surface area facilitates water and gas exchange. Most plants have small leaves, modified leaves (spines), or no leaves at all. The main food-producing organ is not the leaf but the stem, which is often green and nonwoody. Thick, waxy stems and cuticles, seen in succulents such as cacti and agaves, also help conserve water. Spines and thorns (modified branches) protect against predators and also minimize water loss.

1. The passage refers to the spines and thorns of desert plants as

 I. genetically evolved structural adaptations that protect against predation

 II. genetic modifications that aid in the reduction of water loss structures that do not participate directly in food production

 III. structures that do not participate directly in food production

 ① I only
 ② III only
 ③ I and II only
 ④ II and III only
 ⑤ I, II, and III

2. The author suggests that the guard cells of desert plants act to do which of the following?

 I. Facilitate gas and water exchange between the plants and their surroundings

 II. Cause the stomata of desert plants to remain closed during daytime hours

 III. Respond to sudden, heavy rainfalls by forcing the plants' stomata to open

 ① I only
 ② II only
 ③ III only
 ④ I and II only
 ⑤ I, II, and III

3. The passage suggests that which of the following weather-related conditions would most benefit plants with shallow root systems?

 ① An unusually prolonged drought
 ② A windstorm
 ③ A flash flood
 ④ A light spring rain
 ⑤ A winter snowfall

KAPLAN

4. The adaptations of desert plants to their environment would tend to support the statement that

   ① the rate of genetic evolution is greater in the desert than in more temperate surroundings

   ② structures in a plant that usually perform one function may, under certain conditions, perform different functions

   ③ while the amount of leaf surface area is critical for a desert plant, it is much less so for plants in most other environments

   ④ desert plants do not have many physiological and behavioral traits in common with other plants

   ⑤ desert plants could probably adapt to life in a variety of harsh ecosystems

Historians have long known that there were two sides to the Populist movement of the 1890s: a progressive side, embodying the protests of farmers against big business, and a darker side, marked by a distrust of Easterners, immigrants, and intellectuals. In the 1950s, one school of U.S. social thinkers constructed a parallel between this dark side of Populism and the contemporary anti-communist crusade spearheaded by Wisconsin Senator Joseph McCarthy, which attacked liberalism, Eastern intellectuals, and civil liberties in general. To Seymour Martin Lipset, McCarthyism represented "the sour dregs of Populism"; to Edward Shils, McCarthyism, like Populism, exemplified "the ambiguous American impulse toward 'direct democracy.'"

Noting that McCarthyism and Populism had both found their strongest support in the agrarian Midwest, Lipset argued that voters who backed agrarian protest movements during earlier economic crises had supported McCarthy in the post-World War II period of prosperity. "It would be interesting to know," Lipset wrote, "what percentage of those who supported the isolationist but progressive Bob La Follette in Wisconsin now backs McCarthy." But, in the eyes of these writers, the appeal of McCarthyism extended beyond the agrarian base of Populism to include urban groups such as industrial workers. Lipset claimed that "the lower classes, especially the workers," had backed McCarthy. In a more sweeping fashion, Lewis Feuer claimed that "it was the American lower classes . . . who gave their overwhelming support to the attacks in recent years on civil liberties."

Writing a few years later, political scientist Michael Paul Rogin challenged these superficially plausible notions, contending that they merely embodied the writers' own assumptions about the supposed intolerance of lower-class groups, rather than a valid interpretation of McCarthyism. Rogin critically examined their assertions by the simple method of testing them against the evidence. He tested Lipset's claims about the continuity of McCarthyism and earlier agrarian protest movements by breaking down statewide voting statistics on a county-by-county and precinct-by-precinct basis. He found that Wisconsin counties that had voted strongly for Progressives before World War II did not support McCarthy; McCarthy's support was concentrated in his home region and in ethnic German areas that had been traditionally conservative. The old Progressive vote had in fact gone to McCarthy's opponents, the Democrats.

To test Lipset's generalizations about McCarthy's support among lower-class groups, Rogin attempted to determine whether industrial workers had, in fact, backed McCarthy. Correlating income and employment statistics with voting records, Rogin found that the greater the employment in industry in a given Wisconsin county, the lower was McCarthy's share of the vote. Rogin concluded that the thesis of "McCarthyism as Populism" should be judged "not as the product of science but as a . . . venture into conservative political theory."

5. The author would probably assert that Populism and McCarthyism

   ① were basically similar

   ② were completely opposite in character

   ③ were responses to, respectively, agrarian and industrial conditions

   ④ were essentially dissimilar movements that shared some common features

   ⑤ each had both a progressive and a darker side

6. It can be inferred that Rogin's most serious criticism of Lipset, Feuer, and Shils's methodology would probably be that they

    ① reached incorrect conclusions about McCarthy

    ② equated support for McCarthyism with anti-intellectualism

    ③ placed too much emphasis on the dual character of Populism

    ④ failed to examine the evidence that could support or weaken their conclusions

    ⑤ offered a theory that could not easily be tested

7. Rogin studied the class character of Wisconsin voters in order to

    I.   challenge the idea that less affluent socioeconomic groups supported McCarthy

    II. explain the underlying causes of the links between Populism and McCarthyism

    III. account for important changes in voting patterns during the twentieth century

    ① I only

    ② III only

    ③ I and II only

    ④ II and III only

    ⑤ I, II, and III

8. It can be inferred that both Lipset and Rogin made which of the following assumptions about voter support for McCarthy?

    ① The voting patterns of industrial workers are representative of lower-class political preferences.

    ② Industrial workers usually vote for conservative political candidates.

    ③ Supporters of McCarthy were almost exclusively of lower-class origin.

    ④ Lower-class voters generally tend to vote in favor of civil rights measures.

    ⑤ Voters in Midwestern counties are typical of American voters elsewhere.

9. According to the passage, Rogin concluded that the writings of Lipset, Shils, and Feuer

    ① intentionally distorted historical evidence

    ② were flawed by political presuppositions

    ③ lent support to attacks on civil liberties

    ④ took an overly statistical approach to historical evidence

    ⑤ were marked by an anti-intellectual bias

10. The author is primarily concerned with

    ① comparing positions in a political debate

    ② advocating the use of statistical methods in historical research

    ③ examining the similarities between two political movements

    ④ explaining why historical conclusions should be revised according to later discoveries

    ⑤ describing an instance of flawed historiography

KAPLAN

ANSWERS

Desert Plants Passage

Topic and Scope: Desert plants and the adaptations that help them survive.

Purpose and Main Idea: This is a descriptive passage. The author is not concerned with attacking or defending a viewpoint; instead, she wants to detail how plants survive in arid environments. Basically, we have a shopping list of plant adaptations.

Paragraph Structure: In paragraph 1, we find out how desert plants have evolved traits that help them survive, with illustrations of these traits. Paragraph 2 provides more adaptations.

1.   Choice (5)

Reread the section of the passage about spines and thorns (paragraph 2) to answer this question. Take the statements one at a time.

Statement I is true. Spines and thorns, which are identified in the second paragraph as modified leaves and branches, are among the adaptations that the plants have developed to help them cope with the environment.

Statement II is true. In the last sentence, it's stated that spines and thorns help minimize water loss.

Statement III is true. The third sentence of the second paragraph says that most of a desert plant's food is produced in its stem, not in its leaves, so it's pretty clear that spines and thorns have little or nothing to do with food production.

2.   Choice (4)

This is another detail question. Reread the section on the functioning of guard cells, mentioned in the sentence that concludes paragraph 1. This sentence discusses two closely related plant features: the stomata and the guard cells. You read first that daytime closing of the stomata is an adaptation that helps to minimize daytime water loss. The second half of the sentence clearly implies that it's the guard cells that control this opening and closing of the stomata. Now, take the statements one at a time.

Statement I is true. The guard cells force the stomata to close during the day, to minimize water loss, and they later cause the stomata to open when conditions for gas

exchange between the plant and its environment are more favorable. So they must facilitate gas and water exchange.

Statement II is clearly suggested by the reference to guard cells forcing the stomata to close during the day.

Statement III is unjustified. Nothing links the functioning of guard cells to sudden downpours.

3.   Choice (3)

The question stem is looking for the weather-related condition that would especially benefit plants with shallow root systems. Shallow root systems are mentioned up in the second sentence, and the point is that these specially adapted roots allow desert plants to take advantage of heavy, irregular flows of water. The only choice that comes close to this is a flash flood.

Choice (1) and (2) are impossible; neither drought nor windstorms involve water.

Choice (4) won't work because a light rain doesn't fit with the idea of a large, sudden quantity of water.

Choice (5) is out, since this choice doesn't suggest water flows at all.

4.   Choice (2)

The second paragraph contains several examples of structures that in desert plants perform different functions than those they normally perform in plants in other environments. Spines and thorns in desert plants are leaves and branches, modified to reduce water loss. And as a result of their lack of normal leaves, most desert plants produce their food in their green, fleshy stems. This fits well with choice (2).

Choices (1), (4), and (5) are beyond the scope of the passage—there's no information to support any of these statements.

Choice (3) is out. While the passage does indicate that a small leaf surface area is a critical factor for desert plants, nothing suggests that leaf surface area isn't critical for plants in most other environments.

McCarthyism Passage

Topic and Scope: McCarthyism, specifically from who it drew its support.

Purpose and Main Idea: The author claims that although some would argue that McCarthyism drew its support from those who supported Populism and from industrialized workers, later research does not support this contention.

Paragraph Structure: Paragraph 1 presents the idea that McCarthyism represents an offshoot of Populism. Paragraph 2 describes the theories of Lipset, Shils, and Feuer, who claim that McCarthyism drew its support from Populism's base in the agrarian Midwest and extended it to industrial workers. Paragraph 3 describes the case against this theory; according to Rogin, counties in the Midwest that voted Populist did not vote for McCarthy. Paragraph 4 details Rogin's case against the ideas presented in the second paragraph—statistics show that industrialized workers did not in fact vote for McCarthy. The passage concludes by supporting the case against a linkage of McCarthyism with Populism.

5. Choice (4)

This question covers the broad outline of the passage, so treat it as a global question and look to your purpose and main idea. Choice (4) best describes the author's attitude toward McCarthyism and Populism—although they were superficially similar, they were essentially dissimilar.

Choice (1) is an *au contraire* choice; it actually states the case against the author's views.

Choice (2) is too harsh. The first paragraph does draw some parallels between both movements.

Choice (3) is partly right, but partly wrong. Populism was, partially at least, a response to the conditions of farmers, but nowhere is it suggested that McCarthyism was a response to industrial conditions. The passage suggests quite the contrary: As described in the last paragraph, Rogin showed that McCarthyism had little support from workers employed in industry.

Choice (5) is out, as it's never suggested that McCarthyism has a progressive side. Only Populism is described (in the first sentence) as having both of these, a progressive and a darker side.

6. Choice (4)

The substance of Rogin's criticism of Lipset, Feuer, and Shils is explained in the last two paragraphs. The second sentence of the third paragraph says what Rogin did: He "critically examined their assertions by the simple method of testing them against the evidence." This really tells you all you need to know to pick the right choice, choice (4). If you missed this, both of these last two paragraphs are

spent describing how Rogin showed that grass roots voting patterns in both rural Wisconsin counties and more industrial Wisconsin counties failed to support the claims made by Lipset, Feuer, and Shils about who really did and didn't support McCarthy. What Rogin and the author are clearly suggesting is that Lipset, Feuer, and Shils failed to do their homework properly.

Choice (1) doesn't work, because Rogin never really quarrels with any descriptions of McCarthy. The quarrel is with the misrepresentation of lower-class voters and the real nature of Populism.

Choice (2) doesn't work, since the passage never describes Rogin as disagreeing with the idea that McCarthyism is linked to anti-intellectualism.

Choice (3) is wrong since it seems that Lipset, Feuer, and Shils seemingly placed too *little* emphasis on the dual nature of Populism. They failed to perceive the continuity of the *progressive* aspects of Populism among voters in Wisconsin.

Choice (5) is contradicted: Rogin *was* able to submit the conclusions of the three writers to a test—a devastating one—by taking a close look at the voting patterns in Wisconsin counties.

7. Choice (1)

The stem is asking why Rogin studied the class character of Wisconsin voting patterns. Primarily, he did this to check to see if the voting patterns supported or contradicted the arguments of Lipset, Feuer, and Shils. They argued that lower-class farmers and industrial workers provided crucial voter support for both Populism and McCarthyism, and Rogin performed his study of voting patterns in order to challenge their conclusions, by showing that lower-class farmers and workers in fact did not give their votes to McCarthy. Statement I reflects this.

Statement II is wrong since Rogin was out to disprove the alleged links between Populism and McCarthyism, not explain them.

Statement III is way beyond the scope of the passage.

8. Choice (1)

In the last half of the second paragraph the passage indicates that Lipset argued that lower-class support of McCarthy included urban industrial workers, which he describes as "the lower classes, especially the workers."

The last paragraph describes the study in which Rogin found that voters in counties with high industrial employment tended to vote against McCarthy. Rogin used this study to support his counterassertion that McCarthy in fact did not enjoy extensive support among the lower classes. Thus, an assumption made by both men is that voters among industrial workers can be classified as lower-class voters.

Choice (2) is out; Rogin's overall thesis is to argue that lower-class voters voted more progressively than Lipset, Feuer, and Shils admit.

Choice (3) clearly isn't an assumption of Rogin's, who suggests something quite different: McCarthy lacked extensive support among lower classes.

Choice (4) is beyond the scope of the passage. There's not enough information to conclude that either scholar assumed this.

Choice (5) has no support, since neither Lipset nor Rogin is described in this passage as arguing that Midwestern voters are representative of more general political patterns among American voters.

9. Choice (2)

This is a detail question, and since it asks you "[a]ccording to the passage," it will be a paraphrase of something that appears within it. Correct choice (2) paraphrases the first sentence of the third paragraph and the concluding sentence of the passage. Rogin's overall charge against Lipset, Feuer, and Shils is that they not only reach faulty conclusions but are politically biased against the lower classes from the very beginning. It's this latter charge that's summed up in choice (2).

Choice (1) goes too far. Rogin never charges deliberate falsification of evidence by the three men.

Choice (3) is out. Never does Rogin imply that the men's viewpoints will support attacks on civil liberties.

Choice (4) puts things backwards. It's Rogin who makes scrupulous use of statistical analysis. This is what Lipset, Feuer, and Shils failed to do.

Choice (5) is out since Rogin never suggests that the writings of Lipset, Feuer, and Shils were essentially anti-intellectual. Rogin might say that are intellectually or professionally incompetent, since he believes their research methods lack credibility, but this choice distorts this idea.

10. Choice (5)

For this global question, go to your purpose and main idea. The author's main purpose is to describe the rebuff to the views on McCarthyism expressed in the second paragraph. The author states that these conclusions were not based on real evidence, and suggested that they were shaped by preconceived prejudices. These are flaws in historical methodology, choice (4).

Choice (1) uses the wrong verb. The author is not comparing the views; rather, he is supporting one particular view, that of Rogin.

Choice (2) goes for a detail—Rogin's research methods. And choice (3) distorts the author's point of view that the two movements were fundamentally dissimilar.

Choice (4) is out because, although the author would agree with it, it does not address the main point of the passage.

PART THREE

Analytical Writing

Chapter 6: **Strategies for GRE Writing**

WHAT TO EXPECT

The Analytical Writing Measure consists of two timed essay sections. The first is what (ETS) calls an "Issue" essay: You'll be shown two essay topics—each a sentence or paragraph that expresses an opinion on an issue of general interest. You must choose one of the two topics. You then have 45 minutes to plan and write an essay that communicates your own view on the issue. Whether you agree or disagree with the opinion on the screen is irrelevant: What matters is that you support your view with relevant examples and statements.

The second of the two writing tasks is the "Argument" essay. This time, you will be shown a paragraph that argues a certain point. You will then be given 30 minutes to assess that argument's logic. As with the "Issue" essay, it won't matter whether you agree with what you see on the screen.

 **STYLE POINTS**

Effective GRE style is:

- Concise
- Forceful
- Correct

How the Computer-Based Essays Are Administered

At the start of the computer-based Analytical Writing section, you will be given a brief tutorial on how to use the word processor. If you aren't comfortable with complex word processing programs, don't worry. The program you'll use on the GRE is quite simple, as the only commands you'll use are cut, paste, and undo. You'll be well acquainted with the program's commands by the time you start writing.

 KEEP IT SIMPLE

Write your essay in a clear, straightforward manner. Keep word choice, sentence structure, and your argument simple (but not simplistic).

THE FOUR BASIC PRINCIPLES OF GRE WRITING

GRE writing is a simple, two-stage process: First you decide what you want to say about a topic, and then you figure out how to say it. If your writing style isn't clear, your ideas won't come across, no matter how brilliant they are. Good GRE English is not only grammatical but also clear and concise, and by using some basic principles, you'll be able to express your ideas clearly and effectively in both of your essays.

Your Control of Language Is Important

Writing that is grammatical, concise, direct, and persuasive displays the "superior control of language" (as the test makers term it) that earns top GRE Writing Assessment. To achieve effective GRE style in your essays, you should pay attention to the following points.

Grammar

Your writing must follow the rules of standard written English. If you're not confident of your mastery of grammar, brush up before the test.

THE BASIC PRINCIPLES OF GRE WRITING

1. Use language effectively.
2. Keep it simple.
3. Don't worry excessively about making minor errors.
4. Keep sight of your goal.

Diction

Diction means word choice. For example, do you use the words *affect* and *effect* correctly? Be careful with such commonly confused words as *precede/proceed*, *principal/principle*, *whose/who's*, and *stationary/stationery*.

Syntax

Syntax refers to sentence structure. Do you construct your sentences so that your ideas are clear and understandable? Do you vary your sentence structure, sometimes using simple sentences and other times using sentences with clauses and phrases?

It's Better to Keep Things Simple

Perhaps the single most important thing to bear in mind when writing GRE essays is to keep everything simple. This rule applies to word choice, sentence structure, and organization. If you obsess about how to spell an unusual word, you can lose your flow of thought. The more complicated your sentences are, the more likely it is that they will be plagued by errors. The more complex your organization gets, the more likely it is that your argument will get bogged down in convoluted sentences that obscure your point. But keep in mind that simple does not mean simplistic. A clear, straightforward approach can still be sophisticated and convey perceptive insights.

Minor Grammatical Flaws Won't Torpedo Your Score

Many test takers mistakenly believe that they'll lose points because of a few mechanical errors such as misplaced commas, misspellings, or other minor glitches. Occasional mistakes of this type will not dramatically affect your GRE essay score. In fact, the test makers' description of a top-scoring essay acknowledges that there may be minor grammatical flaws. The essay graders understand that you are writing first-draft essays. They will not be looking to take points off for minor errors, provided you don't make them consistently. However, if your essays are littered with misspellings and grammar mistakes, then the graders may conclude that you have a serious communication problem.

To write an effective essay, you must be concise, forceful, and correct. An effective essay wastes no words, makes its point in a clear, direct way, and conforms to the generally accepted rules of grammar and form.

Keep Sight of Your Goal

Remember, your goal isn't to become a prize-winning stylist. It's to write two solid essays that will convince admissions officers you can write well enough to clearly communicate your ideas to a reader—or academic colleague. GRE essay graders don't expect rhetorical flourishes, but they do expect effective expression.

This chapter will give you the chance to sharpen your GRE writing skills.

THE KAPLAN FIVE-STEP METHOD FOR THE ANALYTICAL WRITING MEASURE

Here's the deal: You have a limited amount of time to show the graduate school admissions people that you can think logically and express yourself in clearly written English. They don't care how many syllables you can cram into a sentence or how fancy your phrases are. They care that you're making sense. Whatever you do, don't try to hide beneath a lot of hefty words and abstractions. Just make sure that everything you say is clearly written and relevant to the topic. Get in there, state your main points, back them up, and get out.

❶ **Digest the issue/argument.**
  - Read it through to get a sense of the scope of the matter.
  - Note any terms that are ambiguous and need defining.
  - Frame the issue/argument.

❷ **Select the points you will make.**
  - In the "Analysis of Issue" essay, think of the arguments for both sides and make a decision as to which side you will support or the exact extent to which you agree with the stated position.
  - In the "Analysis of Argument" essay, identify all the important gaps between the evidence and the conclusion. Think of remedies for the problems you discover.

❸ **Organize your argument.**
  - Outline your essay.
  - Lead with your best arguments.
  - Think about how the essay as a whole will flow.

❹ **Write/type your essay.**
  - Be direct.
  - Use paragraph breaks to make your essay easier to read.
  - Make transitions, link related ideas; it will help your writing flow.
  - Finish strongly.

❺ **Proofread your work.**
- Save enough time to read through the entire essay.
- Have a sense of the errors you are liable to make.

As explained before, the two essay types you'll meet on the GRE, the Issue and the Argument, require generally similar tasks. You must analyze a subject, take an informed position, and explain that position in writing. The two essay types, however, require different specific tasks.

 WHAT'S YOUR JOB?

For both essay types, you must:
- **Analyze a topic.**
- **Take a position.**
- **Explain your position.**

THE ISSUE ESSAY

Analysis of Issue questions have two basic parts: the stimulus, and the question stem. The stimulus is the first paragraph, which outlines the issue for you to analyze; the question stem is the second paragraph, giving you instructions about your essay task.

The Stimulus

Expect a sentence or two that discuss a broad, general issue, sometimes presenting two competing points of view, sometimes only one. While the issue will be one upon which reasonable people could disagree, it will not bring up an emotionally charged religious or social issue. You won't be expected to have prior knowledge of any specific subject matter.

The first sentence or two will introduce the general issue itself and express a point of view. If two viewpoints are expressed, sometimes a Keyword—such as *but, however, yet*—will signal the introduction of a contrasting point of view; sometimes, as in the statement above, this transition won't be quite as explicit. The last part of the stimulus will then discuss the opposing view on the issue. If only one viewpoint is discussed, there will be terms in the opinion as stated that make it extreme or overly broad. There may also be an additional statement that elaborates on it more fully.

The Question Stem

The stem will ask you to take a position on the issue and will instruct you to explain your position convincingly, using reasons or examples to back up your assertions.

The directions for the issue essay will be something similar to this:

> **Directions:** You will have 45 minutes to plan and write an essay that communicates your perspective on a given topic. Choose from the two topics provided. No other topics are admissible for this essay.

The topic is a short quotation that expresses an issue of general interest. Write an essay that agrees with, refutes, or qualifies the quotation, and support your opinion with relevant information drawn from your academic studies, reading, observation, or other experiences.

Feel free to consider the issue for a few minutes before planning your response and beginning your writing. Be certain that your ideas are fully developed and organized logically, and make sure you have enough time left to review and revise what you've written.

The topic could take the form of a single-sentence quotation or it might be in paragraph form. Either way, it will state an argument for which one or more counterarguments could be constructed. In short, the topic will present a point of view. Your job is to form an opinion on the topic and make a case for that opinion.

The topics you see in the Issue section might be similar to these:

> *The invention of gunpowder is the single most destructive achievement in history.*

> *If extraterrestrial beings whose intelligence was comparable to humans' visited Earth, they would judge humans by their potential and achievements rather than by their weaknesses and mistakes.*

> *The drawbacks to the use of nuclear power mean that it is not a long-term solution to the problem of meeting ever-increasing energy needs.*

> **TIP! WRITING AN EFFECTIVE ISSUE ESSAY**
>
> An effective Issue Essay takes a stand, supports it with relevant personal insight, and presents it coherently. Take a few minutes to consider your topic and develop arguments for and against its position. Then decide which side you want to take.

Applying the Kaplan Five-Step Method to the Issue Essay

Let's use the Kaplan Five-Step method on one of the sample issue topics we saw before:

The drawbacks to the use of nuclear power mean that it is not a long-term solution to the problem of meeting ever-increasing energy needs.

❶ **Digest the issue.**

It's simple enough. The person who wrote this believes that nuclear power is not a suitable replacement for other forms of energy.

> **THE KAPLAN METHOD FOR THE WRITING ASSESSMENT**
>
> 1. Digest the issue.
> 2. Select a position.
> 3. Organize your argument.
> 4. Compose your essay.
> 5. Proofread your work.

❷ **Select the points you will make.**

Your job, as stated in the directions, is to decide whether or not you agree and explain your decision. Some would argue that the use of nuclear power is too dangerous, while others would say that we can't afford not to use it. So which side do you take? Remember, this isn't about showing the admissions people what your deep-seated beliefs about the environment are—it's about showing that you can formulate an argument and write it down. Quickly think through the pros and cons of each side, and choose the side for which you have the most relevant things to say. For this topic, that process might go something like this:

Arguments for the use of nuclear power:

- Inexpensive compared to other forms of energy
- Fossil fuels will eventually be depleted
- Solar power still too problematic and expensive

Arguments against the use of nuclear power:

- Radioactive byproducts are deadly.
- Safer alternatives like nuclear fusion may be viable in the future
- Solar power already in use

Again, it doesn't matter which side you take. Let's say that in this case you decide to argue against nuclear power. Remember, the question is asking you to argue why the cons of nuclear power outweigh the pros—the inadequacy of this power source is the end you're arguing toward, so don't list it as a supporting argument.

❸ Organize your argument.

You've already begun to think out your arguments—that's why you picked the side you did in the first place. Now's the time to write them all out, including ones that weaken the opposing side.

Nuclear power is not a viable alternative to other sources of energy because:

- Radioactive, spent fuel has leaked from storage sites (too dangerous)
- Reactor accidents can be catastrophic—Three Mile Island, Chernobyl (too dangerous)
- More research into solar power will bring down its cost (weakens opposing argument)
- Solar-powered homes and cars already exist (alternatives proven viable)
- No serious effort to research other alternatives like nuclear fusion (better alternatives lie undiscovered)
- Energy companies don't spend money on alternatives; no vested interest (better alternatives lie undiscovered)

❹ Compose your essay.

Remember, open up with a general statement and then assert your position. From there, get down your main points. Your essay for this assignment might look like the following:

Sample Essay 1

At first glance, nuclear energy may seem to be the power source for the future. It's relatively inexpensive, it doesn't produce smoke, and its fuel supply is virtually inexhaustible. But a close examination of the issue reveals that nuclear energy is more problematic and dangerous than other forms of energy production.

A main reason that nuclear energy is undesirable is the problem of radioactive waste storage. Highly toxic fuel left over from nuclear fission remains toxic for thousands of years, and the spills and leaks from existing storage sites are hazardous and costly to clean up. Even more appalling is the prospect of accidents at the reactor itself: Incidents at the Three Mile Island and Chernobyl power plants have proven that the consequences of a nuclear meltdown can be catastrophic and have consequences that are felt worldwide.

Environmental and health problems aside, the bottom line for the production of energy is profit. Nuclear power is a business just like any other, and the large companies that produce this country's electricity and gas claim they can't make alternatives like solar power affordable. Yet—largely due to incentives from the federal government—there exist today homes that are heated by solar power, and cars that are fueled by the sun have already hit the streets. If the limited resources that have been devoted to energy alternatives have already produced working models, a more intensive effort is likely to make those alternatives less expensive and problematic.

Options like solar power, hydroelectric power, and nuclear fusion are far better in the long run in terms of cost and safety. The only money required for these alternatives is for the materials required to harvest them: Sunlight, water, and the power of the atom are free. They also don't produce any toxic byproducts for which long-term storage—a hidden cost of nuclear power—must be found. And, with the temporary exception of nuclear fusion, these sources of energy are already being harnessed today.

While there are arguments to be made for both sides, it is clear that the drawbacks to the use of nuclear power are too great. If other alternatives are explored more seriously than they have been in the past, safer and less expensive sources of power will undoubtedly prove to be better alternatives.

❺ **Proofread your work.**

Take that last couple of minutes to catch any glaring errors.

THE ARGUMENT ESSAY

Analysis of Argument question stems are just a variation on the same theme: stimulus and question stem. Same basic idea as in Analysis of Issue questions—the stimulus provides information and the question stem tells you how to analyze this information.

The Stimulus

This time you're given an expressed point of view—an "argument"—that contains a conclusion and supporting evidence. Here the writer tries to persuade you of something—her conclusion—by citing some evidence. You should read the "arguments" in Analysis of Argument questions with a critical eye; be on the lookout for assumptions—the way the writer moves from evidence to conclusion.

The Question Stem

Question stems will require you to decide how convincing you find the argument. To make your case, first analyze the argument itself and evaluate its use of evidence; second, explain how a different approach or more information would make the argument itself better (or possibly worse).

Now let's look at how you might approach the other type of essay topic, the Argument. The directions for this section will probably look something like this:

Directions: You will have 30 minutes to plan and write a critique of an argument presented in the form of a short passage. You will be asked to consider the logical soundness of the argument by:

- Identifying and analyzing the argument's important points
- Organizing, developing, and expressing your ideas
- Supporting your ideas with relevant reasons and/or examples
- Demonstrating a knowledge of standard written English

 **TIP! WRITING AN EFFECTIVE ARGUMENT ESSAY**

In Argument Essays, the author has already drawn a conclusion; you need to determine the validity or inadequacy of his or her reasoning. An effective Argument Essay assesses the conclusion and evidence in the argument, analyzing if for flaws and proposing improvements. And remember, there is no "right" answer. You can take either side in an Argument Essay–just analyze it well.

Feel free to consider the issue for a few minutes before planning your response and beginning your writing. Be certain that your ideas are fully developed and organized logically, and make sure you have enough time left to review and revise what you've written.

The author of an argument topic is trying to persuade you of something—his conclusion—by citing some evidence. So look for these two basic components of an argument: a conclusion and supporting evidence. You should be on the lookout for assumptions—the ways the writer makes the leap from evidence to conclusion.

The topics you see in the Argument section may be similar to these:

The problem of poorly trained teachers that has plagued the state public school system is bound to become a good deal less serious in the future. The state has initiated comprehensive guidelines that oblige state teachers to complete a number of required credits in education and educational psychology at the graduate level before being certified.

The commercial airline industry in the country of Freedonia has experienced impressive growth in the past three years. This trend will surely continue in the years to come, since the airline industry will benefit from recent changes in Freedonian society: Incomes are rising, most employees now receive more vacation time, and interest in travel is rising, as shown by an increase in media attention devoted to foreign cultures and tourist attractions.

Insurance policies guaranteeing the policyholder's income if he or she becomes permanently disabled will surely provide the insurance industry with a popular and profitable product. The cost to a worker who is at average risk is very little, and the benefits paid to the disabled far outweigh this cost.

Applying the Kaplan Five-Step Method to an Argument Essay

Let's use the Kaplan Five-Step Method on the Analysis of an Argument topic we saw before:

The problem of poorly trained teachers that has plagued the state public school system is bound to become a good deal less serious in the future. The state has initiated comprehensive guidelines that oblige state teachers to complete a number of required credits in education and educational psychology at the graduate level before being certified.

Explain how logically persuasive you find this argument. In discussing your viewpoint, analyze the argument's line of reasoning and its use of evidence. Also explain what, if anything, would make the argument more valid and convincing or help you to better evaluate its conclusion.

❶ **Digest the argument.**

First, identify the conclusion—the point the argument's trying to make. Here, the conclusion is:

The problem of poorly trained teachers that has plagued the state public school system is bound to become a good deal less serious in the future.

Next, identify the evidence—the basis for the conclusion. Here, the evidence is:

The state has initiated comprehensive guidelines that oblige state teachers to complete a number of required credits in education and educational psychology at the graduate level before being certified.

Finally, sum up the argument in your own words:

The problem of badly trained teachers will become less serious because they'll be getting better training.

Explain how logically persuasive you find this argument. In explaining your viewpoint, analyze the argument's line of reasoning and its use of evidence. Also explain what, if anything, would make the argument more valid and convincing or would help you to better evaluate its conclusion.

- Credits in education will improve teachers' classroom performance.
- Present bad teachers haven't already met this standard of training.
- Current poor teachers will not still be teaching in the future, or will have to be trained, too.

❷ **Select the points you will make.**

Analyze the use of evidence in the argument.

Determine whether there's anything relevant that's not discussed:

- Whether the training will actually address the cause of the problems
- How to either improve or remove the poor teachers now teaching

Also determine what types of evidence would make the argument stronger or more logically sound. In this case, we need some new evidence supporting the assumptions:

- Evidence verifying that this training will make better teachers.
- Evidence making it clear that present bad teachers haven't already had this training.
- Evidence suggesting why all or many bad teachers won't still be teaching in the future (or why they'll be better trained).

 KEY POINT

In attacking the argument, remember to:

- Jot down the conclusion
- Identify the evidence
- Sum up the essential argument in your own words

 WRITE ON!

In writing your essay, cover each point in your outline and employ the four basic principles of GRE writing.

❸ **Organize your arguments.**

For an essay on this topic, your opening sentence might look like this:

The writer concludes that the present problem of poorly trained teachers will become less severe in the future because of required course work in education and psychology.

 ESSAY STRUCTURE

A two-paragraph essay may be the most natural format for your response. However, consider using a third or fourth if you wish to discuss a number of different features of an argument.

Then use your notes as a working outline. Remember to lead with your best arguments. You might also recommend new evidence you'd like to see and explain why.

The argument says that:

The problem of poorly trained teachers will become less serious with better training.

It assumes that:

- Course work in education will improve teachers' classroom performance.
- Present bad teachers haven't already met this standard of classroom training.
- Current poor teachers will not be teaching in the future or will get training, too.

❹ **Compose your essay.**

Begin typing or writing your essay now. Keep in mind the basic principles of writing that we discussed earlier. And remember the following issues:

What assumptions are made by the author?

- Are these assumptions valid? Why or why not?
- What additional information or evidence would make the argument stronger?

Your essay might look something like this:

Sample Essay 2

The writer concludes that the present problem of poorly trained teachers will become less severe in the future because of required credits in education and psychology. However, the conclusion relies on assumptions for which there is no clear evidence.

First, the writer assumes that the required courses will make better teachers. In fact, the courses might be entirely irrelevant to the teachers' failings. If, for example, the prevalent problem is cultural and linguistic gaps between teacher and student, graduate-level courses that do not address these specific issues probably won't do much good. The argument that the courses will improve teachers would be strengthened if the writer provided evidence that the training will be relevant to the problems.

In addition, the writer assumes that current poor teachers have not already had this training. In fact, the writer doesn't mention whether or not some or all of the poor teachers have had similar training. The argument would be strengthened considerably if the writer provided evidence that current poor teachers have not had training comparable to the new requirements.

Finally, the writer assumes that poor teachers currently working will either stop teaching in the future or will have received training. The writer provides no evidence, though, to indicate that this is the case. As the argument stands, it's highly possible that only brand-new teachers will receive the training, and the bright future to which the writer refers is decades away. Only if the writer provides evidence that all teachers in the system will receive training—and will then change their teaching methods accordingly—does the argument hold.

❺ **Proofread your work.**

Save a few minutes to go back over your essay and catch any obvious errors.

PRACTICE ESSAYS

Directions: Write an essay on each of the topics below. While writing, pay particular attention to making your essay concise, forceful, and grammatically correct. After you've finished with each essay, proofread to catch your errors. Allow yourself 45 minutes to complete the first essay and 30 minutes to complete the second essay.

Essay Topic 1: Issue

Some people believe that second-language fluency is crucial to individual development and international accord, and maintain that language training should begin very early. Others feel that second-language fluency is not necessary to most Americans, and that elementary school should be devoted to basic skills.

Which argument do you find more compelling, the case for early foreign language learning or the opposing viewpoint? Explain your position using relevant reasons or examples drawn from your own experience, observations, or reading.

Essay Topic 2: Argument

Many lives might be saved if inoculations against cow flu were routinely administered to all people in areas in which the disease is detected. However, since there is a small possibility that a person will die as a result of the inoculations, we cannot permit inoculations against cow flu to be routinely administered.

Explain how logically persuasive you find this argument. In discussing your viewpoint, analyze the argument's line of reasoning and its use of evidence. Also explain what, if anything, would make the argument more valid or convincing or help you to better evaluate its conclusion.

GRE ANALYTICAL WRITING SCORING

Holistic scoring uses a single letter or a number—on the GRE it's a number—to provide an overall evaluation of an essay as a whole. A holistic score emphasizes the interrelation of different thinking and writing qualities in an essay (such as content, organization, or syntax) and tries to denote the unified effect that all of these elements combine to produce. Although the GRE writing tests consist of two different essays, a single combined score is reported, representing the average of your scores for the two essays.

Each of the two essay tasks requires a different type of response and so has a slightly different set of grading criteria. But both kinds of topic require similar essay qualities. The list below, based on information from the Graduate Record Examinations Board, will give you a general idea of the guidelines a GRE grader will have in mind when reading your essays.

6: "Outstanding" Essay

- Insightfully presents and convincingly supports an opinion on the issue or a critique of the argument.
- Ideas are very clear, well organized and logically connected.
- Shows superior control of language: grammar, stylistic variety, and accepted conventions of writing; minor flaws may occur.

5: "Strong" Essay

- Presents well-chosen examples and strongly supports an opinion on the issue or a critique of the argument.
- Ideas are generally clear and well organized; connections are logical.
- Shows solid control of language: grammar, stylistic variety, and accepted conventions of writing; minor flaws may occur.

4: "Adequate" Essay

- Presents and adequately supports an opinion on the issue or a critique of the argument.
- Ideas are fairly clear and adequately organized; logical connections are satisfactory.
- Shows satisfactory control of language: grammar, stylistic variety, and accepted conventions of writing; some flaws may occur.

3: "Limited" Essay

- Succeeds only partially in presenting and supporting an opinion on the issue or a critique of the argument.
- Ideas may be unclear and poorly organized.
- Shows less than satisfactory control of language: contains significant mistakes in grammar, usage, and sentence structure.

2: "Weak" Essay

- Shows little success in presenting and supporting an opinion on the issue or a critique of the argument.
- Ideas lack clarity and organization.
- Meaning is impeded by many serious mistakes in grammar, usage, and sentence structure.

1: **"Fundamentally Deficient" Essay**
- Fails to present a coherent opinion and/or evidence on the issue or a critique of the argument.
- Ideas are seriously unclear and disorganized.
- Lacks meaning due to widespread severe mistakes in grammar, usage, and sentence structure.

0: **"Unscorable" Essay**
- Completely ignores topic.

You Be the Evaluator

You've now seen what both essay topic types look like, and you know more about the criteria used to evaluate essays. With this information in mind, review your own practice essays and see how you think they measure up.

For this exercise, it's not critical that you assign the "right" grade. It's more important that you understand whether the essays are well written and how well they fulfill the required tasks.

GRE WRITING STYLE

Be Concise

- Cut out words, phrases, and sentences that do not add any information or serve a purpose.
- Watch out for repetitive phrases such as *refer back* or *serious crisis*.
- Don't use conjunctions to join sentences that would be more effective as separate sentences.

Be Forceful

- Avoid jargon and pompous language; it won't impress anybody.
- Avoid clichés and overused terms or phrases. (For example, *beyond the shadow of a doubt*.)
- Don't be vague. Avoid generalizations and abstractions when more specific words would be clearer. (For example, write *a waste of time and money* instead of *pointless temporal and financial expenditure*.)
- Don't use weak sentence openings. Avoid beginning a sentence with "There is" or "There are."
- Don't refer to yourself needlessly. Avoid pointless phrases like *in my personal opinion*.
- Don't be monotonous: Vary sentence length and style.
- Use transitions to connect sentences and make your essay easy to follow. Paragraphs should clarify the different parts of your essay.

Be Correct

- Stick to the rules of standard written English.

PART FOUR

Vocabulary Builder

Chapter 7: **Increasing Your GRE Vocabulary**

BEFORE YOU GET STARTED

A strong vocabulary is the greatest asset that you can bring to the GRE Verbal Section. Antonyms, which make up a quarter of the Verbal Section, are a direct test of your vocabulary skills. The other types of short Verbal questions (Analogics and Sentence Completions) also require you to understand the meanings of a large number of words.

So, how do you start improving your vocabulary? Don't say to yourself, "I'm going to get ready for the GRE by opening the dictionary and starting on page 1." In real life, the dictionary is the single most useful verbal tool there is. But the GRE is not real life, and for the purposes of preparing for the GRE, the dictionary is overkill. It includes a lot more words than you need to look at, including all those everyday words you already know and all those esoteric words that will never appear on the GRE.

Building up a good vocabulary takes time, a lifetime for most people. However, you can increase your GRE vocabulary quickly. There are a couple of reasons for this:

1. The GRE tests the same words over and over again.

If you know the words that the GRE loves, you have a big head start in increasing your GRE vocabulary. We have included the words that appear most often on the GRE in chapter 8, "Top GRE Words." Start learning the meanings of these words as soon as you can.

2. The GRE does not test the exact definitions of words. If you have some idea of what the word means, you can usually get to the answer.

You don't need to know the exact definitions of words to get a good verbal score on the GRE. It's better to know something about ten words than everything about one word. This is why learning words in groups is such a powerful technique. We have included common word groups for the GRE in chapter 9, "GRE Word Groups."

Knowing the meanings of common word roots can be helpful in two ways. First, knowing the meaning of word roots can help you guess at the meanings of unfamiliar words you encounter on the GRE. Second, when you're learning new vocabulary, it's more effective to study words in groups rather than one by one. Learning groups of words that are related by a common root will help you to learn more words faster. We have included a list of common GRE word roots in chapter 10.

TIP! SIGN UP FOR FREE "WORD OF THE DAY" EMAILS

As you study for the GRE, consider signing up for a free "Word of the Day" email service, such as those offered by dictionary.com, the Oxford English Dictionary (oed.com), or the New York Times (nytimes.com). They send a high-level vocabulary word with its definition, a context sentence, and its etymology to your inbox daily.

Once you've looked over the top GRE words and the chapters on word roots and word groups, you can hone your skills using our opposite drills in chapter 11. Finally, chapter 12 includes a minidictionary that gives you the definitions of thousands of GRE words. Use it whenever you encounter an unfamiliar word in your study.

BASICS OF VOCABULARY BUILDING

The way most people build their vocabulary is by reading words in context. Reading is ultimately the best way to increase your vocabulary, although it also takes the most time. Of course, some types of reading material contain more GRE vocabulary words than others. You should get into the habit of reading high-level publications, such as the *Wall Street Journal,* the *Economist,* and the *New York Times.* (Because you'll have to read from the computer screen on Test Day, we recommend that you read these publications online, if possible. And if you read lengthy articles that require scrolling through, so much the better.)

 TIP! READ THE NEWSPAPER DAILY

Read the newspaper daily, concentrating on articles covering topics with which you are unfamiliar. Jot down each article's main idea and the author's tone and purpose. This way, you can practice overcoming the hurdle of reading unfamiliar or difficult material.

When you come across words you don't know and can't figure out from the context, look them up in the dictionary and make a note of them. It sounds tedious, but it's definitely worth the time and effort come Test Day. The words you encounter during your prep can be found in the GRE Minidictionary in chapter 12. This handy reference tool contains thousands of words that you might find on the GRE.

Note that you will find nothing on pronunciation in the minidictionary. Pronunciation is not tested on the GRE, so we don't recommend spending study time learning how to pronounce words. Some people, however, find it much easier to remember the meaning of a word if they have the sound of the word in their heads. If you're such a person, then use the dictionary to figure out how to pronounce words you're not familiar with.

PARTS OF SPEECH

The GRE never directly tests your ability to classify words by part of speech, but you'll do better if you can distinguish nouns, adjectives, and verbs.

Nouns

A noun names a person, place, or thing. A noun answers the questions "who," "where," or "what." A noun can function as the subject ("The *soliloquy* was eloquent") or object of a verb ("He wrote an eloquent *soliloquy*").

If you know the meaning of the word, you can tell if it's a noun by thinking about the way it would be used in a sentence:

- If the word can function as the subject of a sentence, it's a noun.
- If it can be replaced by a pronoun like *he, she, it,* or *they,* it's a noun.

- If you can put an article like *the, a, an,* or *some* in front of it, it's a noun.
- If it has a plural form (usually the ending *-s*), it's a noun. If it has a possessive form (usually the ending *-'s*), it's a noun.
- If you don't know the meaning of a word, but it has one of the following suffixes, then it's probably a noun:

-ACY	-HOOD	-OGY
-AGE	-ICE	-OR
-ANCE	-ICS	-RY
-ANCY	-ISM	-SHIP
-DOM	-IST	-SION
-ENCE	-ITY	-TION
-ENCY	-MENT	-TUDE
-ERY	-NESS	-URE

Adjectives

An adjective describes a noun, answering the questions "what kind," "which one," or "how many." In a sentence, you will generally find adjectives right in front of the nouns they describe ("The book is full of *sophomoric* humor") or after a form of the verb be or some other linking verb ("The book's humor is *sophomoric*").

If you know the meaning of a word, you can tell if it's an adjective by thinking about the way the word would be used in a sentence. If the word can be used to describe a noun, it's an adjective. Most adjectives have comparative and superlative forms *(rife, rifer, rifest* and *sanguine, more sanguine, most sanguine)*. Most adjectives can be turned into adverbs by adding *-ly (intemperately)*.

If you don't know the meaning of a word, but it has one of the following suffixes, then it's probably an adjective:

-ABLE	-FUL	-IVE
-AL	-IBLE	-LESS
-ANE	-IC	-OSE
-ANT	-ILE	-OUS
-AR	-INE	
-ENT	-ISH	

Verbs

A verb is a word that represents an action or state of being. Every sentence must have at least one verb. The main verb usually comes right after the subject (*"They squander* their fortunes"), but sometimes is separated from the subject ("The *contestant* with the second highest vote total *wins* the consolation prize") and sometimes even precedes the subject ("Quickly *flow* the *years.*")

If you know the meaning of the word, you can tell if it's a verb by thinking about the way the word would be used in a sentence. If, with the addition of an *-s*, it can follow a pronoun like *he* or *it* and make a sentence, it's a verb ("He *panders*"). If it has a past form ending in *-ed (pandered)* and a progressive form ending in *-ing (pandering),* it's a verb.

If you don't know the meaning of a word, but it has one of the following suffixes, then it's probably a verb:

-EN	-IFY
-ESCE	-IZE

Split-Personality Words

Remember that many words in the English language can function as more than one part of speech. Here's a single word used as a noun, adjective, and verb:

As the test tube rested overnight, some *precipitate* formed. (noun)

It would be better to proceed with caution than to take *precipitate* action. (adjective)

Passage of the resolution could well *precipitate* rebellion. (verb)

When you see a word all by itself in an analogy or an antonym, with no sentence to show you the word in use, you may not be able to tell at first what part of speech it is. For example, if you see the word brook out of context, don't assume you're looking at a noun. It can also be a verb, as in: "She would brook no interference with her intentions." Instead, look at the answer choices or the other word in an analogy's stem. They should make it pretty clear what meaning they are testing.

Chapter 8: **Top GRE Words**

Some words appear on the GRE more than others. The following words all turn up regularly on the test, although some turn up more than others. You should start by learning these words, and the groups of words that have similar meanings to them.

The top 12 words on the GRE are:

ANOMALY	ASSUAGE	ENIGMA
EQUIVOCAL	ERUDITE	FERVID
LUCID	OPAQUE	PLACATE
PRECIPITATE	PRODIGAL	ZEAL

The next 20 most popular words are:

ABSTAIN	ADULTERATE	APATHY
AUDACIOUS	CAPRICIOUS	CORROBORATE
DESICCATE	ENGENDER	EPHEMERAL
GULLIBLE	HOMOGENOUS	LACONIC
LAUDABLE	LOQUACIOUS	MITIGATE
PEDANT	PRAGMATIC	PROPRIETY
VACILLATE	VOLATILE	

The next 20 most popular words after these are:

ADVOCATE	ANTIPATHY	BOLSTER
CACOPHONY	DERIDE	DISSONANCE
ENERVATE	EULOGY	GARRULOUS
INGENUOUS	LETHARGIC	MALLEABLE
MISANTHROPE	OBDURATE	OSTENTATION
PARADOX	PHILANTHROPIC	PREVARICATE
VENERATE	WAVER	

200 TOP GRE WORDS IN CONTEXT

ABATE: to reduce in amount, degree, or severity

As the hurricane's force ABATED, the winds dropped and the sea became calm.

Words with similar meanings:

EBB	LAPSE	LET UP
MODERATE	RELENT	SLACKEN
SUBSIDE	WANE	

ABSCOND: to leave secretly

The patron ABSCONDED from the restaurant without paying his bill by sneaking out the back door.

Words with similar meanings:

DECAMP	ESCAPE	FLEE

ABSTAIN: to choose not to do something

During Lent, practicing Catholics ABSTAIN from eating meat.

Words with similar meanings:

FORBEAR	REFRAIN	WITHHOLD

ABYSS: an extremely deep hole

The submarine dove into the ABYSS to chart the previously unseen depths.

Related words:

ABYSSAL: pertaining to great depth

ABYSMAL: extremely bad

Words with similar meanings:

CHASM	VOID

ADULTERATE: to make impure

The restaurateur made his ketchup last longer by ADULTERATING it with water.

Related words:

UNADULTERATED: pure

ADULTERY: an illicit relationship; an affair

Words with similar meanings:

DOCTOR

ADVOCATE: to speak in favor of

The vegetarian ADVOCATED a diet containing no meat.

Related words:

ADVOCACY: active support for

Words with similar meanings:

BACK	CHAMPION	SUPPORT

AESTHETIC: concerning the appreciation of beauty

Followers of the AESTHETIC Movement regarded the pursuit of beauty as the only true purpose of art.

Related words:

AESTHETE: someone unusually sensitive to beauty

AESTHETICISM: concern with beauty

Words with similar meanings:

ARTISTIC	TASTEFUL

AGGRANDIZE: to increase in power, influence, and reputation

The supervisor sought to AGGRANDIZE himself by claiming that the achievements of his staff were actually his own.

Words with similar meanings:

AMPLIFY	APOTHEOSIZE	AUGMENT
DIGNIFY	ELEVATE	ENLARGE
ENNOBLE	EXALT	GLORIFY
MAGNIFY	SWELL	UPLIFT
WAX		

ALLEVIATE: to make more bearable:

Taking aspirin helps to ALLEVIATE a headache.

Words with similar meanings:

ALLAY	ASSUAGE	COMFORT
EASE	LESSEN	LIGHTEN
MITIGATE	PALLIATE	RELIEVE

AMALGAMATE: to combine; to mix together

Giant Industries AMALGAMATED with Mega Products to form Giant-Mega Products Incorporated.

Related words:

AMALGAM: a mixture, especially of two metals

Words with similar meanings:

ADMIX	BLEND	COMBINE
COMMINGLE	COMMIX	COMPOUND
FUSE	INTERMINGLE	INTERMIX
MERGE	MINGLE	MIX

AMBIGUOUS: doubtful or uncertain; able to be interpreted several ways

The directions he gave were so AMBIGUOUS that we disagreed on which way to turn.

Related words:

AMBIGUITY: the quality of being ambiguous

Words with similar meanings:

CLOUDY	DOUBTFUL	DUBIOUS
EQUIVOCAL	NEBULOUS	INDETERMINATE
OBSCURE	UNCLEAR	VAGUE

AMELIORATE: to make better; to improve

The doctor was able to AMELIORATE the patient's suffering using painkillers.

Words with similar meanings:

AMEND	BETTER	IMPROVE
PACIFY	UPGRADE	

ANACHRONISM: something out of place in time

The aged hippie used ANACHRONISTIC phrases like *groovy* and *far out* that had not been popular for years.

Words with similar meanings:

ARCHAISM	INCONGRUITY

ANALOGOUS: similar or alike in some way; equivalent to

In a famous argument for the existence of God, the universe is ANALOGOUS to a mechanical timepiece, the creation of a divinely intelligent "clockmaker."

Related words:

ANALOGY: a similarity between things that are otherwise dissimilar

ANALOGUE: something that is similar in some way to something else

Words with similar meanings:

ALIKE	COMPARABLE	CORRESPONDING
EQUIVALENT	HOMOGENEOUS	PARALLEL
SIMILAR		

ANOMALY: deviation from what is normal

Albino animals may display too great an ANOMALY in their coloring to attract normally colored mates.

Related words:

ANOMALOUS: deviating from what is normal

Words with similar meanings:

ABERRANCE	ABERRATION	ABNORMALITY
DEVIANCE	DEVIATION	IRREGULARITY
PRETERNATURALNESS		

ANTAGONIZE: to annoy or provoke to anger

The child discovered that he could ANTAGONIZE the cat by pulling its tail.

Related words:

ANTAGONISTIC: tending to provoke conflict

ANTAGONIST: someone who fights another

Words with similar meanings

CLASH	CONFLICT	INCITE
IRRITATE	OPPOSE	PESTER
PROVOKE	VEX	

ANTIPATHY: extreme dislike

The ANTIPATHY between the French and the English regularly erupted into open warfare.

Words with similar meanings:

ANIMOSITY	ANIMUS	ANTAGONISM
AVERSION	ENMITY	HOSTILITY
REPELLENCE		

APATHY: lack of interest or emotion

The APATHY of voters is so great that less than half the people who are eligible to vote actually bother to do so.

Words with similar meanings:

COOLNESS	DISINTEREST	DISREGARD
IMPASSIVITY	INDIFFERENCE	INSENSIBILITY
LASSITUDE	LETHARGY	LISTLESSNESS
PHLEGM	STOLIDITY	UNCONCERN
UNRESPONSIVENESS		

ARBITRATE: to judge a dispute between two opposing parties

Since the couple could not come to agreement, a judge was forced to ARBITRATE their divorce proceedings.

Related words:

ARBITRATION: a process by which a conflict is resolved

ARBITRATOR: a judge

Words with similar meanings:

ADJUDGE	ADJUDICATE	DECIDE
DETERMINE	JUDGE	MODERATE
REFEREE	RULE	

ARCHAIC: ancient, old-fashioned

Her ARCHAIC Commodore computer could not run the latest software.

Related words:

ARCHAISM: an outdated word or phrase

Words with similar meanings:

ANCIENT	ANTEDILUVIAN	ANTIQUE
BYGONE	DATED	DOWDY
FUSTY	OBSOLETE	OLD-FASHIONED
OUTDATED	OUTMODED	PASSÉ
PREHISTORIC	STALE	SUPERANNUATED
SUPERSEDED	VINTAGE	

ARDOR: intense and passionate feeling

Bishop's ARDOR for landscape was evident when he passionately described the beauty of the scenic Hudson Valley.

Related words:

ARDENT: expressing ardor; passionate

Words with similar meanings:

DEVOTION	ENTHUSIASM	FERVENCY
FERVIDITY	FERVIDNESS	FERVOR
FIRE	PASSION	ZEAL
ZEALOUSNESS		

ARTICULATE: able to speak clearly and expressively

She is such an ARTICULATE defender of labor that unions are among her strongest supporters.

Words with similar meanings

ELOQUENT	EXPRESSIVE	FLUENT
LUCID	SILVER-TONGUED	SMOOTH-SPOKEN

ASSUAGE: to make something unpleasant less severe

Like many people, Philip Larkin used alcohol to ASSUAGE his sense of meaninglessness and despair.

Words with similar meanings:

ALLAY	ALLEVIATE	APPEASE
COMFORT	CONCILIATE	EASE
LIGHTEN	MITIGATE	MOLLIFY
PACIFY	PALLIATE	PLACATE
PROPITIATE	RELIEVE	SOOTHE
SWEETEN		

ATTENUATE: to reduce in force or degree; to weaken

The Bill of Rights ATTENUATED the traditional power of government to change laws at will.

Words with similar meanings:

DEBILITATE	DEVITALIZE	DILUTE
ENERVATE	ENFEEBLE	RAREFY
SAP	THIN	UNDERMINE
UNDO	UNNERVE	WATER
WEAKEN		

AUDACIOUS: fearless and daring

"And you, your majesty, may kiss my bum!" replied the AUDACIOUS peasant.

Related words:

AUDACITY: the quality of being audacious

Words with similar meanings:

ADVENTURESOME	AGGRESSIVE	ASSERTIVE
BOLD	BRAVE	COURAGEOUS
DARING	DAUNTLESS	DOUGHTY
FEARLESS	GALLANT	GAME
HEROIC	INTREPID	METTLESOME
PLUCKY	STOUT	STOUTHEARTED
UNAFRAID	UNDAUNTED	VALIANT
VALOROUS	VENTURESOME	VENTUROUS

AUSTERE: severe or stern in appearance; undecorated

The lack of decoration makes Zen temples seem AUSTERE to the untrained eye.

Related words:

AUSTERITY: severity, especially poverty

Words with similar meanings:

BLEAK	DOUR	GRIM
HARD	HARSH	SEVERE

BANAL: predictable, clichéd, boring

He used BANAL phrases like *Have a nice day* or *Another day, another dollar.*

Related words:

BANALITY: the quality of being banal

Words with similar meanings:

BLAND	BROMIDIC	CLICHÉD
COMMONPLACE	FATUOUS	HACKNEYED
INNOCUOUS	INSIPID	JEJUNE
MUSTY	PLATITUDINOUS	PROSAIC
QUOTIDIAN	SHOPWORN	STALE
STEREOTYPIC	THREADBARE	TIMEWORN
TIRED	TRITE	VAPID
WORN-OUT		

BOLSTER: to support; to prop up

The presence of giant footprints BOLSTERED the argument that Sasquatch was in the area.

Words with similar meanings:

BRACE	BUTTRESS	PROP
SUPPORT	SUSTAIN	UNDERPIN
UPHOLD		

BOMBASTIC: pompous in speech and manner

Mussolini's speeches were mostly BOMBASTIC; his boasting and outrageous claims had no basis in fact.

Related words:

BOMBAST: pompous speech or writing

Words with similar meanings:

BLOATED	DECLAMATORY	FUSTIAN
GRANDILOQUENT	GRANDIOSE	HIGH-FLOWN
MAGNILOQUENT	OROTUND	PRETENTIOUS
RHETORICAL	SELF-IMPORTANT	

CACOPHONY: harsh, jarring noise

The junior high orchestra created an almost unbearable CACOPHONY as they tried to tune their instruments.

Words with similar meanings:

DISCORD	CHAOS	DISHARMONY
NOISE	CLAMOR	DIN

CANDID: impartial and honest in speech

The observations of a child can be charming since they are CANDID and unpretentious.

Words with similar meanings:

DIRECT	FORTHRIGHT	FRANK
HONEST	OPEN	SINCERE
STRAIGHT	STRAIGHTFORWARD	UNDISGUISED

CAPRICIOUS: changing one's mind quickly and often

Queen Elizabeth I was quite CAPRICIOUS; her courtiers could never be sure which of their number would catch her fancy.

Related words:

CAPRICE: whim, sudden fancy

Words with similar meanings:

ARBITRARY	CHANCE	CHANGEABLE
ERRATIC	FICKLE	INCONSTANT
MERCURIAL	RANDOM	WHIMSICAL
WILLFUL		

CASTIGATE: to punish or criticize harshly

Americans are amazed at how harshly the authorities in Singapore CASTIGATE perpetrators of what would be considered minor crimes in the United States.

Words with similar meanings:

ADMONISH	CHASTISE	CHIDE
REBUKE	REPRIMAND	REPROACH
REPROVE	SCOLD	TAX
UPBRAID		

CATALYST: something that brings about a change in something else

The imposition of harsh taxes was the CATALYST that finally brought on the revolution.

Related words:

CATALYZE: to bring about a change in something else

CAUSTIC: biting in wit

Dorothy Parker gained her reputation for CAUSTIC wit from her cutting, yet clever, insults.

Words with similar meanings:

ACERBIC	BITING	MORDANT
TRENCHANT		

CHAOS: great disorder or confusion

In most religious traditions, God created an ordered universe from CHAOS.

Related words:

CHAOTIC: jumbled, confused

Words with similar meanings:

CLUTTER	CONFUSION	DISARRANGEMENT
DISARRAY	DISORDER	DISORDERLINESS
DISORGANIZATION	JUMBLE	MESS
MUDDLE	SCRAMBLE	SNARL
TOPSY-TURVINESS	TURMOIL	

CHAUVINIST: someone prejudiced in favor of a group to which he or she belongs

The attitude that men are inherently superior to women and therefore must be obeyed is common among male CHAUVINISTS.

Words with similar meanings:

PARTISAN

CHICANERY: deception by means of craft or guile

Dishonest used car salesmen often use CHICANERY to sell their beat-up old cars.

Words with similar meanings:

ARTIFICE	CONNIVING	CRAFTINESS
DECEPTION	DEVIOUSNESS	MISREPRESENTATION
PETTIFOGGERY	SHADINESS	SNEAKINESS
SOPHISTRY	SUBTERFUGE	UNDERHANDEDNESS

COGENT: convincing and well reasoned

Swayed by the COGENT argument of the defense, the jury had no choice but to acquit the defendant.

Related words:

COGITATE: to think deeply

Words with similar meanings:

CONVINCING	PERSUASIVE	SOLID
SOUND	TELLING	VALID

CONDONE: to overlook, pardon, or disregard

Some theorists believe that failing to prosecute minor crimes is the same as CONDONING an air of lawlessness.

Words with similar meanings:

EXCULPATE	EXCUSE	PARDON
REMIT		

CONVOLUTED: intricate and complicated

Although many people bought *A Brief History of Time*, few could follow its CONVOLUTED ideas and theories.

Words with similar meanings:

BYZANTINE	COMPLEX	ELABORATE
INTRICATE	KNOTTY	LABYRINTHINE
PERPLEXING	TANGLED	

CORROBORATE: to provide supporting evidence

Fingerprints CORROBORATED the witness's testimony that he saw the defendant in the victim's apartment.

Words with similar meanings:

AUTHENTICATE	BACK	BEAR OUT
BUTTRESS	CONFIRM	SUBSTANTIATE
VALIDATE	VERIFY	

CREDULOUS: too trusting; gullible

Although some 4-year-olds believe in the Easter Bunny, only the most CREDULOUS 9-year-olds also believe in him.

Related words:

CREDULITY: the quality of being credulous

Words with similar meanings:

NAIVE	SUSCEPTIBLE	TRUSTING

CRESCENDO: steadily increasing volume or force

The CRESCENDO of tension became unbearable as Evel Knievel prepared to jump his motorcycle over the school buses.

DECORUM: appropriateness of behavior or conduct; propriety

The countess complained that the vulgar peasants lacked the DECORUM appropriate for a visit to the palace.

Related words:

DECOROUS: conforming to acceptable standards

Words with similar meanings:

CORRECTNESS	DECENCY	ETIQUETTE
MANNERS	MORES	PROPRIETY
SEEMLINESS		

DEFERENCE: respect, courtesy

The respectful young law clerk treated the Supreme Court justice with the utmost DEFERENCE.

Related words:

DEFER: to delay; to show someone deference
DEFERENT: courteous and respectful

Words with similar meanings:

COURTESY	HONOR	HOMAGE
OBEISANCE	RESPECT	REVERENCE
VENERATION		

DERIDE: to speak of or treat with contempt; to mock

The awkward child was often DERIDED by his "cooler" peers.

Related words:

DERISION: mockery and taunts
DERISIVE: in a mocking manner

Words with similar meanings:

GIBE	JEER	MOCK
RIDICULE	SCOFF	SNEER
TAUNT		

DESICCATE: to dry out thoroughly

After a few weeks of lying on the desert's baking sands, the cow's carcass became completely DESICCATED.

Related words:

DESICCANT: something that removes water from another substance

Words with similar meanings:

DRY	PARCH	DEHYDRATE

DESULTORY: jumping from one thing to another; disconnected

Diane had a DESULTORY academic record; she had changed majors 12 times in 3 years.

Words with similar meanings:

AIMLESS	DISCONNECTED	ERRATIC
HAPHAZARD	INDISCRIMINATE	OBJECTLESS
PURPOSELESS	RANDOM	STRAY
UNCONSIDERED	UNPLANNED	

DIATRIBE: an abusive, condemnatory speech

The trucker bellowed a DIATRIBE at the driver who had cut him off.

Words with similar meanings:

FULMINATION	HARANGUE	INVECTIVE
JEREMIAD	MALEDICTION	OBLOQUY
TIRADE		

DIFFIDENT: lacking self-confidence

Steve's DIFFIDENT manner during the job interview stemmed from his nervous nature and lack of experience in the field.

Words with similar meanings:

BACKWARD	BASHFUL	COY
DEMURE	MODEST	RETIRING
SELF-EFFACING	SHY	TIMID

DILATE: to make larger; to expand

When you enter a darkened room, the pupils of your eyes DILATE to let in more light.

Words with similar meanings:

AMPLIFY	DEVELOP	ELABORATE
ENLARGE	EXPAND	EXPATIATE

DILATORY: intended to delay

The congressman used DILATORY measures to delay the passage of the bill.

Words with similar meanings:

DRAGGING	FLAGGING	LAGGARD
LAGGING	SLOW	SLOW-FOOTED
SLOW-GOING	SLOW-PACED	TARDY

DILETTANTE: someone with an amateurish and superficial interest in a topic

Jerry's friends were such DILETTANTES that they seemed to have new jobs and hobbies every week.

Words with similar meanings:

AMATEUR	DABBLER	SUPERFICIAL
TYRO		

DIRGE: a funeral hymn or mournful speech

Melville wrote the poem A DIRGE for James McPherson for the funeral of a Union general who was killed in 1864.

Words with similar meanings:

ELEGY	LAMENT

DISABUSE: to set right; to free from error

Galileo's observations DISABUSED scholars of the notion that the Sun revolved around the Earth.

Words with similar meanings:

CORRECT	UNDECEIVE

DISCERN: to perceive; to recognize

It is easy to DISCERN the difference between butter and butter-flavored topping.

Related words:

DISCERNMENT: taste and cultivation

Words with similar meanings:

CATCH	DESCRY	DETECT
DIFFERENTIATE	DISCRIMINATE	DISTINGUISH
ESPY	GLIMPSE	KNOW
SEPARATE	SPOT	SPY
TELL		

DISPARATE: fundamentally different; entirely unlike

Although the twins appear to be identical physically, their personalities are DISPARATE.

Words with similar meanings:

DIFFERENT	DISSIMILAR	DIVERGENT
DIVERSE	VARIANT	VARIOUS

DISSEMBLE: to present a false appearance; to disguise one's real intentions or character

The villain could DISSEMBLE to the police no longer—he admitted the deed and tore up the floor to reveal the body of the old man.

Words with similar meanings:

ACT	AFFECT	ASSUME
CAMOUFLAGE	CLOAK	COUNTERFEIT
COVER UP	DISGUISE	DISSIMULATE
FAKE	FEIGN	MASK
MASQUERADE	POSE	PRETEND
PUT ON	SHAM	SIMULATE

DISSONANCE: a harsh and disagreeable combination, often of sounds

Cognitive DISSONANCE is the inner conflict produced when long-standing beliefs are contradicted by new evidence.

Words with similar meanings:

CLASH	CONTENTION	DISCORD
DISSENSION	DISSENT	DISSIDENCE
FRICTION	STRIFE	VARIANCE

DOGMA: a firmly held opinion, often a religious belief

Linus' central DOGMA was that children who believed in the Great Pumpkin would be rewarded.

Words with similar meanings:

CREED	DOCTRINE	TEACHING
TENET		

DOGMATIC: dictatorial in one's opinions

The dictator was DOGMATIC—he, and only he, was right.

Words with similar meanings:

AUTHORITARIAN	BOSSY	DICTATORIAL
DOCTRINAIRE	DOMINEERING	IMPERIOUS
MAGISTERIAL	MASTERFUL	OVERBEARING
PEREMPTORY		

DUPE: to deceive; a person who is easily deceived

Bugs Bunny was able to DUPE Elmer Fudd by dressing up as a lady rabbit.

Words with similar meanings:

BEGUILE	BETRAY	BLUFF
COZEN	DECEIVE	DELUDE
FOOL	HOODWINK	HUMBUG
MISLEAD	TAKE IN	TRICK

ECLECTIC: selecting from or made up from a variety of sources

Budapest's architecture is an ECLECTIC mix of eastern and western styles.

Words with similar meanings:

SELECTIVE   CATHOLIC   BROAD

EFFICACY: effectiveness

The EFFICACY of penicillin was unsurpassed when it was first introduced; the drug completely eliminated almost all bacterial infections for which it was administered.

Related words:

EFFICACIOUS: effective; productive

Words with similar meanings:

DYNAMISM	EFFECTIVENESS	EFFICIENCY
FORCE	POWER	PRODUCTIVENESS
PROFICIENCY	STRENGTH	VIGOR

ELEGY: a sorrowful poem or speech

Although Thomas Gray's "ELEGY Written in a Country Churchyard" is about death and loss, it urges its readers to endure this life, and to trust in spirituality.

Related words:

ELEGIAC: like an elegy; mournful

Words with similar meanings:

DIRGE   LAMENT

ELOQUENT: persuasive and moving, especially in speech

The Gettysburg Address is moving not only because of its lofty sentiments but also because of its ELOQUENT words.

Words with similar meanings:

ARTICULATE	EXPRESSIVE	FLUENT
MEANINGFUL	SIGNIFICANT	SMOOTH-SPOKEN

EMULATE: to copy; to try to equal or excel

The graduate student sought to EMULATE his professor in every way, copying not only how she taught, but also how she conducted herself outside of class.

Words with similar meanings:

APE   IMITATE   SIMULATE

ENERVATE: to reduce in strength

The guerrillas hoped that a series of surprise attacks would ENERVATE the regular army.

Related words:

UNNERVE: to deprive of strength or courage

Words with similar meanings:

| DEBILITATE | ENFEEBLE | SAP |
| WEAKEN | | |

ENGENDER: to produce, cause, or bring about

His fear and hatred of clowns was ENGENDERED when he witnessed the death of his father at the hands of a clown.

Words with similar meanings:

| BEGET | GENERATE | PROCREATE |
| PROLIFERATE | REPRODUCE | SPAWN |

ENIGMA: a puzzle; a mystery

Speaking in riddles and dressed in old robes, the artist gained a reputation as something of an ENIGMA.

Words with similar meanings:

| CONUNDRUM | PERPLEXITY |

ENUMERATE: to count, list, or itemize

Moses returned from the mountain with tablets on which the commandments were ENUMERATED.

Words with similar meanings:

| CATALOG | INDEX | TABULATE |

EPHEMERAL: lasting a short time

The lives of mayflies seem EPHEMERAL to us, since the flies' average life span is a matter of hours.

Words with similar meanings:

| EVANESCENT | FLEETING | MOMENTARY |
| TRANSIENT | | |

EQUIVOCATE: to use expressions of double meaning in order to mislead

When faced with criticism of his policies, the politician EQUIVOCATED and left all parties thinking he agreed with them.

Related words:

EQUIVOCAL: undecided; trying to deceive

EQUIVOCATION: the act or state of equivocating

Words with similar meanings:

| AMBIGUOUS | EVASIVE | WAFFLING |

ERRATIC: wandering and unpredictable

The plot seemed predictable until it suddenly took a series of ERRATIC turns that surprised the audience.

Related words:

ERRANT: straying, mistaken, roving

Words with similar meanings:

| CAPRICIOUS | INCONSTANT | IRRESOLUTE |
| WHIMSICAL | | |

ERUDITE: learned, scholarly, bookish

The annual meeting of philosophy professors was a gathering of the most ERUDITE, well-published individuals in the field.

Related words:

ERUDITION: extensive knowledge or learning

Words with similar meanings:

| SCHOLASTIC | LEARNED | WISE |

ESOTERIC: known or understood by only a few

Only a handful of experts are knowledgeable about the ESOTERIC world of particle physics.

Words with similar meanings:

| ABSTRUSE | ARCANE | OBSCURE |

ESTIMABLE: admirable

Most people consider it ESTIMABLE that Mother Teresa spent her life helping the poor of India.

Related words:

ESTEEM: high regard

Words with similar meanings:

ADMIRABLE	COMMENDABLE	CREDITABLE
HONORABLE	LAUDABLE	MERITORIOUS
PRAISEWORTHY	RESPECTABLE	VENERABLE
WORTHY		

EULOGY: speech in praise of someone

His best friend gave the EULOGY, outlining his many achievements and talents.

Words with similar meanings:

| COMMEND | EXTOL | LAUD |

EUPHEMISM: use of an inoffensive word or phrase in place of a more distasteful one

The funeral director preferred to use the EUPHEMISM "sleeping" instead of the word "dead."

Words with similar meanings:

| CIRCUMLOCUTION | WHITEWASH |

EXACERBATE: to make worse

It is unwise to take aspirin to try to relieve heartburn; instead of providing relief, the drug will only EXACERBATE the problem.

Words with similar meanings:

| ANNOY | AGGRAVATE | INTENSIFY |
| IRRITATE | PROVOKE | |

EXCULPATE: to clear from blame; prove innocent

The adversarial legal system is intended to convict those who are guilty and to EXCULPATE those who are innocent.

Words with similar meanings:

| ABSOLVE | ACQUIT | CLEAR |
| EXONERATE | VINDICATE | |

EXIGENT: urgent; requiring immediate action

The patient was losing blood so rapidly that it was EXIGENT to stop the source of the bleeding.

Words with similar meanings:

| CRITICAL | IMPERATIVE | NEEDED |
| URGENT | | |

EXONERATE: to clear of blame

The fugitive was EXONERATED when another criminal confessed to committing the crime.

Words with similar meanings:

| ABSOLVE | ACQUIT | CLEAR |
| EXCULPATE | VINDICATE | |

EXPLICIT: clearly stated or shown; forthright in expression

The owners of the house left a list of EXPLICIT instructions detailing their house-sitters' duties, including a schedule for watering the house plants.

Related words:

EXPLICABLE: capable of being explained

EXPLICATE: to give a detailed explanation

Words with similar meanings:

CANDID	FRANK	STRAIGHTFORWARD
UNEQUIVOCAL		

FANATICAL: acting excessively enthusiastic; filled with extreme, unquestioned devotion

The stormtroopers were FANATICAL in their devotion to the Emperor, readily sacrificing their lives for him.

Words with similar meanings:

EXTREMIST	FIERY	FRENZIED
ZEALOUS		

FAWN: to grovel

The understudy FAWNED over the director in hopes of being cast in the part on a permanent basis.

Words with similar meanings:

BOOTLICK	GROVEL	PANDER
TOADY		

FERVID: intensely emotional; feverish

The fans of Maria Callas were particularly FERVID, doing anything to catch a glimpse of the great opera singer.

Related words:

FERVENT: enthusiastic

FERVOR: passion

Words with similar meanings:

BURNING	IMPASSIONED	PASSIONATE
VEHEMENT	ZEALOUS	

FLORID: excessively decorated or embellished

The palace had been decorated in an excessively FLORID style; every surface had been carved and gilded.

Words with similar meanings:

BAROQUE	ELABORATE	FLAMBOYANT
ORNATE	OSTENTATIOUS	ROCOCO

FOMENT: to arouse or incite

The protesters tried to FOMENT feeling against the war through their speeches and demonstrations.

Words with similar meanings:

AGITATE	IMPASSION	INFLAME
INSTIGATE	KINDLE	

FRUGALITY: a tendency to be thrifty or cheap

Scrooge McDuck's FRUGALITY was so great that he accumulated enough wealth to fill a giant storehouse with money.

Words with similar meanings:

ECONOMICAL	PARSIMONY	PRUDENCE
SPARING		

GARRULOUS: tending to talk a lot

The GARRULOUS parakeet distracted its owner with its continuous talking.

Words with similar meanings:

EFFUSIVE	LOQUACIOUS

GREGARIOUS: outgoing, sociable

She was so GREGARIOUS that when she found herself alone she felt quite sad.

Words with similar meanings:

AFFABLE	CONGENIAL	COMMUNICATIVE
SOCIABLE		

GUILE: deceit or trickery

Since he was not fast enough to catch the roadrunner on foot, the coyote resorted to GUILE in an effort to trap his enemy.

Related words:

GUILELESS: innocent, without trickery

Words with similar meanings:

ARTIFICE	CHICANERY	CONNIVERY
DUPLICITY		

GULLIBLE: easily deceived

The con man pretended to be a bank officer so as to fool GULLIBLE bank customers into giving him their account information.

Related words:

GULL: a person who is easily tricked

Words with similar meanings:

CREDULOUS	EXPLOITABLE	NAIVE

HOMOGENOUS: of a similar kind

The class was fairly HOMOGENOUS, since almost all of the students were senior journalism majors.

Related words:

HOMOGENIZED: thoroughly mixed together

Words with similar meanings:

CONSISTENT	STANDARDIZED	UNIFORM
UNVARYING		

ICONOCLAST: one who opposes established beliefs, customs, and institutions

His lack of regard for traditional beliefs soon established him as an ICONOCLAST.

Words with similar meanings:

MAVERICK	NONCONFORMIST	REBEL
REVOLUTIONARY		

IMPERTURBABLE: not capable of being disturbed

The counselor had so much experience dealing with distraught children that she seemed IMPERTURBABLE, even when faced with the wildest tantrums.

Related words:

PERTURB: to disturb greatly

Words with similar meanings:

COMPOSED	DISPASSIONATE	IMPASSIVE
SERENE	STOICAL	

IMPERVIOUS: impossible to penetrate; incapable of being affected

A good raincoat will be IMPERVIOUS to moisture.

Words with similar meanings:

RESISTANT	IMPREGNABLE

IMPETUOUS: quick to act without thinking

It is not good for an investment broker to be IMPETUOUS, since much thought should be given to all the possible options.

Related words:

IMPETUS: impulse

Words with similar meanings:

IMPULSIVE	PRECIPITATE	RASH
RECKLESS	SPONTANEOUS	

IMPLACABLE: unable to be calmed down or made peaceful

His rage at the betrayal was so great that he remained IMPLACABLE for weeks.

Related words:

PLACATE: to make peaceful

Words with similar meanings:

INEXORABLE	INTRANSIGENT	IRRECONCILABLE
RELENTLESS	REMORSELESS	UNFORGIVING
UNRELENTING		

INCHOATE: not fully formed; disorganized

The ideas expressed in Nietzsche's mature work also appear in an INCHOATE form in his earliest writing.

Words with similar meanings:

AMORPHOUS	INCOHERENT	INCOMPLETE
UNORGANIZED		

INGENUOUS: showing innocence or childlike simplicity

She was so INGENUOUS that her friends feared that her innocence and trustfulness would be exploited when she visited the big city.

Related words:

INGÉNUE: a naive girl or young woman

DISINGENUOUS: giving a false impression of innocence

Words with similar meanings:

ARTLESS	GUILELESS	INNOCENT
NAIVE	SIMPLE	UNAFFECTED

INIMICAL: hostile, unfriendly

Even though a cease-fire had been in place for months, the two sides were still INIMICAL to each other.

Words with similar meanings:

ADVERSE	ANTAGONISTIC	DISSIDENT
RECALCITRANT		

INNOCUOUS: harmless

Some snakes are poisonous, but most species are INNOCUOUS and pose no danger to humans.

Words with similar meanings:

BENIGN	HARMLESS	INOFFENSIVE

INSIPID: lacking interest or flavor

The critic claimed that the painting was INSIPID, containing no interesting qualities at all.

Words with similar meanings:

BANAL	BLAND	DULL
STALE	VAPID	

INTRANSIGENT: uncompromising; refusing to be reconciled

The professor was INTRANSIGENT on the deadline, insisting that everyone turn the assignment in at the same time.

Words with similar meanings:

IMPLACABLE	INEXORABLE	IRRECONCILABLE
OBDURATE	OBSTINATE	REMORSELESS
RIGID	UNBENDING	UNRELENTING
UNYIELDING		

INUNDATE: to overwhelm; to cover with water

The tidal wave INUNDATED Atlantis, which was lost beneath the water.

Words with similar meanings:

DELUGE	DROWN	ENGULF
FLOOD	SUBMERGE	

IRASCIBLE: easily made angry

Attila the Hun's IRASCIBLE and violent nature made all who dealt with him fear for their lives.

Related words:

IRATE: angry

Words with similar meanings:

CANTANKEROUS	IRRITABLE	ORNERY
TESTY		

LACONIC: using few words

She was a LACONIC poet who built her reputation on using words as sparingly as possible.

Words with similar meanings:

CONCISE	CURT	PITHY
TACITURN	TERSE	

LAMENT: to express sorrow; to grieve

The children continued to LAMENT the death of the goldfish weeks after its demise.

Words with similar meanings:

BEWAIL	DEPLORE	GRIEVE
MOURN		

LAUD: to give praise; to glorify

Parades and fireworks were staged to LAUD the success of the rebels.

Related words:

LAUDABLE: worth of praise

LAUDATORY: expressing praise

Words with similar meanings:

ACCLAIM	APPLAUD	COMMEND
COMPLIMENT	EXALT	EXTOL
HAIL	PRAISE	

LAVISH: to give unsparingly (v.); extremely generous or extravagant (adj.)

She LAVISHED the puppy with so many treats that it soon become overweight and spoiled.

Words with similar meanings:

BESTOW	CONFER	EXTRAVAGANT
EXUBERANT	LUXURIANT	OPULENT
PRODIGAL	PROFUSE	SUPERABUNDANT

LETHARGIC: acting in an indifferent or slow, sluggish manner

The clerk was so LETHARGIC that, even when the store was slow, he always had a long line in front of him.

Words with similar meanings:

APATHETIC	LACKADAISICAL	LANGUID
LISTLESS	TORPID	

LOQUACIOUS: talkative

She was naturally LOQUACIOUS, which was a problem in situations in which listening was more important than talking.

Related words:

ELOQUENCE: powerful, convincing speaking

LOQUACITY: the quality of being loquacious

Words with similar meanings:

EFFUSIVE	GARRULOUS	VERBOSE

LUCID: clear and easily understood

The explanations were written in a simple and LUCID manner so that students were immediately able to apply what they learned.

Related words:

LUCIDITY: clarity

LUCENT: glowing with light

Words with similar meanings:

CLEAR	COHERENT	EXPLICIT
INTELLIGIBLE	LIMPID	

LUMINOUS: bright, brilliant, glowing

The park was bathed in LUMINOUS sunshine that warmed the bodies and the souls of the visitors.

Related words:

ILLUMINATE: to shine light on

LUMINARY: an inspiring person

Words with similar meanings:

INCANDESCENT	LUCENT	LUSTROUS
RADIANT	RESPLENDENT	

MALINGER: to evade responsibility by pretending to be ill

A common way to avoid the draft was by MALINGERING—pretending to be mentally or physically ill so as to avoid being taken by the Army.

Related words:

LINGER: to be slow in leaving

Words with similar meanings:

SHIRK	SLACK

MALLEABLE: capable of being shaped

Gold is the most MALLEABLE of precious metals; it can easily be formed into almost any shape.

Words with similar meanings:

ADAPTABLE	DUCTILE	PLASTIC
PLIABLE	PLIANT	

METAPHOR: a figure of speech comparing two different things; a symbol

The METAPHOR "a sea of troubles" suggests a lot of troubles by comparing their number to the vastness of the sea.

Related words:

METAPHORICAL: standing as a symbol for something else

Words with similar meanings:

ANALOGY   COMPARISON

METICULOUS: extremely careful about details

To find all the clues at the crime scene, the investigators METICULOUSLY examined every inch of the area.

Words with similar meanings:

CONSCIENTIOUS   PRECISE   SCRUPULOUS

MISANTHROPE: a person who dislikes others

The character Scrooge in *A Christmas Carol* is such a MISANTHROPE that even the sight of children singing makes him angry.

MITIGATE: to soften; to lessen

A judge may MITIGATE a sentence if she decides that a person committed a crime out of need.

Words with similar meanings:

ALLAY	ALLEVIATE	ASSUAGE
EASE	LIGHTEN	MODERATE
MOLLIFY	PALLIATE	TEMPER

MOLLIFY: to calm or make less severe

Their argument was so intense that is was difficult to believe any compromise would MOLLIFY them.

Words with similar meanings:

APPEASE	ASSUAGE	CONCILIATE
PACIFY		

MONOTONY: lack of variation

The MONOTONY of the sound of the dripping faucet almost drove the research assistant crazy.

Related words:

MONOTONE: a sound that is made at the same tone or pitch

Words with similar meanings:

DRONE	TEDIUM

NAIVE: lacking sophistication or experience

Having never traveled before, the hillbillies were more NAIVE than the people they met in Beverly Hills.

Related words:

NAIVETÉ: the state of being naive

Words with similar meanings:

ARTLESS	CREDULOUS	GUILELESS
INGENUOUS	SIMPLE	UNAFFECTED

OBDURATE: hardened in feeling; resistant to persuasion

The President was completely OBDURATE on the issue, and no amount of persuasion would change his mind.

Words with similar meanings:

INFLEXIBLE	INTRANSIGENT	RECALCITRANT
TENACIOUS	UNYIELDING	

OBSEQUIOUS: overly submissive and eager to please

The OBSEQUIOUS new associate made sure to compliment her supervisor's tie and agree with him on every issue.

Related words:

OBEISANCE: a physical show of respect or submission, such as a bow

Words with similar meanings:

COMPLIANT	DEFERENTIAL	SERVILE
SUBSERVIENT		

OBSTINATE: stubborn, unyielding

The OBSTINATE child could not be made to eat any food that he disliked.

Words with similar meanings:

INTRANSIGENT	MULISH	PERSISTENT
PERTINACIOUS	STUBBORN	TENACIOUS

OBVIATE: to prevent; to make unnecessary

The river was shallow enough to wade across at many points, which OBVIATED the need for a bridge.

Words with similar meanings:

FORESTALL   PRECLUDE   PROHIBIT

OCCLUDE: to stop up; to prevent the passage of

A shadow is thrown across the Earth's surface during a solar eclipse, when the light from the sun is OCCLUDED by the moon.

Words with similar meanings:

BARRICADE   BLOCK   CLOSE
OBSTRUCT

ONEROUS: troublesome and oppressive; burdensome

The assignment was so extensive and difficult to manage that it proved ONEROUS to the team in charge of it.

Words with similar meanings:

ARDUOUS   BACKBREAKING   BURDENSOME
CUMBERSOME   DIFFICULT   EXACTING
FORMIDABLE   HARD   LABORIOUS
OPPRESSIVE   RIGOROUS   TAXING
TRYING

OPAQUE: impossible to see through; preventing the passage of light

The heavy buildup of dirt and grime on the windows almost made them OPAQUE.

Related words:

OPACITY: the quality of being obscure and indecipherable

Words with similar meanings:

OBSCURE

OPPROBRIUM: public disgrace

After the scheme to embezzle the elderly was made public, the treasurer resigned in utter OPPROBRIUM.

Words with similar meanings:

DISCREDIT   DISGRACE   DISHONOR
DISREPUTE   IGNOMINY   INFAMY
OBLOQUY   SHAME

OSTENTATION: excessive showiness

The OSTENTATION of the Sun King's court is evident in the lavish decoration and luxuriousness of his palace at Versailles.

Related words:

OSTENSIBLE: apparent

Words with similar meanings:

CONSPICUOUSNESS	FLASHINESS	PRETENTIOUSNESS
SHOWINESS		

PARADOX: a contradiction or dilemma

It is a PARADOX that those most in need of medical attention are often those least able to obtain it.

Words with similar meanings:

AMBIGUITY	INCONGRUITY

PARAGON: model of excellence or perfection

She is the PARAGON of what a judge should be: honest, intelligent, hardworking, and just.

Words with similar meanings:

APOTHEOSIS	IDEAL	QUINTESSENCE
STANDARD		

PEDANT: someone who shows off learning

The graduate instructor's tedious and excessive commentary on the subject soon gained her a reputation as a PEDANT.

Related words:

PEDANTIC: making an excessive display of learning

PERFIDIOUS: willing to betray one's trust

The actress's PERFIDIOUS companion revealed all of her intimate secrets to the gossip columnist.

Related words:

PERFIDY: deceit, treachery

Words with similar meanings:

DISLOYAL	FAITHLESS	TRAITOROUS
TREACHEROUS		

PERFUNCTORY: done in a routine way; indifferent

The machinelike bank teller processed the transaction and gave the waiting customer a PERFUNCTORY smile.

Words with similar meanings:

APATHETIC	AUTOMATIC	MECHANICAL

PERMEATE: to penetrate

This miraculous new cleaning fluid is able to PERMEATE stains and dissolve them in minutes!

Related words:

IMPERMEABLE: unable to be permeated

Words with similar meanings:

IMBUE	INFUSE	SUFFUSE

PHILANTHROPY: charity; a desire or effort to promote goodness

New York's Metropolitan Museum of Art owes much of its collection to the PHILANTHROPY of private collectors who willed their estates to the museum.

Related words:

PHILANTHROPIST: someone who is generous and desires to promote goodness

Words with similar meanings:

HUMANITARIANISM	ALTRUISM

PLACATE: to soothe or pacify

The burglar tried to PLACATE the snarling dog by saying, "Nice doggy," and offering it a treat.

Related words:

PLACID: tolerant; calm

IMPLACABLE: unable to be made peaceful

Words with similar meanings:

APPEASE	CONCILIATE	MOLLIFY

PLASTIC: able to be molded, altered, or bent

The new material was very PLASTIC and could be formed into products of vastly different shape.

Words with similar meanings:

ADAPTABLE	DUCTILE	MALLEABLE
PLIANT		

PLETHORA: excess

Assuming that more was better, the defendant offered the judge a PLETHORA of excuses.

Words with similar meanings:

GLUT	OVERABUNDANCE	SUPERFLUITY
SURFEIT		

PRAGMATIC: practical as opposed to idealistic

While daydreaming gamblers think they can get rich by frequenting casinos, PRAGMATIC gamblers realize that the odds are heavily stacked against them.

Related words:

PRAGMATISM: a practical approach to problem solving

Words with similar meanings:

RATIONAL   REALISTIC

PRECIPITATE: to throw violently or bring about abruptly; lacking deliberation

Upon learning that the couple married after knowing each other only two months, friends and family members expected such a PRECIPITATE marriage to end in divorce.

Related words:

PRECIPITOUS: very steep

PRECIPICE: a steep cliff

PRECIPITATION: weather phenomena, like rain or snow, that fall from the sky

Words with similar meanings:

ABRUPT	HASTY	HEADLONG
HURRIED	ILL-CONSIDERED	IMPETUOUS
IMPULSIVE	PROMPT	RASH
RECKLESS	SUDDEN	

PREVARICATE: to lie or deviate from the truth

Rather than admit that he had overslept again, the employee PREVARICATED and claimed that heavy traffic had prevented him from arriving at work on time.

Words with similar meanings:

EQUIVOCATE   LIE   PERJURE

PRISTINE: fresh and clean; uncorrupted

Since concerted measures had been taken to prevent looting, the archeological site was still PRISTINE when researchers arrived.

Words with similar meanings:

INNOCENT   UNDAMAGED

PRODIGAL: lavish, wasteful

The PRODIGAL Son quickly wasted all of his inheritance on a lavish lifestyle devoted to pleasure.

Related words:

PRODIGALITY: excessive or reckless spending

Words with similar meanings:

EXTRAVAGANT	LAVISH	PROFLIGATE
SPENDTHRIFT	WASTEFUL	

PROLIFERATE: to increase in number quickly

Although he only kept two guinea pigs initially, they PROLIFERATED to such an extent that he soon had dozens.

Related words:

PROLIFIC: very productive or highly able to reproduce rapidly

Words with similar meanings:

BREED	MULTIPLY	PROCREATE
PROPAGATE	REPRODUCE	SPAWN

PROPITIATE: to conciliate; to appease

The management PROPITIATED the irate union by agreeing to raise wages for its members.

Related words:

PROPITIOUS: advantageous, favorable

Words with similar meanings:

APPEASE	CONCILIATE	MOLLIFY
PACIFY	PLACATE	

PROPRIETY: correct behavior; obedience to rules and customs

The aristocracy maintained a high level of PROPRIETY, adhering to even the most minor social rules.

Related words:

APPROPRIATE: suitable for a particular occasion or place

Words with similar meanings:

DECENCY	DECORUM	MODESTY
SEEMLINESS		

PRUDENCE: wisdom, caution, or restraint

The college student exhibited PRUDENCE by obtaining practical experience along with her studies, which greatly strengthened her résumé.

Related words:

PRUDE: someone who is excessively concerned with propriety

PRUDISH: prissy and puritanical

Words with similar meanings:

ASTUTENESS	CIRCUMSPECTION	DISCRETION
FRUGALITY	JUDICIOUSNESS	PROVIDENCE
THRIFT		

PUNGENT: sharp and irritating to the senses

The smoke from the burning tires was extremely PUNGENT.

Words with similar meanings:

ACRID	CAUSTIC	PIQUANT
POIGNANT	STINGING	

QUIESCENT: motionless

Many animals are QUIESCENT over the winter months, minimizing activity in order to conserve energy.

Related words:

QUIESCENCE: state of rest or inactivity

Words with similar meanings:

DORMANT	LATENT

RAREFY: to make thinner or sparser

Since the atmosphere RAREFIES as altitudes increase, the air at the top of very tall mountains is too thin to breathe.

Related words:

RAREFACTION: the process of making something less dense

Words with similar meanings:

ATTENUATE	THIN

REPUDIATE: to reject the validity of

The old woman's claim that she was Russian royalty was REPUDIATED when DNA tests showed she was of no relation to them.

Words with similar meanings:

DENY	DISAVOW	DISCLAIM
DISOWN	RENOUNCE	

RETICENT: silent, reserved

Physically small and RETICENT in her speech, Joan Didion often went unnoticed by those upon whom she was reporting.

Words with similar meanings:

COOL	INTROVERTED	LACONIC
STANDOFFISH	TACITURN	UNDEMONSTRATIVE

RHETORIC: effective writing or speaking

Lincoln's talent for RHETORIC was evident in his beautifully expressed Gettysburg Address.

Words with similar meanings:

ELOQUENCE	ORATORY

SATIATE: to satisfy fully or overindulge

His desire for power was so great that nothing less than complete control of the country could SATIATE it.

Related words:

SATE: to fully satisfy or overindulge

INSATIABLE:

incapable of being satisfied

Words with similar meanings:

CLOY	GLUT	GORGE
SURFEIT		

SOPORIFIC: causing sleep or lethargy

The movie proved to be so SOPORIFIC that soon loud snores were heard throughout the theater.

Related words:

SOPOR: deep sleep

Words with similar meanings:

HYPNOTIC	NARCOTIC	SLUMBEROUS
SOMNOLENT		

SPECIOUS: deceptively attractive; seemingly plausible but fallacious

The student's SPECIOUS excuse for being late sounded legitimate, but was proved otherwise when his teacher called his home.

Words with similar meanings:

ILLUSORY	OSTENSIBLE	PLAUSIBLE
SOPHISTICAL	SPURIOUS	

STIGMA: a mark of shame or discredit

In *The Scarlet Letter*, Hester Prynne was required to wear the letter "A" on her clothes as a public STIGMA for her adultery.

Related words:

STIGMATIZE: to disgrace; to label with negative terms or reputation

Words with similar meanings:

BLEMISH	BLOT	OPPROBRIUM
STAIN	TAINT	

STOLID: unemotional; lacking sensitivity

The prisoner appeared STOLID and unaffected by the judge's harsh sentence.

Words with similar meanings:

APATHETIC	IMPASSIVE	INDIFFERENT
PHLEGMATIC	STOICAL	UNCONCERNED

SUBLIME: lofty or grand

The music was so SUBLIME that it transformed the rude surroundings into a special place.

Related words:

SUBLIMATE: to elevate or convert into something of higher worth

SUBLIMINAL: existing outside conscious awareness

Words with similar meanings:

AUGUST	EXALTED	GLORIOUS
GRAND	MAGNIFICENT	MAJESTIC
NOBLE	REGAL	RESPLENDENT
SUPERB		

TACIT: done without using words

Although not a word had been said, everyone in the room knew that a TACIT agreement had been made about which course of action to take.

Related words:

TACITURN: silent, not talkative

Words with similar meanings:

IMPLICIT	IMPLIED	UNDECLARED
UNSAID	UNUTTERED	

TACITURN: silent, not talkative

The clerk's TACITURN nature earned him the nickname "Silent Bob."

Related words:

TACIT: done without using words

Words with similar meanings:

      LACONIC   RETICENT

TIRADE: long, harsh speech or verbal attack

    Observers were shocked at the manager's TIRADE over such a minor mistake.

Words with similar meanings:

DIATRIBE	FULMINATION	HARANGUE
OBLOQUY	REVILEMENT	VILIFICATION

TORPOR: extreme mental and physical sluggishness

    After surgery, the patient experienced TORPOR until the anesthesia wore off.

Related words:

TORPID: sluggish, lacking movement

Words with similar meanings:

      APATHY   LANGUOR

TRANSITORY: temporary, lasting a brief time

    The reporter lived a TRANSITORY life, staying in one place only long enough to cover the current story.

Related words:

TRANSIT: to pass through; to change or make a transition

TRANSIENT: passing quickly in and out of existence; one who stays a short time

Words with similar meanings:

EPHEMERAL	EVANESCENT	FLEETING
IMPERMANENT	MOMENTARY	

VACILLATE: to sway physically; to be indecisive

    The customer held up the line as he VACILLATED between ordering chocolate chip or rocky road ice cream.

Words with similar meanings:

DITHER	FALTER	FLUCTUATE
OSCILLATE	WAVER	

VENERATE: to respect deeply

    In a traditional Confucian society, the young VENERATE their elders, deferring to the elders' wisdom and experience.

Related words:

VENERABLE: old, worthy of respect

Words with similar meanings:

ADORE	HONOR	IDOLIZE
REVERE		

VERACITY: filled with truth and accuracy

She had a reputation for VERACITY, so everyone trusted her description of events.

Related words:

VERITY: truth

VERACIOUS: truthful, accurate

Words with similar meanings:

CANDOR	EXACTITUDE	FIDELITY
PROBITY		

VERBOSE: wordy

The professor's answer was so VERBOSE that his student forgot what the original question had been.

Related words:

VERBALIZE: to put into words

VERBATIM: to quote using the exact words, word for word

VERBIAGE: lots of words that are usually superfluous

Words with similar meanings:

LONG-WINDED	LOQUACIOUS	PROLIX
SUPERFLUOUS		

VEX: to annoy

The old man who loved his peace and quiet was VEXED by his neighbor's loud music.

Related words:

VEXATION: a feeling of irritation

Words with similar meanings:

ANNOY	BOTHER	CHAFE
EXASPERATE	IRK	NETTLE
PEEVE	PROVOKE	

VOLATILE: easily aroused or changeable; lively or explosive

His VOLATILE personality made it difficult to predict his reaction to anything.

Words with similar meanings:

CAPRICIOUS	ERRATIC	FICKLE
INCONSISTENT	INCONSTANT	MERCURIAL
TEMPERAMENTAL		

WAVER: to fluctuate between choices

If you WAVER too long before making a decision about which testing site to register for, you may not get your first choice.

Words with similar meanings:

DITHER	FALTER	FLUCTUATE
OSCILLATE	VACILLATE	

WHIMSICAL: acting in a fanciful or capricious manner; unpredictable

The ballet was WHIMSICAL, delighting the children with its imaginative characters and unpredictable sets.

Related words:

WHIM: a fancy or sudden notion

Words with similar meanings:

CAPRICIOUS	ERRATIC	FLIPPANT
FRIVOLOUS		

ZEAL: passion, excitement

She brought her typical ZEAL to the project, sparking enthusiasm in the other team members.

Related words:

ZEALOT: a fanatic

Words with similar meanings:

ARDENCY	FERVOR	FIRE
PASSION		

Chapter 9: **GRE Word Groups**

Learning words in groups is an efficient way of increasing your GRE vocabulary, since the GRE often tests only that you have a general sense of what a word means. Say you saw the following question on the test:

DENOUNCE:

    (A) blaspheme

    (B) acclaim

    (C) permit

    (D) gather

    (E) assist

If you looked up *denounce* in a dictionary, you'd see something like this:

de•nounce (dĭ-nouns′) *transitive verb,* de•nounced, de•nounc•ing, de•nounc•es [Middle English: *denouncen, denounsen,* fr. Latin *denoncier,* fr. *de + nuntiare* to report, announce, fr. *nuntius* messenger]

1. To declare (a person, an idea, behavior, a philosophy) to be censurable or evil; stigmatize or accuse, especially publicly and indignantly; inveigh against openly

2. *archaic* to announce in a public, formal, and solemn manner: to declare or publish something disastrous

3. to inform against: declare or expose a lawbreaker to the authorities

4a. *obsolete* to indicate or portend

4b. *archaic* to announce in a warning or threatening manner

5. to proclaim formally and publicly the ending of a treaty or pact

6. *Mexican Law* to offer for record legal notice of a claim for a mining concession on land held by the government

Synonym see CRITICIZE

Do you need to know all this to answer the question? No—all you need to know is that *denounce* means something like criticize. And in the time it took you to learn the meaning of denounce from the dictionary, you could have memorized a whole list of other words that also mean something like *criticize (aspersion, belittle, berate, calumny, castigate, decry, defamation, denounce, deride/derisive, diatribe, rebuke,* etcetera).

And the answer to the above question? Well, that would be drawn from the list of words that mean *praise (acclaim, accolade, aggrandize, encomium, eulogize, extol, fawn, laud/laudatory, venerate/ veneration,* etcetera.)

This is why learning words in groups is a better general strategy for beefing up your GRE vocabulary than working slowly through the dictionary.

Just remember, the categories in which these words are listed are GENERAL and not to be taken for the exact definitions of the words.

BOLD

audacious	courageous	dauntless

CHANGING QUICKLY

capricious	mercurial	volatile

HESITATE

dither	oscillate	teeter
vacillate	waver	

ACT QUICKLY

abrupt	apace	headlong
impetuous	precipitate	

INNOCENT/INEXPERIENCED

credulous	gullible	ingenuous
naive	novitiate	tyro

DIFFICULT TO UNDERSTAND

abstruse	ambiguous	arcane
bemusing	cryptic	enigmatic
esoteric	inscrutable	obscure
opaque	paradoxical	perplexing
recondite	turbid	

EASY TO UNDERSTAND

articulate	cogent	eloquent
evident	limpid	lucid
pellucid		

SMART/LEARNED

astute	canny	erudite
perspicacious		

CRITICIZE/CRITICISM

aspersion	belittle	berate
calumny	castigate	decry
defamation	denounce	deride/derisive
diatribe	disparage	excoriate
gainsay	harangue	impugn
inveigh	lambaste	objurgate
obloquy	opprobrium	pillory
rebuke	remonstrate	reprehend
reprove	revile	tirade
vituperate		

CAROUSAL

bacchanalian	depraved	dissipated
iniquity	libertine	libidinous
licentious	reprobate	ribald
salacious	sordid	turpitude

TRUTH

candor/candid	fealty	frankness
indisputable	indubitable	legitimate
probity	sincere	veracious
verity		

FALSEHOOD

apocryphal	canard	chicanery
dissemble	duplicity	equivocate
erroneous	ersatz	fallacious
feigned	guile	mendacious
mendacity	perfidy	prevaricate
specious	spurious	

BITING (as in wit or temperament)

acerbic	acidulous	acrimonious
asperity	caustic	mordant
mordacious	trenchant	

PRAISE

acclaim	accolade	aggrandize
encomium	eulogize	extol
fawn	laud/laudatory	venerate

HARMFUL

baleful	baneful	deleterious
inimical	injurious	insidious
minatory	perfidious	pernicious

TIMID/TIMIDITY

craven	diffident	pusillanimous
recreant	timorous	trepidation

BORING

banal	fatuous	hackneyed
insipid	mundane	pedestrian
platitude	prosaic	quotidian
trite		

WEAKEN

adulterate	enervate	exacerbate
inhibit	obviate	stultify
undermine	vitiate	

ASSIST

abet	advocate	ancillary
bolster	corroborate	countenance
espouse	mainstay	munificent
proponent	stalwart	sustenance

HOSTILE

antithetic	churlish	curmudgeon
irascible	malevolent	misanthropic
truculent	vindictive	

STUBBORN

implacable	inexorable	intractable
intransigent	obdurate	obstinate
recalcitrant	refractory	renitent
untoward	vexing	

BEGINNING/YOUNG

burgeoning	callow	engender
inchoate	incipient	nascent

GENEROUS/KIND

altruistic	beneficent	clement
largess	magnanimous	munificent
philanthropic	unstinting	

GREEDY

avaricious	covetous	mercenary
miserly	penurious	rapacious
venal		

TERSE

compendious	curt	laconic
pithy	succinct	taciturn

OVERBLOWN/WORDY

bombastic	circumlocution	garrulous
grandiloquent	loquacious	periphrastic
prolix	rhetoric	turgid
verbose		

DICTATORIAL

authoritarian	despotic	dogmatic
hegemonic	hegemony	imperious
peremptory	tyrannical	

HATRED

abhorrence	anathema	antagonism
antipathy	detestation	enmity
loathing	malice	odium
rancor		

BEGINNER/AMATEUR

dilettante	fledgling	neophyte
novitiate	proselyte	tyro

LAZY/SLUGGISH

indolent	inert	lackadaisical
languid	lassitude	lethargic
phlegmatic	quiescent	slothful
torpid		

PACIFY/SATISFY

ameliorate	appease	assuage
defer	mitigate	mollify
placate	propitiate	satiate
slake		

FORGIVE

absolve	acquit	exculpate
exonerate	expiate	palliate
redress	vindicate	

POOR

destitute	esurient	impecunious
indigent		

FAVORING/NOT IMPARTIAL

ardor/ardent	doctrinaire	fervid
partisan	tendentious	zealot

DENYING OF SELF

abnegate	abstain	ascetic
Spartan	stoic	temperate

WALKING ABOUT

ambulatory	itinerant	peripatetic

INSINCERE

disingenuous	dissemble	fulsome
ostensible	unctuous	

PREVENT/OBSTRUCT

discomfit	encumber	fetter
forfend	hinder	impede
inhibit	occlude	

ECCENTRIC/DISSIMILAR

aberrant	anachronism	anomalous
eclectic	esoteric	discrete
iconoclast		

FUNNY

chortle	droll	facetious
flippant	gibe	jocular
levity	ludicrous	raillery
riposte	simper	

SORROW

disconsolate	doleful	dolor
elegiac	forlorn	lament
lugubrious	melancholy	morose
plaintive	threnody	

DISGUSTING/OFFENSIVE

defile	fetid	invidious
noisome	odious	putrid
rebarbative		

WITHDRAWAL/RETREAT

abeyance	abjure	abnegation
abortive	abrogate	decamp
demur	recant	recidivism
remission	renege	rescind
retrograde		

DEATH/MOURNING

bereave	cadaver	defunct
demise	dolorous	elegy
knell	lament	macabre
moribund	obsequies	sepulchral
wraith		

COPY

counterpart	emulate	facsimile
factitious	paradigm	precursor
quintessence	simulated	vicarious

EQUAL

equitable	equity	tantamount

UNUSUAL

aberration	anomaly	iconoclast
idiosyncrasy		

WANDERING

discursive	expatiate	forage
itinerant	peregrination	peripatetic
sojourn		

GAPS/OPENINGS

abatement	aperture	fissure
hiatus	interregnum	interstice
lull	orifice	rent
respite	rift	

HEALTHY

beneficial	salubrious	salutary

ABBREVIATED COMMUNICATION

abridge	compendium	cursory
curtail	syllabus	synopsis
terse		

WISDOM

adage	aphorism	apothegm
axiom	bromide	dictum
epigram	platitude	sententious
truism		

FAMILY

conjugal	consanguine	distaff
endogamous	filial	fratricide
progenitor	scion	

NOT A STRAIGHT LINE

askance	awry	careen
carom	circuitous	circumvent
gyrate	labyrinth	meander
oblique	serrated	sidle
sinuous	undulating	vortex

INVESTIGATE

appraise	ascertain	assay
descry	peruse	

TIME/ORDER/DURATION

anachronism	antecede	antedate
anterior	archaic	diurnal
eon	ephemeral	epoch
fortnight	millennium	penultimate
synchronous	temporal	

BAD MOOD

bilious	dudgeon	irascible
pettish	petulant	pique
querulous	umbrage	waspish

EMBARRASS

abash	chagrin	compunction
contrition	diffidence	expiate
foible	gaucherie	rue

HARDHEARTED

asperity	baleful	dour
fell	malevolent	mordant
sardonic	scathing	truculent
vitriolic	vituperation	

NAG

admonish	cavil	belabor
enjoin	exhort	harangue
hector	martinet	remonstrate
reproof		

PREDICT

augur	auspice	fey
harbinger	portentous	presage
prescient	prognosticate	

LUCK

adventitious	amulet	auspicious
fortuitous	kismet	nemesis
optimum	portentous	propitiate
propitious	providential	talisman

NASTY

fetid	noisome	noxious

HARSH-SOUNDING

assonance	cacophony	din
dissonant	raucous	strident

PLEASANT-SOUNDING

euphonious	harmonious	melodious
sonorous		

Chapter 10: **Word Root List**

INTRODUCTION TO THE WORD ROOT LIST

The following list presents some of the commonest word roots—mostly Greek and Latin—that appear in English. Learning to recognize these word roots is a great help in expanding your vocabulary. Many seemingly difficult words yield up their meanings easily when you recognize the word roots that make them up. *Excrescence*, for example, contains the roots *ex-*, meaning out or out of, and *cresc-*, meaning to grow; once you know this, the meaning of *excrescence*, an outgrowth (whether normal, such as hair, or abnormal, such as a wart) is easily deduced.

The list concentrates on Latin and Greek roots because these are the most frequently used to form compound words in English, and because they tend not to be self-explanatory to the average reader. Each entry gives the root in the most common form or forms in which it appears in English, with a very brief definition. (The definition does not cover all the shades of meaning of the given root, only the most important or the most broadly applicable.) The rest of the entry is a list of some of the common English words derived from this root; this list is only intended to provide a few examples of such words, and does not even come close to being exhaustive. Some words will naturally be found under more than one entry. The words themselves are not defined. We hope the Word Root List will encourage you to turn to the GRE Minidictionary, chapter 12, or, better yet, to a good dictionary.

A, AN	**NOT, WITHOUT**
	amoral, anarchy, anomalous, anonymous, aseptic, asexual, atheism, atrophy, averse
AB	**FROM, AWAY, APART**
	abdicate, abduct, abhor, abject, abnormal, abrupt, absent, abuse
ABLE, IBLE	**CAPABLE OF, WORTHY OF**
	changeable, durable, laudable, indubitable, inevitable, infallible, irreducible, tolerable, variable
AC, ACR	**SHARP, SOUR**
	acerbic, acetate, acid, acrid, acrimony, acumen, acute
ACOU	**HEARING**
	acoustic
AD, A	**TO**
	(Often *d* is dropped and the first letter to which a is prefixed is doubled.) adapt, adequate, adumbrate, advocate, accede, adduce, affiliate, aggregate, allocate, annunciation, appall, arrest, assiduous, attract
AMBI, AMPHI	**BOTH, ON BOTH SIDES, AROUND**
	ambidextrous, ambient, ambiguous, ambition, ambivalent, amphibian, amphitheater
AMBL, AMBUL	**WALK**
	amble, ambulance, ambulatory, perambulator, preamble
ANIM	**MIND, SPIRIT, BREATH**
	animadversion, animal, animate, animosity, equanimity, magnanimity, pusillanimous, unanimity
ANT, ANTE	**BEFORE**
	ancient, antecedent, antechamber, antediluvian, anterior, anticipate, antiquity
ANTI, ANT	**AGAINST, OPPOSITE**
	antagonism, anticlimax, antidote, antipathy, antiphony, antipodes, antithesis
AQUA, AQUE	**WATER**
	aquamarine, aquarium, aquatic, aquatint, aqueduct, subaqueous
ARD	**BURN**
	ardent, ardor, arson

AUTO, AUT   SELF

autism, autobiography, autocracy, autograph, automaton, autonomous, autopsy

BEL, BELL   BEAUTIFUL

belle, embellish

BELL, BELLI   WAR

antebellum, bellicose, belligerent, rebellion

BEN, BEN   WELL, GOOD

benediction, benefactor, benevolent, benign

BI, BIN   TWO

bicameral, bicycle, bifocals, bifurcate, bilateral, binoculars, binomial, biped, combination

BON, BOUN   GOOD, GENEROUS

bonus, bountiful, bounty, debonair

BREW, BRID   SHORT, SMALL

abbreviate, abridge, brevet, breviary, breviloquent, brevity, brief

BURS   PURSE, MONEY

bursar, bursary, disburse, reimburse

CARN   FLESH

carnage, carnal, carnival, carnivorous, charnel, incarnate

CAUS, CAUT   BURN

caustic, cauterize, cautery, encaustic, holocaust

CED, CESS   YIELD, GO

abscess, accede, access, accessory, ancestor, antecedent, cession, concede, exceed, excess, intercede, precede, proceed, recede, recess, recession, secede, succeed

CELER   SPEED

accelerate, celerity, decelerate

CENT   HUNDRED, HUNDREDTH

cent, centennial, bicentennial, centigrade, centigram, centiliter, centimeter, centipede, century, percent

CHROM   COLOR

chromatic, chrome, chromosome, monochromatic

CHRON   TIME

anachronism, chronic, chronicle, chronological, chronometer, synchronize

CIRCUM   AROUND

circumference, circumlocution, circumnavigate, circumspect, circumstance

CO, COM, CON   WITH, TOGETHER

coeducation, coefficient, coincide, communicate, communist, compare, concert, concubine, conflict, cooperate, correspond

CONTRA,   AGAINST
CONTRO,
COUNTER   contradict, contrary, controversy, counter, counteract, counterattack, counterfeit, countermand, counterpart, counterpoint, encounter

CORD, CARD   HEART

accord, cardiac, cardiograph, cardiology, concord, cordial, discord, record

CORP, CORS   BODY

corporate, corps, corpse, corpulent, corpus, corpuscle, corset, incorporation

COSM   ORDER, UNIVERSE, WORLD

cosmetic, cosmic, cosmology, cosmonaut, cosmopolitan, cosmos, microcosm

CRED   TRUST, BELIEVE

accredit, credentials, credible, credit, creditable, credo, credulity, creed, incredible, incredulous

CRYPT   HIDE

apocryphal, crypt, cryptic, cryptography

CULP   FAULT, BLAME

culpable, culprit, inculpate, exculpate

CUMB, CUB   LIE DOWN

concubine, cubicle, incubate, incubus, incumbent, recumbent, succubus, succumb

CYN, CAN   DOG

canine, cynic

DE	**DOWN, OUT, AWAY FROM, APART**
	dehydrate, deject, depend, deport, depress, descend, describe, devalue
DELE	**ERASE**
	dele, delete, indelible
DEXT	**RIGHT HAND, RIGHT SIDE**
	ambidextrous, dexterity, dexterous
DI	**DAY**
	dial, diary, dismal, diurnal, meridian, quotidian
DI, DIS	**AWAY, APART**
	disagreeable, discard, discern, disdain, dismay, dismiss, distant, diverge
DIA	**THROUGH, ACROSS**
	diadem, diagnosis, diagonal, diagram, dialect, dialogue, diameter, diaphanous, diaphragm, diarrhea, diatribe
DIC, DICT, DIT	**SPEAK**
	abdicate, addict, benediction, condition, contradict, dedicate, dictate, dictator, diction, dictionary, dictum, ditto, edict, indicate, indict, interdict, malediction, predicament, predicate, predict, valedictorian, verdict
DOL	**GRIEVE**
	condole, condolence, doleful, dolor, indolent
DORM	**SLEEP**
	dormant, dormitory
DORS	**BACK**
	dorsal, endorse
DUC, DUCT	**LEAD**
	adduce, conduce, conduit, deduce, duct, duke, educate, induction, misconduct, produce, reduce, seduce, traduce, viaduct
DULC	**SWEET**
	dulcet, dulcified, dulcimer
DUR	**HARD, LASTING**
	dour, durable, duration, duress, during, endure, obdurate, perdurable

E, EX, EC	**OUT**	

eliminate, emanate, eradicate, erase, evade, evict, evince, exact, excavate, except, excerpt, excise excite, exclusive, excommunicate, excrescence, execute, exhale, exile, exit

EGO	**SELF**

ego, egocentric, egoism, egotist

EQU	**EQUAL**

adequate, equable, equal, equation, equator, equilibrium, equinox, equivocate

ERR	**WANDER**

aberration, err, errant, erratic, erroneous, error

EU	**WELL, GOOD**

eugenics, eulogy, euphemism, euphony, euphoria, euthanasia

FAL	**LIABLE TO ERR TO DECEIVE**

default, fail, fallacy false, faux pas, infallible

FATU	**FOOLISH**

fatuity, fatuous, infatuate

FERN	**BOIL**

effervescent, fervent, fervid, fervor

FID, FI	**FAITH**

affiance, affidavit, confidant, fealty, fidelity, fiducial, fiduciary

FLAGR, FULG, FULM	**BURN, SHINE**

conflagration, effulgent, flagrant, fulgent, fulminate, refulgent

FLECT, FLEX	**BEND, TURN**

circumflex, deflect, flex, flexible, inflection, reflect

FUG	**FLEE**

centrifuge, fugitive, fugue, refuge, refugee, subterfuge

FUM	**SMOKE**

fume, fumigate, perfume

GEN	**BIRTH, CLASS, KIN**

congenital, degenerate, engender, eugenics, gender, gene, general, generation, generosity, genesis, genetics, genial, genital, genius, gentle, gentile, gentility, gentry, ingenious, ingenuity, ingenuous, progenitor, progeny, regenerate

GNO, GNI, COGN, CONN	**KNOW**
	agnostic, cognition, cognizance, diagnosis, gnomic, ignore, incognito, prognosis, quaint, recognize, reconnaissance, reconnoiter
GRAM, GRAPH	**WRITE, DRAW**
	anagram, diagram, epigram, epigraph, grammar, grammarian, gramophone, graph, graphic, graphite, phonograph, photograph, program, telegram
GREG	**FLOCK**
	aggregate, congregate, egregious, gregarious, segregate
HAP	**BY CHANCE**
	haphazard, hapless, happen, happily, happy, mayhap, mishap
HEMI	**HALF**
	hemiptera, hemisphere, hemistich
HETERO	**OTHER**
	heterodox, heterodyne, heterogeneous, heterosexual
HOL	**WHOLE**
	catholic, holistic, holocaust, hologram, holograph
HOMO	**SAME (from Greek)**
	homogeneous, homogenize, homologue, homonym, homophone, homoptera, homosexual, homotype
HUM	**EARTH**
	exhume, humble, humility, posthumous
ICON	**IMAGE, IDOL**
	icon, iconic, iconoclast, iconography, iconology
IM, IN	**NOT**
	immature, immutable, imperfect, improvident, indigestible, inhospitable, innocuous, intolerant
N, IM, I	**IN, ON**
	(Often *n* is dropped and the first letter to which *i* is prefixed is doubled.) illuminate, incantation, induct, infer, imbibe, immigrate, impact, irrigate
INTER	**BETWEEN, AMONG**
	intercept, interchange, interfere, interject, interpret, interval

INTRA	**INSIDE, WITHIN**
	intramural, intrastate, intravenous
IT, ITER	**WAY, JOURNEY**
	ambition, circuit, initial, itinerant, itinerary, reiterate, transit
JOC	**JOKE**
	jocose, jocular, jocularity, jocund, joke
JOUR	**DAY**
	adjourn, journal, journey
JUD	**JUDGE**
	adjudicate, judiciary, judicious, prejudice
JUNCT, JUG	**JOIN**
	adjunct, conjugal conjunction, injunction, junction, junta, subjugate, subjunctive
JUR	**LAW**
	abjure, adjure, conjure, injure, juridical, jurisdiction, jurisprudence, jurist, jury, perjury
JUV	**YOUNG**
	juvenile, juvenilia, rejuvenate
LAUD	**PRAISE**
	applaud, cum laude, laud, laudable, laudatory, plaudits
LAV, LAU, LU	**WASH**
	ablution, laundry, lava, lavatory, lave
LAX, LAK, LEAS, LES	**LOOSE**
	lax, laxative, laxity, lease, leash, lessee, lessor, relax, release
LEG, LEC, LEX	**READ, SPEAK**
	dialect, lectern, lecture, legend, legible, lesson, lexicographer, lexicon
LEV	**LIGHT**
	alleviation, elevate, leaven, lever, levitate, levity, levy, relieve
LIBER	**FREE**
	delivery, illiberal, liberal, liberality, liberate, libertine, livery

LIG, LI	**TIE, BIND**
	ally, league, liable, liaison, lien, ligament, ligature, oblige, religion, rely
LING, LANG	**TONGUE**
	bilingual, language, linguistics
LITH	**STONE**
	acrolith, lithography, lithoid, lithology, lithotomy, megalith, monolith
LOG, LOQU	**SPEECH, THOUGHT**
	biology, circumlocution, colloquial, dialogue, ecology, elocution, eloquent, geology, grandiloquent, interlocutor, locution, logic, loquacious, monologue, obloquy, soliloquy, ventriloquism, zoology
LUX, LUC	**LIGHT**
	elucidate, lucid, lucubrate, luster, pellucid, translucent
MACRO	**GREAT, LONG**
	macrobiotics, macrocephalous, macrocosm
MAG, MAX, MAJ, MAS	**GREAT**
	magistrate, magnanimous, magnate, magnificent, magnify, magniloquent, magnitude, majesty, major, majority, master, maxim, maximum, mistress
MAL	**BAD**
	maladroit, malady, malediction, malefactor, malevolence, malice, malinger
MAN, MANU	**HAND**
	amanuensis, emancipation, manacle, manage, maneuver, manifest, manipulate, manner, manual, manufacture, manuscript
MAND, MEND	**COMMAND, ORDER**
	command, countermand, demand, mandate, mandatory, recommend, remand, reprimand
MEDI	**MIDDLE**
	immediate, intermediate, mean, media, median, mediate, medieval, mediocre, medium, medius
MEGA	**LARGE, GREAT**
	megalithic, megalomania, megalopolis, megaphone, megaton
MICRO	**VERY SMALL**
	microbe, microcosm, micron, microorganism, microphone, microscope

MIS	BAD, WRONG, HATE
	misadventure, misanthropist, misapply, miscarry, mischance, mischief, misconstrue, miscount, misfit, misinterpret
MOLL	SOFT
	emollient, mild, mollify, mollusk
MON, MONO	ONE
	monarchy, monastic, monism, monk, monochord, monograph, monogram, monograph, monolithic, monologue, monomania, monosyllable, monotonous
MOR, MORT	DEATH
	amortize, immortal, morbid, moribund, mortality, mortgage, mortification, mortuary
MOT, MOV, MOM, MOB	MOVE
	automobile, demote, immovable, locomotion, mob, mobile, mobility, mobilize, momentous, momentum, motion, motive, motor, move, mutiny, promote, removable
MULT	MANY
	multiplex, multiply, multitudinous
MUT	CHANGE
	commute, immutable, mutability, mutation, mutual, permutation, transmute
NASC, NAT, GNA	BIRTH
	cognate, innate, nascent, natal, native, natural, nature, pregnant, Renaissance
NAU, NAV	SHIP, SAILOR
	astronaut, cosmonaut, circumnavigate, nauseous, nautical, naval, nave, navy
NEO	NEW
	neolithic, neologism, neophyte, neoplasm
NIHIL	NOTHING, NONE
	annihilate, nihilism
NOCT, NOX	NIGHT
	equinox, noctambulent, nocturnal, nocturne
NOX, NOC	HARM
	innocent, innocuous, internecine, noxious, nuisance, obnoxious, pernicious

NOM, NYM **NEC**	NAME anonymous, antonym, cognomen, denominator, homonym, misnomer, nomenclature, nominal, nominate, noun, pronoun, pseudonym, renowned, synonym
NON	NOT nonconformist, nonentity, nonpareil, nonpartisan
NOV	NEW innovate, nova, novel, novelty, novice, novitiate, renovate
NULL	NOTHING annul, null, nullify, nullity
OB	AGAINST obdurate, object, obliterate, oblong, obloquy, obstacle, obstreperous, obstruct
OMNI	ALL omnibus, omnipotent, omnipresent, omniscient, omnivorous
ONER	BURDEN exonerate, onerous, onus
OSS, OSTE	BONE osseous, ossicle, ossiferous, ossify, ostectomy, ossuary, osteopathy
PALP	FEEL palpable, palpate, palpitation
PAN, PANT	ALL panacea, pandemic, pandemonium, panegyric, panoply, panorama, pantheon, pantomime
PATH	SUFFER, FEEL apathy, antipathy, empathy, pathetic, pathology, pathos, sympathy
PEC	MONEY impecunious, peculation, pecuniary
PED, POD	FOOT arthropod, expedient, impede, pedal, pedestal, pedestrian, pedigree, pediment, tripod

PED	**CHILD, EDUCATION**
	encyclopedia, pedagogue, pedant, pediatrician
PEL	**DRIVE, PUSH**
	appellate, appellation, compel, dispel, expel, impel, propel
PENE, PEN	**ALMOST**
	antepenult, peninsula, penult, penultimate, penumbra
PERI	**AROUND**
	pericardium, perihelion, perimeter, perineum, periphery, periscope
PHIL	**LOVE**
	bibliophile, necrophilia, philanthropy, philately, philharmonic, philogyny, philology, philosophy
PHOB	**FEAR**
	claustrophobia, hydrophobia, phobia, phobic, xenophobia
PHON	**SOUND**
	antiphony, euphony, megaphone, phonetics, phonograph, polyphony, saxophone, symphony, telephone
PLAC	**PLEASE**
	complacent, implacable, placate, placebo, placid
PLEN, PLET, PLE	**FILL, FULL**
	accomplishment, complement, complete, deplete, implement, plenary, plenipotentiary, plenitude, plenty, replenish, replete, supplement
POLY	**MANY**
	polyandry, polygamy, polyglot, polygon, polyhedron, polynomial, polysyllable, polytechnic, polytheism
PORT	**CARRY**
	comport, deportment, disport, export, import, important, portable, portage, porter, portfolio, portly, purport, rapport, reporter, supportive, transport
POST	**BEHIND, AFTER**
	posterior, posterity, postern, posthumous, postmeridian, postmortem, postpone, postprandial, postscript, postwar, preposterous
POT	**DRINK**
	potable, potation, potion

PRE   **BEFORE, IN FRONT**

preamble, precaution, preclude, precocity, precursor, predecessor, predict, preface, prefigure, prelate, premonition, prescribe, president

PRIM, PRI   **FIRST**

primary, primal, prime, primeval, primordial, pristine

PRO   **IN FRONT, BEFORE**

problem, proboscis, procedure, proceed, proclaim, proclivity, procrastinate, procure, propound, prostrate, protest

PROP, PROX   **NEAR**

approximate, propinquity, proximate, proximity

PROTO, PROT   **FIRST**

protagonist, protocol, prototype, protozoan

PSEUDO,   **FALSE**
  PSEUD

pseudepigrapha, pseudoclassic, pseudomorph, pseudonym, pseudopod, pseudoscientific

PUG, PUN   **HIT, PRICK**

expunge, impugn, poignant, pugilist, pugnacious, punch, punctual, punctuate, pungent, repugnant

PYR   **FIRE**

pyre, pyromania, pyrometer, pyrosis, pyrotechnic

QUAD, QUAR,   **FOUR**
  QUAT

quadrant, quadrille, quadrinomial, quadruple, quadruplets, quart, quarter, quaternary

QUIE, QUIT   **QUIET, TEST**

acquiesce, acquit, coy, disquiet, quiescent, quiet, quietude, quietus, quit, requiem, requital, tranquil

QUINT, QUIN   **FIVE**

quincunx, quinquennial, quintessence, quintile, quintillion, quintuple

RADI, RACI,   **ROOT, BRANCH**
  RAMI

deracinate, eradicate, radical, radish, ramification, ramiform, ramify

RE   **BACK, AGAIN**

recline, refer, regain, remain, reorganize, repent, request

RECT	STRAIGHT, RIGHT
	correct, direct, erect, rectangle, rectify, rectilinear, rectitude, rector
REG	KING, RULE
	interregnum, realm, regal, regent, regicide, regime, regiment, region, regular, regulate
RETRO	BACKWARD
	retroactive, retroflex, retrograde, retrospective
RUB, RUD	RED
	rouge, rubella, rubicund, rubric, ruby, ruddy, russet
RUD	CRUDE
	erudite, rude, rudimentary, rudiments
SACER, SACR, SANCT	HOLY
	consecration, desecrate, execrate, sacerdotal, sacrament, sacred, sacrifice, sacrilege, sacristy, sacrosanct, saint, sanctify, sanctimonious, sanction, sanctity, sanctuary, sanctum
SAG, SAP, SAV	TASTE, THINK
	insipid, sagacious, sagacity, sage, sapid, sapient, savant, savor
SAL	SALT
	salary, saline
SALU, SALV	HEALTH, SAVE
	safe, salubrious, salutary, salute, salvage, salvation, salve, savior
SAN	HEALTHY
	sane, sanitarium, sanitation, sanity
SANG	BLOOD
	consanguinity, sanguinary, sanguine
SAT	ENOUGH
	asset, dissatisfied, insatiable, sate, satiate, satisfy, saturate
SCRIB, SCRIV, SCRIPT	WRITE
	ascribe, circumscription, conscript, describe, indescribable, inscription, postscript, prescribe, proscribe, scribble, scribe, script, scripture, scrivener, subscribe, transcription

SE	DOWN, OUT, AWAY, APART
	secede, seclude, secret, secrete, secure, sedition, seduce, segregate, select, separate
SED, SID	SIT
	assiduous, dissident, insidious, preside, reside, residue, seance, sedate, sedative, sedentary, sediment, sedulous, session, siege, subside, supersede
SEM	SEED, SOW
	disseminate, semen, seminal, seminar, seminary
SEMI	HALF
	semicircle, semicolon, semiconscious, semifluid
SEN	OLD
	senate, senescent, senile, senior, sire
SEQU, SECU, SUE, SUI	FOLLOW
	consecutive, consequent, execute, executive, non sequitur, obsequious, obsequy, persecute, prosecution, pursue, sequel, sequence, subsequent, sue, suitable, suite, suitor
SINU, SIN	BEND, FOLD
	cosine, insinuate, sine, sinuous, sinus
SOL	SUN
	parasol, solar, solarium, solstice
SOL	ALONE
	desolate, isolate, sole, soliloquize, solipsism, solitude, solo
SOMN	SLEEP
	insomnia, somnambulist, somniferous, somniloquist, somnolent
SOPH	WISDOM
	philosopher, sophism, sophist, sophisticated, sophistry, sophomore
SPEC, SPIC	LOOK, SEE
	aspect, auspicious, circumspect, conspicuous, despicable, expect, inspect, introspection, perspective, perspicacious, perspicuous, prospectus, respectable, retrospect, specimen, spectacle, spectator, specter, spectrum, suspect, suspicious

SPIR **BREATH**

aspire, conspire, expire, inspire, perspire, respirator, spirit, spiritual, sprightly, sprite, suspire, transpire

STRICT, STRING, STRAN **TIGHT**

astringency, constrain, constrict, district, restriction, strain, strait, strangle, strict, stringent

SUA **PLEASE**

assuage, dissuade, persuade, persuasive, suasion, suave, sweet

SUB **UNDER**

subdivide, subdue, subjugate, subjunctive, sublunary, submarine, submerge, subordinate, subpoena, subscribe, subside, substitute, subterfuge, subterranean, suburb

SUMM **HIGHEST**

consummate, sum, summary, summit

SUPER, SUR **ABOVE**

insuperable, superabound, superannuated, superb, supercharge, supercilious, superficial, superfluous, superior, superlative, supernatural, supernumerary, supervise, surmount, surpass, surrealism, survey

SURG, SOURC, SURRECT **RISE**

insurgent, insurrection, resource, resurge, resurrection, source, surge

SYM, SYN **TOGETHER**

symbiosis, symmetry, sympathy, symposium, synonym, synthesis

TACIT **SILENT**

reticent, tacit, taciturn

TACT, TAG, TAM, TANG **TOUCH**

contact, contagious, contamination, contiguous, cotangent, intact, intangible, integral, tact, tactile, tangent, tangential

TEST **BEAR WITNESS**

attest, contest, detest, intestate, protest, testament, testify, testimonial

THERM **HEAT**

diathermy, thermal, thermesthesia, thermometer, thermonuclear, thermophilic, thermos, thermostat

TIM   **FEAR**

intimidate, timid, timidity, timorous

TORP   **STIFF, NUMB**

torpedo, torpid, torpor

TORQ, TORT,   **TWIST**
TOR

contort, distort, extort, retort, torch, torment, torque, torsion, tort, tortuous, torture

TOX   **POISON**

antitoxin, intoxication, toxemia, toxic, toxicology, toxin

TRANS   **ACROSS, BEYOND**

intransigent, transcend, transcontinental, transcribe, transient, transmit, transpire, transport

ULT   **LAST, BEYOND**

penultimate, ulterior, ultimate, ultimatum, ultramarine, ultramontane, ultraviolet

UMBR   **SHADOW**

adumbrate, penumbra, somber, umber, umbrage, umbrella

UN   **NOT**

unaccustomed, unruly, unseen, untold, unusual

UND   **WAVE**

abound, abundance, inundate, redundant, undulant, undulate

UNI, UN   **ONE**

reunion, unanimous, unicorn, uniform, union, unison, unit, unite, unity, universe

URB   **CITY**

exurbanite, suburban, urban, urbane, urbanity, urbanization

VAL, VAIL   **STRENGTH, USE, WORTH**

ambivalent, avail, convalescent, countervailing, equivalent, evaluate, invalid, prevalent, valediction, valiant, valid, valor, value

VER   **TRUE**

aver, veracious, verdict, verify, verily, verisimilitude, verity, very

VERB   **WORD**

adverb, proverb, verb, verbal, verbalize, verbatim, verbose, verbiage

VERD	**GREEN**
	verdant, verdigris, verdure
VIL	**BASE, MEAN**
	revile, vile, vilification, vilify
VIRU	**POISON**
	virulence, virulent, viruliferous, virus
VIT, VIV	**LIFE**
	convivial, revival, revive, survive, vital, vitality, vivacious, vivid, viviparous, vivisection
VOC, VOU	**CALL, WORD**
	advocacy, advocate, avow, convocation, convoke, equivocal, evoke, invocation, invoke, provoke, revoke, vocabulary, vocal, vocalist, vocation, vociferous, vouch, vouchsafe
VOL	**FLY**
	volant, volatile, volley
VOLU, VOLV	**ROLL, TURN**
	circumvolve, convolution, devolve, evolve, involution, revolt, revolve, voluble, volume, voluminous, volute

Chapter 11: **Opposite Drills**

Each of the word lists below relates to two concepts that are opposite in meaning. The words in each list relate to one of the concepts or its opposite. Try to sort out which category each word belongs in. For each word, check the oval under the appropriate concept. If you don't know the meaning of a word, make your best guess using roots, charge (whether the word sounds "good" or "bad"), prefixes, or context to help you.

No definitions are provided. Look up words that you are unsure of in chapter 12, GRE Minidictionary.

HAPPY		SAD
●	BLITHE	○
○	DISCONSOLATE	●
○	DISPIRITED	●
○	DOLDRUMS	●
○	DOLOROUS	●
●	EBULLIENT	○
●	EUPHORIC	○
●	FELICITY	○
●	PROVIDENT	○
●	RUE	✗
○	WOE	●

Answer key on page 257.

TRUE		FALSE	TRUE		FALSE
●	APOCRYPHAL	✗	●	FRANKNESS	○
○	CALUMNY	●	○	GUILE	●
●	CANARD	✗	●	INDISPUTABLE	○
●	CANDOR	○	●	INDUBITABLE	○
○	CHICANERY	●	●	LEGITIMATE	○
○	DISSEMBLE	●	○	MALINGER	●
○	DISSIMULATE	●	●	MENDACIOUS	✗
○	DUPE	●	●	MENDACITY	✗
●	DUPLICITY	✗	○	PERFIDY	●
○	EQUIVOCATE	●	○	PREVARICATE	●
○	ERRONEOUS	●	●	PROBITY	○
●	ERSATZ	✗	●	SINCERE	○
○	FALLACIOUS	●	○	SPECIOUS	●
●	FEALTY	○	○	SPURIOUS	●
○	FEIGNED	●	●	VERACIOUS	○
○	FOIST	●	●	VERITY	○

Answer key on page 258.

AGREEMENT		DISAGREEMENT	AGREEMENT		DISAGREEMENT
●	ACCORD	○	○	DETRACTOR	●
○	ALTERCATE	●	○	DIFFER	●
○	ALTERCATION	●	○	DISPARAGE	●
○	ANTITHETIC	●	○	DISPUTE	●
●	ASKANCE	⊗	○	DISSENT	●
●	ASSENT	○	●	EXCORIATE	⊗
○	AVERSE	●	○	FEUD	●
○	BICKER	●	●	HARMONY	○
●	CAVIL	⊗	○	INIMICAL	●
●	CONCORD	○	○	MOOT	●
●	CONCUR	○	●	POLEMIC	⊗
●	CONSENSUS	○	○	QUIBBLE	●
●	CONSONANCE	○	●	RAPPORT	○
○	CONTENTION	●	○	SQUABBLE	●
○	CONTENTIOUS	●	⊗	UNANIMITY	●
○	CONTRADICT	●	○	WRANGLE	●

Answer key on page 259.

ATTRACTION OR LIKE		REPULSION OR DISLIKE	ATTRACTION OR LIKE		REPULSION OR DISLIKE
○	ABHOR	◉	◉	ENCHANT	○
○	ABOMINATE	◉	◉	ENTICE	○
◉	AFFINITY	○	◉	ESCHEW	⊗
◉	ALLURE	○	⊗	INVEIGLE	◉
◉	ANATHEMA	⊗	○	LOATH	◉
○	ANTIPATHY	◉	○	PARRY	⊗
○	BANE	◉	◉	PENCHANT	○
⊗	BEGUILE	◉	◉	PREDILECTION	○
◉	BENT	○	◉	PROCLIVITY	○
◉	CHARM	○	◉	PROPENSITY	○
○	DISSUADE	◉	○	RANCOR	◉
◉	DRAW	○	○	REVILE	◉
◉	ELICIT	○	○	SPURN	◉

Answer key on page 260.

BRAVERY OR CONFIDENCE		FEAR OR CAUTION
⊗	APLOMB	⬤
◯	APPREHENSION	⬤
⬤	AUDACIOUS	◯
⬤	AUDACITY	◯
⬤	CHARY	⊗
◯	CIRCUMSPECTION	⬤
◯	CRAVEN	⬤
⬤	DAUNTLESS	◯
⊗	DOUGHTY	⬤
⬤	GALLANTRY	◯
⬤	GAME	◯
⬤	INTREPID	◯
⬤	METTLESOME	◯
◯	MISGIVING	⬤
⊗	PLUCKY	⬤
◯	PUSILLANIMOUS	⬤
⬤	TEMERITY	◯
◯	TREPIDATION	⬤
⬤	UNDAUNTED	◯
⬤	VALIANT	◯
⬤	VALOROUS	◯

Answer key on page 261.

CALMNESS		AGITATION	CALMNESS		AGITATION
◯	BECALM	◯	◯	NONCHALANT	◯
◯	BLUSTER	◯	◯	PERTURB	◯
◯	COLLECTED	◯	◯	PLACID	◯
◯	COMPOSED	◯	◯	QUIESCENT	◯
◯	COMPOSURE	◯	◯	RAGING	◯
◯	DETACHED	◯	◯	RAIL	◯
◯	DISCOMPOSED	◯	◯	REPOSE	◯
◯	DISPASSIONATE	◯	◯	ROIL	◯
◯	DISQUIETED	◯	◯	RUFFLED	◯
◯	DISTRAUGHT	◯	◯	SEDENTARY	◯
◯	FLURRIED	◯	◯	SERENE	◯
◯	FLUSTER	◯	◯	STAID	◯
◯	FRENETIC	◯	◯	STEADY	◯
◯	FULMINATE	◯	◯	TRANQUIL	◯
◯	FUROR	◯	◯	TUMULTUOUS	◯
◯	IMPERTURBABLE	◯	◯	TURBID	◯
◯	INDOLENT	◯	◯	TURBULENT	◯
◯	INSURGENT	◯	◯	UNRUFFLED	◯
◯	KINETIC	◯	◯	VEHEMENCE	◯
◯	LANGUOR	◯	◯	VERVE	◯
◯	LULL	◯			

Answer key on page 262.

CHANGE		LACK OF CHANGE
◯	CATALYST	◯
◯	COMMUTATION	◯
◯	CONSISTENT	◯
◯	CONSTANT	◯
◯	DETERMINATE	◯
◯	ENTRENCHED	◯
◯	FIXITY	◯
◯	IMMUTABLE	◯
◯	IMPERVIOUS	◯
◯	INERT	◯
◯	INGRAINED	◯
◯	INNOVATIVE	◯
◯	INVARIABLE	◯
◯	INVIOLATE	◯
◯	LODGED	◯
◯	METAMORPHOSIS	◯
◯	MUTABLE	◯
◯	ROOTED	◯
◯	STEADFAST	◯
◯	TRANSFIGURATION	◯
◯	TRANSFORMATION	◯
◯	TRANSLATION	◯
◯	TRANSMOGRIFY	◯
◯	TRANSMUTATION	◯
◯	UNFAILING	◯

Answer key on page 263.

GOODNESS OR MORALITY		EVIL OR IMMORALITY		GOODNESS OR MORALITY		EVIL OR IMMORALITY
●	ALTRUISM	○		○	INVIDIOUS	●
○	BACCHANALIAN	●		○	LASCIVIOUS	●
●	BEATIFIC	○		○	LICENTIOUS	●
●	BENEFICENT	○		○	LURID	●
●	BENIGN	○		○	MISCREANT	●
●	BENISON	○		○	NEFARIOUS	●
●	CLEMENT	○		●	NOBLE	○
●	CONTINENCE	○		●	PERFIDIOUS	✗
○	DEBAUCH	●		●	PROBITY	○
●	DECADENCE	✗		○	PROFLIGATE	●
●	ELEVATED	○		●	PRURIENT	✗
●	ETHICAL	○		●	RAPACITY	✗
●	EXEMPLARY	○		●	RECTITUDE	○
○	FIENDISH	●		●	REPROBATE	✗
○	ILLICIT	●		●	RIGHTEOUS	○
○	INFERNAL	●		✗	TEMPERANCE	●
○	INIQUITOUS	●		●	TURPITUDE	✗
●	INTEGRITY	○		●	VIRTUE	○

Answer key on page 264.

LARGE AMOUNT OR EXCESS		SMALL AMOUNT OR SHORTAGE	LARGE AMOUNT OR EXCESS		SMALL AMOUNT OR SHORTAGE
◯	CAPACIOUS	◯	◯	MYRIAD	◯
◯	CAVALCADE	◯	◯	OPULENCE	◯
✗	CLOYING	◯	◯	OVERABUNDANCE	◯
◯	CORNUCOPIA	◯	◯	PAUCITY	◯
◯	DEARTH	◯	◯	PLETHORA	◯
◯	DEFECT	◯	◯	POVERTY	◯
◯	DEFICIENT	◯	◯	PREPONDERANCE	◯
◯	DILATE	◯	◯	PRIVATION	◯
◯	DISTEND	◯	◯	PRODIGIOUS	◯
◯	EFFUSIVE	◯	◯	PROFUSION	◯
◯	FAMINE	◯	✗	REPLETE	◯
✗	FRAUGHT	◯	◯	SCANTINESS	◯
◯	GLUT	◯	◯	SCARCITY	◯
◯	INSUFFICIENCY	◯	◯	STINTING	◯
◯	MANIFOLD	◯	◯	SUPERABUNDANCE	◯
◯	MEAGER	◯	✗	SUPEREROGATORY	◯
◯	MULTIFARIOUS	◯	◯	SUPERFLUITY	◯
			◯	SURFEIT	◯

Answer key on page 265.

GROW		SHRINK
○	ABATE	⬤
○	ACCRETE	○
⬤	AGGRANDIZE	○
⬤	AMPLIFY	○
⊗	APPEND	⬤
⬤	AUGMENT	○
⬤	BURGEON	○
○	CONSTRICT	⬤
○	CORRODE	⬤
○	DWINDLE	⬤
○	EBB	⬤
○	ERODE	⬤
⬤	ESCALATE	○
⬤	UPSURGE	○
⊗	WANE	⬤
○	WAX	⬤

Answer key on page 266.

GRAND AND IMPORTANT		PETTY OR UNIMPORTANT	GRAND AND IMPORTANT		PETTY OR UNIMPORTANT
◯	ABJECT	◯	◯	MOMENTOUS	◯
◯	APOTHEOSIS	◯	◯	NEGLIGIBLE	◯
◯	ASTRAL	◯	◯	NIGGLING	◯
◯	AUGUST	◯	◯	NONENTITY	◯
◯	CONSEQUENTIAL	◯	◯	OVERWEENING	◯
◯	CONSIDERABLE	◯	◯	PALTRY	◯
◯	DEBASED	◯	◯	PICAYUNE	◯
◯	ELEVATED	◯	◯	PIDDLING	◯
◯	ELOQUENT	◯	◯	PRETENTIOUS	◯
◯	EXALTED	◯	◯	REGAL	◯
◯	FRIVOLOUS	◯	◯	SALIENT	◯
◯	GRANDIOSE	◯	◯	SERVILE	◯
◯	IGNOBLE	◯	◯	SPLENDID	◯
◯	INCONSEQUENTIAL	◯	◯	STATELY	◯
◯	INGLORIOUS	◯	◯	SUBLIME	◯
◯	LOFTY	◯	◯	SUBSTANTIAL	◯
◯	MEANINGFUL	◯	◯	WEIGHTY	◯

Answer key on page 267.

UNLIMITED OR FREE		LIMITED OR CLOSED
⬭	CIRCUMSCRIBED	⬭
⬭	DURESS	⬭
⬭	EMANCIPATED	⬭
⬭	ENCUMBRED	⬭
⬭	FETTERED	⬭
⬭	HERMETIC	⬭
⬭	IMMURE	⬭
⬭	INCOMMUNICADO	⬭
⬭	INDENTURE	⬭
⬭	INSULAR	⬭
⬭	LATITUDE	⬭
⬭	LAXITY	⬭
⬭	LICENSE	⬭
⬭	MANUMISSION	⬭
⬭	MAVERICK	⬭
⬭	OCCLUSION	⬭
⬭	STRICTURE	⬭
⬭	STYMIE	⬭
⬭	THRALL	⬭
⬭	TRAMMELED	⬭
⬭	UNBRIDLED	⬭
⬭	UNFETTERED	⬭
⬭	UNTRAMMELED	⬭
⬭	YOKE	⬭

Answer key on page 268.

YOUTH OR IMMATURITY		OLD AGE OR MATURITY
◯	ABIDING	◯
◯	ANTEDELUVIAN	◯
◯	CALLOW	◯
◯	DOTAGE	◯
◯	GERIATRIC	◯
◯	GREEN	◯
◯	HOARY	◯
◯	INVETERATE	◯
◯	JUVENILE	◯
◯	NEOPHYTE	◯
◯	PUERILE	◯
◯	SENESCENT	◯
◯	SOPHOMORIC	◯
◯	STRIPLING	◯
◯	SUPERANNUATED	◯
◯	TYRO	◯

Answer key on page 269.

PRAISE		CRITICISM	PRAISE		CRITICISM
⬭	ACCLAIM	⬭	⬭	EULOGIZE	⬭
⬭	ACCOLADE	⬭	⬭	EXALT	⬭
⬭	ADULATORY	⬭	⬭	EXTOL	⬭
⬭	APPLAUSE	⬭	⬭	HAIL	⬭
⬭	APPROBATION	⬭	⬭	HOMAGE	⬭
⬭	BOUQUET	⬭	⬭	HONOR	⬭
⬭	CELEBRATE	⬭	⬭	IMPUGN	⬭
⬭	CENSURE	⬭	⬭	KUDOS	⬭
⬭	COMMEND	⬭	⬭	LAUD	⬭
⬭	DEFAME	⬭	⬭	PAEAN	⬭
⬭	DEMEAN	⬭	⬭	PANEGYRIC	⬭
⬭	DENIGRATE	⬭	⬭	PEJORATIVE	⬭
⬭	DENOUNCE	⬭	⬭	PLAUDIT	⬭
⬭	DENUNCIATE	⬭	⬭	TRIBUTE	⬭
⬭	DEPRECATE	⬭	⬭	VENERATE	⬭
⬭	ENCOMIUM	⬭			

Answer key on page 270.

SWIFTNESS OR BRIEFNESS		DELAY OR SLOWNESS
◯	ALACRITY	◯
◯	CELERITY	◯
◯	CURSORY	◯
◯	DALLY	◯
◯	DILATORY	◯
◯	EPHEMERAL	◯
◯	EVANESCENT	◯
◯	EXTEMPORANEOUS	◯
◯	IMPROMPTU	◯
◯	LAGGARD	◯
◯	MERCURIAL	◯
◯	PERFUNCTORY	◯
◯	PERPETUITY	◯
◯	PRECIPITOUS	◯
◯	PROCRASTINATION	◯
◯	PROTRACTED	◯
◯	RETARD	◯
◯	SLUGGISH	◯
◯	TORPID	◯
◯	TRANSIENT	◯

Answer key on page 271.

SUBTLE OR SLIGHT		OBVIOUS
⬭	BLATANT	⬭
⬭	EGREGIOUS	⬭
⬭	FLAGRANT	⬭
⬭	GOSSAMER	⬭
⬭	MANIFEST	⬭
⬭	MODICUM	⬭
⬭	NUANCE	⬭
⬭	OSTENTATIOUS	⬭
⬭	OVERT	⬭
⬭	PATENT	⬭
⬭	RAREFY	⬭
⬭	REFINED	⬭
⬭	SCINTILLA	⬭

Answer key on page 272.

RUDENESS		POLITENESS
◯	ASOCIAL	◯
◯	BOORISH	◯
◯	CHEEKY	◯
◯	CHURLISH	◯
◯	CIVIL	◯
◯	CRASS	◯
◯	DEFERENTIAL	◯
◯	DEMURE	◯
◯	FARTHY	◯
◯	EFFRONTERY	◯
◯	GALLANT	◯
◯	GENTEEL	◯
◯	OBEISANCE	◯
◯	OBLIGING	◯
◯	OBSTREPEROUS	◯
◯	PHILISTINE	◯
◯	PUNCTILIOUS	◯
◯	RAW	◯
◯	SCABROUS	◯
◯	SOLICITOUS	◯
◯	TACTFUL	◯
◯	UNGRACIOUS	◯
◯	UNPOLISHED	◯
◯	VULGAR	◯

Answer key on page 273.

INTELLIGENCE AND ABILITY		STUPIDITY AND CLUMSINESS	INTELLIGENCE AND ABILITY		STUPIDITY AND CLUMSINESS
◯	ACUMEN	◯	◯	INGENIOUS	◯
◯	ASININE	◯	◯	KEN	◯
◯	ASTUTE	◯	◯	MALADROIT	◯
◯	DERANGED	◯	◯	OMNISCIENT	◯
◯	DOLTISH	◯	◯	PERCIPIENT	◯
◯	FATUOUS	◯	◯	PERSPICACIOUS	◯
◯	FINESSE	◯	◯	PRECOCIOUS	◯
◯	FLAIR	◯	◯	PUNDIT	◯
◯	GAUCHE	◯	◯	SAGACIOUS	◯
◯	GULLIBLE	◯	◯	SAPIENT	◯
◯	IGNORAMUS	◯	◯	SIMPLE	◯
◯	IMPOLITIC	◯	◯	UNWITTING	◯
◯	INANE	◯	◯	VACUOUS	◯
◯	INCISIVE	◯	◯	VAPID	◯

Answer key on page 274.

LOUD, LONG, OR A LOT OF SPEECH		QUIET, SHORT, OR ABSENCE OF SPEECH
○	BOMBAST	○
○	CURT	○
○	DUMB	○
○	ELOQUENT	○
○	GARRULOUS	○
○	GRANDILOQUENT	○
○	LACONIC	○
○	LOQUACIOUS	○
○	MUTE	○
○	OROTUND	○
○	PLANGENT	○
○	PROLIX	○
○	RETICENT	○
○	STENTORIAN	○
○	SUCCINCT	○
○	TACIT	○
○	TACITURN	○
○	TERSE	○
○	TURGID	○
○	VERBOSE	○

Answer key on page 275.

CLEAN		DIRTY
◯	ABLUTION	◯
◯	BESMEAR	◯
◯	BESPATTER	◯
◯	DEFILE	◯
◯	GRIMY	◯
◯	GRUBBY	◯
◯	IMMACULATE	◯
◯	PRISTINE	◯
◯	SLOVENLY	◯
◯	SMUTTY	◯
◯	SULLY	◯
◯	UNSOILED	◯
◯	UNSULLIED	◯
◯	VIRGINAL	◯

Answer key on page 276.

TOGETHER OR CONTINUOUS		SEPARATE OR DISCONTINUOUS	TOGETHER OR CONTINUOUS		SEPARATE OR DISCONTINUOUS
○	ABUT	○	○	DISCRETE	○
○	AGGREGATION	○	○	DISJOINTED	○
○	ASUNDER	○	○	DISPERSE	○
○	BIFURCATE	○	○	DISSIPATE	○
○	CABAL	○	○	DIVERGE	○
○	COLLATE	○	○	ESTRANGE	○
○	COLLOQUY	○	○	HIATUS	○
○	COLLUSION	○	○	INCONGRUOUS	○
○	CONCATENATE	○	○	INTERREGNUM	○
○	CONCOMITANT	○	○	INTERSTICE	○
○	CONFLUENCE	○	○	RIFT	○
○	CONJOIN	○	○	SCHISM	○
○	CONSENSUS	○	○	SEQUESTERED	○
○	CONSONANCE	○	○	SYNCHRONOUS	○
○	COTERIE	○	○	SYNTHESIS	○
○	DIFFUSE	○	○	TANDEM	○

Answer key on page 277.

STUBBORN		AGREEABLE
◯	ACCEDE	◯
◯	ACCOMMODATING	◯
◯	ACQUIESCE	◯
◯	AMENABLE	◯
◯	CAPITULATE	◯
◯	COMPLY	◯
◯	CONCEDE	◯
◯	CONTUMACIOUS	◯
◯	DOGMATIC	◯
◯	HIDEBOUND	◯
◯	INTRANSIGENT	◯
◯	OBDURACY	◯
◯	OBLIGING	◯
◯	OBSTINATE	◯
◯	OSSIFIED	◯
◯	PERTINACIOUS	◯
◯	RECALCITRANT	◯
◯	REFRACTORY	◯
◯	UNBENDING	◯
◯	UNSWAYABLE	◯

Answer key on page 278.

OPPOSITE DRILL ANSWER KEYS

HAPPY		SAD
●	BLITHE	○
○	DISCONSOLATE	●
○	DISPIRITED	●
○	DOLDRUMS	●
○	DOLOROUS	●
●	EBULLIENT	○
●	EUPHORIC	○
●	FELICITY	○
●	PROVIDENT	○
○	RUE	●
○	WOE	●

DIS means "not," so here the two *DIS* words mean "not consolate" and "not spirited," that is, "sad." Also, *DOL* means "pain," so *dolorous* and *doldrums* also mean "sad."

TRUE		FALSE	TRUE		FALSE
○	APOCRYPHAL	●	●	FRANKNESS	○
○	CALUMNY	●	○	GUILE	●
○	CANARD	●	●	INDISPUTABLE	○
●	CANDOR	○	●	INDUBITABLE	○
○	CHICANERY	●	●	LEGITIMATE	○
○	DISSEMBLE	●	○	MALINGER	●
○	DISSIMULATE	●	○	MENDACIOUS	●
○	DUPE	●	○	MENDACITY	●
○	DUPLICITY	●	○	PERFIDY	●
○	EQUIVOCATE	●	○	PREVARICATE	●
○	ERRONEOUS	●	●	PROBITY	○
○	ERSATZ	●	●	SINCERE	○
○	FALLACIOUS	●	○	SPECIOUS	●
●	FEALTY	○	○	SPURIOUS	●
○	FEIGNED	●	●	VERACIOUS	○
○	FOIST	●	●	VERITY	○

Notice that *veracious* and *verity* both have to do with truthfulness. (The root VER is from the Latin word for truth.) Perhaps you know that Yale's motto is "Lux et veritas," or "light and truth."

AGREEMENT		DISAGREEMENT	AGREEMENT		DISAGREEMENT
●	ACCORD	○	○	DETRACTOR	●
○	ALTERCATE	●	○	DIFFER	●
○	ALTERCATION	●	○	DISPARAGE	●
○	ANTITHETIC	●	○	DISPUTE	●
○	ASKANCE	●	○	DISSENT	●
●	ASSENT	○	○	EXCORIATE	●
○	AVERSE	●	○	FEUD	●
○	BICKER	●	●	HARMONY	○
○	CAVIL	●	○	INIMICAL	●
●	CONCORD	○	○	MOOT	●
●	CONCUR	○	○	POLEMIC	●
●	CONSENSUS	○	○	QUIBBLE	●
●	CONSONANCE	○	●	RAPPORT	○
○	CONTENTION	●	○	SQUABBLE	●
○	CONTENTIOUS	●	●	UNANIMITY	○
○	CONTRADICT	●	○	WRANGLE	●

Notice that all the words that began with *DIS* had to do with disagreement.

ATTRACTION OR LIKE		REPULSION OR DISLIKE	ATTRACTION OR LIKE		REPULSION OR DISLIKE
○	ABHOR	●	●	ENCHANT	○
○	ABOMINATE	●	●	ENTICE	○
●	AFFINITY	○	○	ESCHEW	●
●	ALLURE	○	●	INVEIGLE	○
○	ANATHEMA	●	○	LOATHe	●
○	ANTIPATHY	●	○	PARRY	●
○	BANE	●	●	PENCHANT	○
●	BEGUILE	○	●	PREDILECTION	○
●	BENT	○	●	PROCLIVITY	○
●	CHARM	○	●	PROPENSITY	○
○	DISSUADE	●	○	RANCOR	●
●	DRAW	○	○	REVILE	●
●	ELICIT	○	○	SPURN	●

When you talk about the pros and cons of a situation, you're talking about the positives and negatives. Notice that the words with *PRO* mean "attraction" or "like."

BRAVERY OR CONFIDENCE		FEAR OR CAUTION
●	APLOMB	○
○	APPREHENSION	●
●	AUDACIOUS	○
●	AUDACITY	○
○	CHARY	●
○	CIRCUMSPECTION	●
○	CRAVEN	●
●	DAUNTLESS	○
●	DOUGHTY	○
●	GALLANTRY	○
●	GAME	○
●	INTREPID	○
●	METTLESOME	○
○	MISGIVING	●
●	PLUCKY	○
○	PUSILLANIMOUS	●
●	TEMERITY	○
○	TREPIDATION	●
●	UNDAUNTED	○
●	VALIANT	○
●	VALOROUS	○

Notice that there are several words in this list with the same roots. For instance, *valiant* and *valorous* both use the root *VAL.* If *intrepid* means "fearless," then *trepidation* must be "fear." And *dauntless* and *undaunted* both mean the same thing.

CALMNESS		AGITATION	CALMNESS		AGITATION
●	BECALM	○	●	NONCHALANT	○
○	BLUSTER	●	○	PERTURB	●
●	COLLECTED	○	●	PLACID	○
●	COMPOSED	○	●	QUIESCENT	○
●	COMPOSURE	○	○	RAGING	●
●	DETACHED	○	○	RAIL	●
○	DISCOMPOSED	●	●	REPOSE	○
●	DISPASSIONATE	○	○	ROIL	●
○	DISQUIETED	●	○	RUFFLED	●
○	FLURRIED	●	●	SEDENTARY	○
○	FLUSTER	●	●	SERENE	○
○	FRENETIC	●	●	STAID	○
○	FULMINATE	●	●	STEADY	○
○	FUROR	●	●	TRANQUIL	○
●	IMPERTURBABLE	○	○	TUMULTUOUS	●
●	INDOLENT	○	○	TURBID	●
○	INSURGENT	●	○	TURBULENT	●
○	KINETIC	●	●	UNRUFFLED	○
●	LANGUOR	○	○	VEHEMENCE	●
●	LULL	○	○	VERVE	●

On this list, you can use "charge" to answer many of these words. Words like *fluster, frenetic, furor, kinetic, perturb,* and *tumultuous* sound agitating, while *becalm, serene,* and *tranquil* all sound calm.

CHANGE		LACK OF CHANGE
●	CATALYST	○
●	COMMUTATION	○
○	CONSISTENT	●
○	CONSTANT	●
○	DETERMINATE	●
○	ENTRENCHED	●
○	FIXITY	●
○	IMMUTABLE	●
○	IMPERVIOUS	●
○	INERT	●
○	INGRAINED	●
●	INNOVATIVE	○
○	INVARIABLE	●
○	INVIOLATE	●
○	LODGED	●
●	METAMORPHOSIS	○
●	MUTABLE	○
○	ROOTED	●
○	STEADFAST	●
●	TRANSFIGURATION	○
●	TRANSFORMATION	○
●	TRANSLATION	○
●	TRANSMOGRIFY	○
●	TRANSMUTATION	○
○	UNFAILING	●

TRANS means "across," so the five words in this list that begin with this root are all words that have to do with change.

GOODNESS OR MORALITY		EVIL OR IMMORALITY	GOODNESS OR MORALITY		EVIL OR IMMORALITY
●	ALTRUISM	○	○	INVIDIOUS	●
○	BACCHANALIAN	●	○	LASCIVIOUS	●
●	BEATIFIC	○	○	LICENTIOUS	●
●	BENEFICENT	○	○	LURID	●
●	BENIGN	○	○	MISCREANT	●
●	BENISON	○	○	NEFARIOUS	●
●	CLEMENT	○	●	NOBLE	○
●	CONTINENCE	○	○	PERFIDIOUS	●
○	DEBAUCH	●	●	PROBITY	○
○	DECADENCE	●	○	PROFLIGATE	●
●	ELEVATED	○	○	PRURIENT	●
●	ETHICAL	○	○	RAPACITY	●
●	EXEMPLARY	○	●	RECTITUDE	○
○	FIENDISH	●	○	REPROBATE	●
○	ILLICIT	●	●	RIGHTEOUS	○
○	INFERNAL	●	●	TEMPERANCE	○
○	INIQUITOUS	●	○	TURPITUDE	●
●	INTEGRITY	○	●	VIRTUE	○

The root *BEN* means "good." Notice that the three words in this list that include this root all mean something having to do with goodness or morality.

LARGE AMOUNT OR EXCESS		SMALL AMOUNT OR SHORTAGE	LARGE AMOUNT OR EXCESS		SMALL AMOUNT OR SHORTAGE
●	CAPACIOUS	○	●	MYRIAD	○
●	CAVALCADE	○	●	opulence	○
●	CLOYING	○	●	OVERABUNDANCE	○
●	CORNUCOPIA	○	○	PAUCITY	●
○	DEARTH	●	●	PLETHORA	○
○	DEFECT	●	○	POVERTY	●
○	DEFICIENT	●	●	PREPONDERANCE	○
●	DILATE	○	○	PRIVATION	●
●	DISTEND	○	●	PRODIGIOUS	○
●	EFFUSIVE	○	●	PROFUSION	○
○	FAMINE	●	●	REPLETE	○
●	FRAUGHT	○	○	SCANTINESS	●
●	GLUT	○	○	SCARCITY	●
○	INSUFFICIENCY	●	○	STINTING	●
●	MANIFOLD	○	●	SUPERABUNDANCE	○
○	MEAGER	●	●	SUPEREROGATORY	○
●	MULTIFARIOUS	○	●	SUPERFLUITY	○
			●	SURFEIT	○

Notice that all the words that start with *SUPER* have to do with excess.

GROW		SHRINK
○	ABATE	●
●	ACCRETE	○
●	AGGRANDIZE	○
●	AMPLIFY	○
●	APPEND	○
●	AUGMENT	○
●	BURGEON	○
○	CONSTRICT	●
○	CORRODE	●
○	DWINDLE	●
○	EBB	●
○	ERODE	●
●	ESCALATE	○
●	UPSURGE	○
●	WANE	○
○	WAX	●

Here you might want to think of clichéd phrases. For instance, an *ebb tide* is a tide that's going out. A *burgeoning debt* is a debt that's increasing at a healthy rate. And the moon has *waxing* (growing) and *waning* (shrinking) phases.

GRAND AND IMPORTANT		PETTY OR UNIMPORTANT	GRAND AND IMPORTANT		PETTY OR UNIMPORTANT
○	ABJECT	●	●	MOMENTOUS	○
●	APOTHEOSIS	○	○	NEGLIGIBLE	●
●	ASTRAL	○	○	NIGGLING	●
●	AUGUST	○	○	NONENTITY	●
●	CONSEQUENTIAL	○	●	OVERWEENING	○
●	CONSIDERABLE	○	○	PALTRY	●
○	DEBASED	●	○	PICAYUNE	●
●	ELEVATED	○	○	PIDDLING	●
●	ELOQUENT	○	●	PRETENTIOUS	○
●	EXALTED	○	●	REGAL	○
○	FRIVOLOUS	●	●	SALIENT	○
●	GRANDIOSE	○	○	SERVILE	●
○	IGNOBLE	●	●	SPLENDID	○
○	INCONSEQUENTIAL	●	●	STATELY	○
○	INGLORIOUS	●	●	SUBLIME	○
●	LOFTY	○	●	SUBSTANTIAL	○
●	MEANINGFUL	○	●	WEIGHTY	○

This is another list in which common phrases can help you figure out the meaning of words. For instance, if someone makes a *salient point*, it's central to an argument. In physics, certain forces, such as air resistance, are often considered *negligible*, or ignored.

UNLIMITED OR FREE		LIMITED OR CLOSED
⭕	CIRCUMSCRIBED	⬤
⭕	DURESS	⬤
⬤	EMANCIPATED	⭕
⭕	ENCUMBRED	⬤
⭕	FETTERED	⬤
⭕	HERMETIC	⬤
⭕	IMMURE	⬤
⭕	INCOMMUNICADO	⬤
⭕	INDENTURE	⬤
⭕	INSULAR	⬤
⬤	LATITUDE	⭕
⬤	LAXITY	⭕
⬤	LICENSE	⭕
⬤	MANUMISSION	⭕
⬤	MAVERICK	⭕
⭕	OCCLUSION	⬤
⭕	STRICTURE	⬤
⭕	STYMIE	⬤
⭕	THRALL	⬤
⭕	TRAMMELED	⬤
⬤	UNBRIDLED	⭕
⬤	UNFETTERED	⭕
⬤	UNTRAMMELED	⭕
⭕	YOKE	⬤

Notice that *trammeled* and *fettered* are joined on this list by untrammeled and unfettered. Also, notice that all the words with *UN* are free.

YOUTH OR IMMATURITY		OLD AGE OR MATURITY
⬭	ABIDING	⬤
⬭	ANTEDELUVIAN	⬤
⬤	CALLOW	⬭
⬭	DOTAGE	⬤
⬭	GERIATRIC	⬤
⬤	GREEN	⬭
⬭	HOARY	⬤
⬭	INVETERATE	⬤
⬤	JUVENILE	⬭
⬤	NEOPHYTE	⬭
⬤	PUERILE	⬭
⬭	SENESCENT	⬤
⬤	SOPHOMORIC	⬭
⬤	STRIPLING	⬭
⬭	SUPERANNUATED	⬤
⬤	TYRO	⬭

This list is full of roots to help you figure things out: *NEO* means "new." *GERI* means "old." *Senescent* comes from the Latin *senex*, which means "old man." *Superannuated* has to do with lots of years.

PRAISE		CRITICISM	PRAISE		CRITICISM
●	ACCLAIM	○	●	EULOGIZE	○
●	ACCOLADE	○	●	EXALT	○
●	ADULATORY	○	●	EXTOL	○
●	APPLAUSE	○	●	HAIL	○
●	APPROBATION	○	●	HOMAGE	○
●	BOUQUET	○	●	HONOR	○
●	CELEBRATE	○	○	IMPUGN	●
○	CENSURE	●	●	KUDOS	○
●	COMMEND	○	●	LAUD	○
○	DEFAME	●	●	PAEAN	○
○	DEMEAN	●	●	PANEGYRIC	○
○	DENIGRATE	●	○	PEJORATIVE	●
○	DENOUNCE	●	●	PLAUDIT	○
○	DENUNCIATE	●	●	TRIBUTE	○
○	DEPRECATE	●	●	VENERATE	○
●	ENCOMIUM	○			

In this exercise, every word that uses *DE,* which can mean "down," as a prefix is negative. For instance, *denounce* means "to speak down" or "to criticize."

SWIFTNESS OR BRIEFNESS		**DELAY OR SLOWNESS**
●	ALACRITY	○
●	CELERITY	○
●	CURSORY	○
○	DALLY	●
○	DILATORY	●
●	EPHEMERAL	○
●	EVANESCENT	○
●	EXTEMPORANEOUS	○
●	IMPROMPTU	○
○	LAGGARD	●
●	MERCURIAL	○
●	PERFUNCTORY	○
○	PERPETUITY	●
●	PRECIPITOUS	○
○	PROCRASTINATION	●
○	PROTRACTED	●
○	RETARD	●
○	SLUGGISH	●
○	TORPID	●
●	TRANSIENT	○

Mercurial is a word based on a mythological figure. Mercury was the messenger of the gods who traveled with winged sandals. Thus, *mercurial* is fast.

SUBTLE OR SLIGHT		OBVIOUS
⬭	BLATANT	⬤
⬭	EGREGIOUS	⬤
⬭	FLAGRANT	⬤
⬤	GOSSAMER	⬭
⬭	MANIFEST	⬤
⬤	MODICUM	⬭
⬤	NUANCE	⬭
⬭	OSTENTATIOUS	⬤
⬭	OVERT	⬤
⬭	PATENT	⬤
⬤	RAREFY	⬭
⬤	REFINED	⬭
⬤	SCINTILLA	⬭

This list has several words that you can probably recognize from when they are used in context. For instance, people often refer to an *"egregious* error" or a *"modicum* of respect."

RUDENESS		POLITENESS
●	ASOCIAL	○
●	BOORISH	○
●	CHEEKY	○
●	CHURLISH	○
○	CIVIL	●
●	CRASS	○
○	DEFERENTIAL	●
○	DEMURE	●
●	EARTHY	○
●	EFFRONTERY	○
○	GALLANT	●
○	GENTEEL	●
○	OBEISANCE	●
○	OBLIGING	●
●	OBSTREPEROUS	○
●	PHILISTINE	○
○	PUNCTILIOUS	●
●	RAW	○
●	SCABROUS	○
○	SOLICITOUS	●
○	TACTFUL	●
●	UNGRACIOUS	○
●	UNPOLISHED	○
●	VULGAR	○

The word *Philistine* comes from a reference to the ancient people of Philistia. These people had a reputation for being smug and ignorant, particularly in the area of art and culture.

INTELLIGENCE AND ABILITY		STUPIDITY AND CLUMSINESS	INTELLIGENCE AND ABILITY		STUPIDITY AND CLUMSINESS
●	ACUMEN	○	●	INGENIOUS	○
○	ASININE	●	●	KEN	○
●	ASTUTE	○	○	MALADROIT	●
○	DERANGED	●	●	OMNISCIENT	○
○	DOLTISH	●	●	PERCIPIENT	○
○	FATUOUS	●	●	PERSPICACIOUS	○
●	FINESSE	○	●	PRECOCIOUS	○
●	FLAIR	○	●	PUNDIT	○
○	GAUCHE	●	●	SAGACIOUS	○
○	GULLIBLE	●	●	SAPIENT	○
○	IGNORAMUS	●	○	SIMPLE	●
○	IMPOLITIC	●	○	UNWITTING	●
○	INANE	●	○	VACUOUS	●
●	INCISIVE	○	○	VAPID	●

Many of these words have roots that can lead you to the answer. *MAL* means "bad," so *maladroit* deals with clumsiness. *OMNI* means "all," and *SCI* means "knowing," so *omniscient* means "all-knowing."

LOUD, LONG, OR A LOT OF SPEECH		QUIET, SHORT, OR ABSENCE OF SPEECH
●	BOMBAST	○
○	CURT	●
○	DUMB	●
●	ELOQUENT	○
●	GARRULOUS	○
●	GRANDILOQUENT	○
○	LACONIC	●
●	LOQUACIOUS	○
○	MUTE	●
●	OROTUND	○
●	PLANGENT	○
●	PROLIX	○
○	RETICENT	●
●	STENTORIAN	○
○	SUCCINCT	●
○	TACIT	●
○	TACITURN	●
○	TERSE	●
●	TURGID	○
●	VERBOSE	○

Notice that there are three different words with the root *LOQU* in this list. *LOQU* means "word, speech," so these three words all have to do with a lot of speech.

CLEAN		DIRTY
●	ABLUTION	○
○	BESMEAR	●
○	BESPATTER	●
○	DEFILE	●
○	GRIMY	●
○	GRUBBY	●
●	IMMACULATE	○
●	PRISTINE	○
○	SLOVENLY	●
○	SMUTTY	●
○	SULLY	●
●	UNSOILED	○
●	UNSULLIED	○
●	VIRGINAL	○

In this case, the sound of the words tell you a lot about the words themselves. If the word sounds dirty, as the words *besmear, bespatter, defile,* or *slovenly* do, you can bet that's what it means.

TOGETHER OR CONTINUOUS		SEPARATE OR DISCONTINUOUS	TOGETHER OR CONTINUOUS		SEPARATE OR DISCONTINUOUS
●	ABUT	○	○	DISCRETE	●
●	AGGREGATION	○	○	DISJOINTED	●
○	ASUNDER	●	○	DISPERSE	●
○	BIFURCATE	●	○	DISSIPATE	●
●	CABAL	○	○	DIVERGE	●
●	COLLATE	○	○	ESTRANGE	●
●	COLLOQUY	○	○	HIATUS	●
●	COLLUSION	○	○	INCONGRUOUS	●
●	CONCATENATE	○	○	INTERREGNUM	●
●	CONCOMITANT	○	○	INTERSTICE	●
●	CONFLUENCE	○	○	RIFT	●
●	CONJOIN	○	○	SCHISM	●
●	CONSENSUS	○	○	SEQUESTERED	●
●	CONSONANCE	○	●	SYNCHRONOUS	○
●	COTERIE	○	●	SYNTHESIS	○
○	DIFFUSE	●	●	TANDEM	○

This list is full of roots. *SYN* means "same"; *CON, COM,* and *COLL* mean "with"; and *DIS* means "away from" or "apart." Use your knowledge of these roots to make your decisions.

STUBBORN		AGREEABLE
⬭	ACCEDE	⬤
⬭	ACCOMMODATING	⬤
⬭	ACQUIESCE	⬤
⬭	AMENABLE	⬤
⬭	CAPITULATE	⬤
⬭	COMPLY	⬤
⬭	CONCEDE	⬤
⬤	CONTUMACIOUS	⬭
⬤	DOGMATIC	⬭
⬤	HIDEBOUND	⬭
⬤	INTRANSIGENT	⬭
⬤	OBDURACY	⬭
⬭	OBLIGING	⬤
⬤	OBSTINATE	⬭
⬤	OSSIFIED	⬭
⬤	PERTINACIOUS	⬭
⬤	RECALCITRANT	⬭
⬤	REFRACTORY	⬭
⬤	UNBENDING	⬭
⬤	UNSWAYABLE	⬭

UN means "not," so *unswayable* and *unbending* both mean "stubborn."

Chapter 12: **GRE Minidictionary**

This Minidictionary provides you with the definitions of many common GRE words. Use this list not only when you work with the vocabulary exercises but whenever you encounter an unfamiliar word anywhere—such as in released tests or everyday reading.

A

ABANDON (n)   total lack of inhibition

ABASE   to humble, disgrace

ABASH   to embarrass

ABATEMENT   decrease, reduction

ABDICATE   to give up a position, right, or power

ABERRANT   atypical, not normal

ABERRATION   something different from the usual or normal

ABET   to aid, act as accomplice

ABEYANCE   temporary suppression or suspension

ABHOR   to loathe, detest

ABIDING   enduring, continuing

ABJECT   miserable, pitiful

ABJURE   to reject, abandon formally

ABLUTION   act of cleansing

ABNEGATE   to deny, renounce

ABOLITIONIST   one who opposes the practice of slavery

ABOMINATE   to hate

ABORTIVE   interrupted while incomplete

ABRIDGE   to condense, shorten

ABROGATE   to abolish or invalidate by authority

ABRUPT   sudden, unexpected

ABSCOND   to depart secretly

ABSOLVE   to forgive, free from blame

ABSTAIN   to refrain deliberately from something

ABSTEMIOUS   moderate in appetite

ABSTRACT (adj)   theoretical; complex, difficult

ABSTRUSE   difficult to comprehend

ABUT   to touch, to be in contact with

ABYSS   an extremely great depth

ACCEDE   to express approval; agree to

ACCESSIBLE   attainable, available; approachable

ACCESSORY   attachment, ornament; accomplice, partner

ACCLAIM   praise

ACCOLADE   praise, distinction

ACCOMMODATING   helpful

ACCORD   to reconcile, come to an agreement

ACCOST   to approach and speak to someone

ACCRETION   growth in size or increase in amount

ACCRUE   to accumulate, grow by additions

ACERBIC   bitter, sharp in taste or temper

ACIDULOUS   sour in taste or manner

ACME   highest point, summit

ACQUIESCE   to agree, comply quietly

ACQUITTAL   release from blame

ACRID   harsh, bitter

ACRIMONY   bitterness, animosity

ACUITY   sharpness

ACUMEN   sharpness of insight

ACUTE   sharp, pointed

ADAGE   old saying or proverb

ADAMANT   uncompromising, unyielding

ADAPT   to accommodate, adjust

ADHERE   to cling or to follow without deviation

ADJACENT   next to

ADJUNCT   something added, attached, or joined

ADMONISH   to caution or reprimand

ADROIT   skillful, accomplished, highly competent

ADULATION   high praise

ADULTERATE   to corrupt or make impure

ADUMBRATE   to sketch, outline in a shadowy way

ADVANTAGEOUS   favorable, useful

ADVENTITIOUS   accidental

ADVERSARIAL   antagonistic, competitive

ADVERSE   unfavorable, unlucky, harmful

ADVOCATE   to speak in favor of

AERIAL   having to do with the air

AERIE   nook or nest built high in the air

AERODYNAMIC   relating to objects moving through the air

AESTHETIC   pertaining to beauty or art

AFFABLE   friendly, easy to approach

AFFECTED (adj)   pretentious, phony

AFFINITY   fondness, liking; similarity

AFFLUENT   rich, abundant

AFFRONT (n)   personal offense, insult

AGENDA   plan, schedule

AGGRANDIZE   to make larger or greater in power

AGGREGATE (n)   collective mass or sum; total

AGGRIEVE   to afflict, distress

AGILE   well coordinated, nimble

AGITATION   commotion, excitement; uneasiness

AGNOSTIC   one doubting that people can know God

AGRARIAN   relating to farming or rural matters

ALACRITY   cheerful willingness, eagerness; speed

ALCHEMY   medieval chemical philosophy based on quest to change metal into gold

ALGORITHM   mechanical problem-solving procedure

ALIAS   assumed name

ALIENATED   distanced, estranged

ALIGNED   precisely adjusted; committed to one side or party

ALLAY   to lessen, ease, or soothe

ALLEGORY   symbolic representation

ALLEVIATE   to relieve, improve partially

ALLITERATION   repetition of the beginning sounds of words

ALLOCATION   allowance, portion, share

ALLURE (v)   to entice by charm; attract

ALLUSION   indirect reference

ALLUSIVENESS   quality of making many indirect references

ALOOF   detached, indifferent

ALTERCATION   noisy dispute

ALTRUISM   unselfish concern for others' welfare

AMALGAM   mixture, combination, alloy

AMBIDEXTROUS   able to use both hands equally well

AMBIGUOUS   uncertain; subject to multiple interpretations

AMBIVALENCE   attitude of uncertainty; conflicting emotions

AMBULATORY   itinerant; related to walking around

AMELIORATE   to make better, improve

AMENABLE   agreeable, cooperative

AMEND   to improve or correct flaws in

AMENITY   pleasantness; something increasing comfort

AMIABLE   friendly, pleasant, likable

AMICABLE   friendly, agreeable

AMITY   friendship

AMORAL   unprincipled, unethical

AMOROUS   strongly attracted to love; showing love

AMORPHOUS   having no definite form

AMORTIZE   to diminish by installment payments

AMPHIBIAN (n)   creature equally at home on land or in water

AMPHITHEATER   arena theater with rising tiers around a central open space

AMPLE   abundant, plentiful

AMPLIFY   to increase, intensify

AMULET   ornament worn as a charm against evil spirits

ANACHRONISM   something chronologically inappropriate

ANACHRONISTIC   outdated

ANALGESIA   a lessening of pain

ANALOGOUS   comparable, parallel

ANARCHY   absence of government or law; chaos

ANATHEMA   ban, curse; something shunned or disliked

ANCILLARY   accessory, subordinate, helping

ANECDOTE   short, usually funny account of an event

ANGULAR   characterized by sharp angles; lean and gaunt

ANIMATION   enthusiasm, excitement

ANIMOSITY   hatred, hostility

ANNUL   to cancel, nullify, declare void, or make legally invalid

ANODYNE   something that calms or soothes pain

ANOINT   to apply oil to, esp. as a sacred rite

ANOMALY   irregularity or deviation from the norm

ANONYMITY   condition of having no name or an unknown name

ANTAGONIST   foe, opponent, adversary

ANTECEDENT (adj)   coming before in place or time

ANTEDATE   dated prior to the actual occurrence

ANTEDILUVIAN   prehistoric, ancient beyond measure

ANTEPENULTIMATE   third from last

ANTERIOR   preceding, previous, before, prior (to)

ANTHOLOGY   collection of literary works

ANTHROPOMORPHIC   attributing human qualities to nonhumans

ANTIPATHY   dislike, hostility; extreme opposition or aversion

ANTIQUATED   outdated, obsolete

ANTIQUITY   ancient times; the quality of being old or ancient

ANTITHESIS   exact opposite or direct contrast

APACE   done quickly

APATHETIC   indifferent, unconcerned

APATHY   lack of feeling or emotion

APERTURE   an opening or hole

APHASIA   inability to speak or use words

APHELION   point in a planet's orbit that is farthest from the sun

APHORISM   old saying or short pithy statement

APLOMB   poise, confidence

APOCRYPHAL   not genuine; fictional

APOSTATE (n)   one who renounces a religious faith

APOSTROPHE   speech to the reader or someone not present; a superscript sign (')

APOTHEGM   a short, instructive saying

APOTHEOSIS   glorification; glorified ideal

APPEASE   to satisfy, placate, calm, pacify

APPEND   to attach

APPLAUSE   praise

APPRAISE   to evaluate the value of something

APPREHENSION   the act of comprehending; fear, foreboding

APPRISE   to give notice of; inform

APPROBATION   praise; official approval

APPROPRIATE (v)   to take possession of

AQUATIC   belonging or living in water

ARABLE   suitable for cultivation

ARBITRARY   depending solely on individual will; inconsistent

ARBITRATOR   mediator, negotiator

ARBOREAL   relating to trees; living in trees

ARBORETUM   place where trees are displayed and studied

ARCANE   secret, obscure, known only to a few

ARCHAIC   antiquated, from an earlier time; outdated

ARCHIPELAGO   large group of islands

ARDENT   passionate, enthusiastic, fervent

ARDOR   great emotion or passion

ARDUOUS   extremely difficult, laborious

ARID   extremely dry or deathly boring

ARRAIGN   to call to court to answer a charge

ARROGATE   to demand, claim arrogantly

ARSENAL   ammunition storehouse

ARTICULATE (adj) well-spoken, expressing oneself clearly

ARTIFACT historical relic, item made by human craft

ARTISAN craftsperson; expert

ARTLESS open and honest

ASCEND to rise or climb

ASCENDANCY state of rising, ascending; power or control

ASCERTAIN to determine, discover, make certain of

ASCETIC (adj) self-denying, abstinent, austere

ASCRIBE to attribute to, assign

ASHEN resembling ashes; deathly pale

ASININE lacking intelligence or sound judgment

ASKANCE scornfully

ASKEW crooked, tilted

ASOCIAL unable or unwilling to interact socially

ASPERITY harshness, roughness

ASPERSION false rumor, damaging report, slander

ASPIRE to have great hopes; to aim at a goal

ASSAIL to attack, assault

ASSAY to analyze or estimate

ASSENT (v) to express agreement

ASSERT to affirm, attest

ASSIDUOUS diligent, persistent, hardworking

ASSIGNATION appointment for lovers' meeting; assignment

ASSIMILATION act of blending in, becoming similar

ASSONANCE resemblance in sound, especially in vowel sounds; partial rhyme

ASSUAGE to make less severe, ease, relieve

ASTRAL exalted, elevated in position; relating to the stars

ASTRINGENT harsh, severe, stern

ASTUTE having good judgment

ASUNDER (adv) into different parts

ASYMMETRICAL not corresponding in size, shape, position, etc.

ATONE to make amends for a wrong

ATROCIOUS monstrous, shockingly bad, wicked

ATROPHY (v) to waste away, wither from disuse

ATTAIN to accomplish, gain

ATTENUATE to make thin or slender; weaken

ATTEST to testify, stand as proof of, bear witness

AUDACIOUS bold, daring, fearless

AUDIBLE capable of being heard

AUDIT (n) formal examination of financial records

AUDITORY having to do with hearing

AUGMENT to expand, extend

AUGURY (adj) prophecy, prediction of events

AUGUST dignified, awe-inspiring, venerable

AUSPICIOUS having favorable prospects, promising

AUSTERE stern, strict, unadorned

AUTHORITARIAN extremely strict, bossy

AUTOCRAT dictator

AUTONOMOUS separate, independent

AUXILIARY supplementary, reserve

AVARICE greed

AVENGE to retaliate, take revenge for an injury or crime

AVER to declare to be true, affirm

AVERSE being disinclined towards something

AVERSION intense dislike

AVERT to turn (something) away; prevent

AVIARY large enclosure housing birds

AVOW to state openly or declare

AWRY crooked, askew, amiss

AXIOM premise, postulate, self-evident truth

B

BACCHANALIAN drunkenly festive

BALEFUL harmful, with evil intentions

BALK (v) to refuse, shirk; prevent

BALLAD folk song, narrative poem

BALM soothing, healing influence

BAN (v) to forbid, outlaw

BANAL trite and overly common

BANE something causing ruin, death, or destruction

BANTER playful conversation

BASE being of low value or position

BASTION fortification, stronghold

BAY (v) to bark, especially in a deep, prolonged way

BEATIFIC   appearing to be saintly, angelic

BECALM   to make calm or still; keep motionless by lack of wind

BECLOUD   to confuse; darken with clouds

BEGUILE   to deceive, mislead; charm

BEHEMOTH   huge creature

BELABOR   to insist repeatedly or harp on

BELATED   late

BELEAGUER   to harass, plague

BELFRY   bell tower, room in which a bell is hung

BELIE   to misrepresent; expose as false

BELITTLE   to represent as unimportant, make light of

BELLICOSE   warlike, aggressive

BELLIGERENT   hostile, tending to fight

BELLOW   to roar, shout

BEMUSE   to confuse, stupefy; plunge deep into thought

BENCHMARK   standard of measure

BENEFACTOR   someone giving aid or money

BENEFICENT   kindly, charitable; doing good deeds; producing good effects

BENEFICIAL   advantageous

BENIGHTED   unenlightened

BENIGN   kindly, gentle or harmless

BENISON   blessing

BENT   a natural inclination towards something

BEQUEATH   to give or leave through a will; to hand down

BERATE   to scold harshly

BEREAVED   suffering the death of a loved one

BESEECH   to beg, plead, implore

BESMEAR   to smear

BESPATTER   to spatter

BESTIAL   beastly, animal-like

BESTOW   to give as a gift

BETOKEN   to indicate, signify, give evidence of

BEVY   group

BIAS   prejudice, slant

BIBLIOGRAPHY   list of books

BIBLIOPHILE   book lover

BICKER   to have a petty argument

BIFURCATE   divide into two parts

BILATERAL   two sided

BILIOUS   bad-natured

BILK   to cheat, defraud

BILLET   board and lodging for troops

BIPED   two-footed animal

BISECT   to cut into two (usually equal) parts

BLANCH   to pale; take the color out of

BLANDISH   to coax with flattery

BLASPHEMOUS   cursing, profane, irreverent

BLATANT   glaring, obvious, showy

BLIGHT (v)   to afflict, destroy

BLITHE   joyful, cheerful, or without appropriate thought

BLUDGEON   to hit as with a short, heavy club

BLUSTER   to boast or make threats loudly

BOISTEROUS   rowdy, loud, unrestrained

BOLSTER   to support; reinforce

BOMBASTIC   using high-sounding but meaningless language

BONANZA   extremely large amount; something profitable

BONHOMIE   good-natured geniality; atmosphere of good cheer

BOON   blessing, something to be thankful for

BOOR   crude person, one lacking manners or taste

BOTANIST   scientist who studies plants

BOUNTIFUL   plentiful

BOUQUET   a bunch of cut flowers

BOURGEOIS   middle class

BOVINE   relating to cows

BRAZEN   bold, shameless, impudent; of or like brass

BREACH   act of breaking, violation

BREVITY   the quality of being brief in time

BRIGAND   bandit, outlaw

BROACH   to mention or suggest for the first time

BROMIDE   a dull, commonplace person or idea

BRUSQUE   rough and abrupt in manner

BUFFET (v)   to strike, hit

BUFFOON   clown or fool

BULWARK   defense wall; anything serving as defense

BURGEON   to sprout or flourish

BURLY   brawny, husky

BURNISH   to polish, make smooth and bright

BURSAR   treasurer

BUSTLE   commotion, energetic activity

BUTT   person or thing that is object of ridicule

BUTTRESS (v)   to reinforce or support

BYWAY   back road

C

CABAL   a secret group seeking to overturn something

CACOPHONOUS   jarring, unpleasantly noisy

CADAVER   dead body

CADENCE   rhythmic flow of poetry; marching beat

CAJOLE   to flatter, coax, persuade

CALAMITOUS   disastrous, catastrophic

CALLOUS   thick-skinned, insensitive

CALLOW   immature, lacking sophistication

CALUMNY   false and malicious accusation, misrepresentation, slander

CANARD   a lie

CANDID   frank or fair

CANDOR   honesty of expression

CANNY   smart; founded on common sense

CANONIZE   to declare a person a saint; raise to highest
honors

CANVASS   to examine thoroughly; conduct a poll

CAPACIOUS   large, roomy; extensive

CAPITULATE   to submit completely, surrender

CAPRICIOUS   impulsive, whimsical, without much thought

CARDIOLOGIST   physician specializing in diseases of the
heart

CAREEN   to lean to one side

CARICATURE   exaggerated portrait, cartoon

CARNAL   of the flesh

CARNIVOROUS   meat-eating

CAROM   to strike and rebound

CARP (v)   to find fault, complain constantly

CARTOGRAPHY   science or art of making maps

CAST (n)   copy, replica

CAST (v)   to fling, to throw

CASTIGATE   to punish, chastise, criticize severely

CATACLYSMIC   disastrous

CATALYST   something causing change without being
changed

CATEGORICAL   absolute, without exception

CATHARSIS   purification, cleansing

CATHOLIC   universal; broad and comprehensive

CAUCUS   smaller group within an organization; a meeting
of such a group

CAULK   to make watertight

CAUSALITY   cause-and-effect relationship

CAUSTIC   biting, sarcastic; able to burn

CAVALCADE   a procession

CAVALIER (adj)   carefree, happy; with lordly disdain

CAVIL   to raise trivial objections

CAVORT   to frolic, frisk

CEDE   to surrender possession of something

CELEBRITY   fame, widespread acclaim

CELERITY   quick moving or acting

CENSORIOUS   severely critical

CENSURE   to criticize or find fault with

CENTRIPETAL   directed or moving towards the
center

CERTITUDE   assurance, certainty

CESSATION   temporary or complete halt

CESSION   act of surrendering something

CHAGRIN   shame, embarrassment, humiliation

CHALICE   goblet, cup

CHAMP (v)   chew noisily

CHAMPION (v)   to defend or support

CHAOS   confusion

CHAOTIC   extremely disorderly

CHARLATAN   quack, fake

CHARM   compelling attractiveness

CHARY   watchful, cautious, extremely shy

CHASTISE   to punish, discipline, scold

CHATTEL   piece of personal property

CHAUVINIST   someone prejudiced in the belief of their kind's superiority

CHEEKY   lacking prudence or discretion

CHERUBIC   sweet, innocent, resembling a cherub angel

CHICANERY   trickery, fraud, deception

CHIDE   to scold, express disapproval

CHIMERICAL   fanciful, imaginary, visionary; impossible

CHOICE (adj)   specially selected, preferred

CHOLERIC   easily angered, short-tempered

CHORTLE   to chuckle

CHROMATIC   relating to color

CHRONICLER   one who keeps records of historical events

CHURLISH   rude

CIRCUITOUS   roundabout

CIRCUMFERENCE   boundary or distance around a circle or sphere

CIRCUMLOCUTION   roundabout, lengthy way of saying something

CIRCUMNAVIGATE   to sail completely around

CIRCUMSCRIBE   to encircle; set limits on, confine

CIRCUMSPECT   cautious, wary

CIRCUMVENT   to go around; avoid

CISTERN   tank for rainwater

CITADEL   fortress or stronghold

CIVIL   polite; relating to citizens

CIVILITY   courtesy, politeness

CLAIRVOYANT (adj)   having ESP, psychic

CLAMOR (n)   noisy outcry

CLAMOR (v)   to make a noisy outcry

CLANDESTINE   secretive, concealed for a darker purpose

CLARITY   clearness; clear understanding

CLAUSTROPHOBIA   fear of small, confined places

CLEAVE   to split or separate; to stick, cling, adhere

CLEMENCY   merciful leniency

CLEMENT   mild

CLOISTER (v)   to confine, seclude

CLOYING   indulging to excess

COAGULATE   to clot or change from a liquid to a solid

COALESCE   to grow together or cause to unite as one

CODDLE   to baby, treat indulgently

COERCE   to compel by force or intimidation

COFFER   strongbox, large chest for money

COGENT   logically forceful, compelling, convincing

COGNATE   related, similar, akin

COGNITION   mental process by which knowledge is acquired

COGNOMEN   family name; any name, especially a nickname

COHABIT   to live together

COHERENT   intelligible, lucid, understandable

COLLATE   to arrange in an order

COLLATERAL   accompanying

COLLECTED   acting calm and composed

COLLOQUIAL   characteristic of informal speech

COLLOQUY   dialog or conversation, conference

COLLUSION   collaboration, complicity, conspiracy

COMELINESS   physical grace and beauty

COMMEND   to compliment, praise

COMMENSURATE   proportional

COMMISSION   fee payable to an agent; authorization

COMMODIOUS   roomy, spacious

COMMONPLACE   ordinary, found every day

COMMUNICABLE   transmittable

COMMUTE   to change a penalty to a less severe one

COMPATRIOT   fellow countryman

COMPELLING (adj)   having a powerful and irresistible effect

COMPENDIOUS   summarizing completely and briefly

COMPENSATE   to repay or reimburse

COMPLACENT   self-satisfied, smug, affable

COMPLAISANT   agreeable, friendly

COMPLEMENT   to complete, perfect

COMPLIANT   submissive and yielding

COMPLICITY   knowing partnership in wrongdoing

COMPOSED   acting calm

COMPOSURE   a calm manner or appearance

COMPOUND (adj)   complex; composed of several parts

COMPOUND (v)   to combine, add to

COMPRESS (v)   to reduce, squeeze

COMPULSIVE   obsessive, fanatic

COMPUNCTION   feeling of uneasiness caused by guilt or regret

COMPUNCTIOUS   feeling guilty or having misgivings

CONCATENATE   linked together

CONCAVE   curving inward

CONCEDE   to yield, admit

CONCEPTUALIZE   to envision, imagine

CONCERN   a matter of importance or worthy of consideration

CONCERTO   musical composition for orchestra and soloist(s)

CONCILIATORY   overcoming distrust or hostility

CONCOMITANT   accompanying something

CONCORD   agreement

CONCUR   to agree

CONDONE   to pardon or forgive; overlook, justify, or excuse a fault

CONDUIT   tube, pipe, or similar passage

CONFECTION   something sweet to eat

CONFISCATE   to appropriate, seize

CONFLAGRATION   big, destructive fire

CONFLUENCE   meeting place; meeting of two streams

CONFOUND   to baffle, perplex

CONGEAL   to become thick or solid, as a liquid freezing

CONGENIAL   similar in tastes and habits

CONGENITAL   existing since birth

CONGLOMERATE   collected group of varied things

CONGRESS   formal meeting or assembly

CONGRUITY   correspondence, harmony, agreement

CONJECTURE   speculation, prediction

CONJOIN   to join together

CONJUGAL   pertaining to marriage

CONJURE   to evoke a spirit, cast a spell

CONNIVE   to conspire, scheme

CONNOISSEUR   a person with refined taste

CONSANGUINEOUS   of the same origin; related by blood

CONSCIENTIOUS   governed by conscience; careful and thorough

CONSECRATE   to declare sacred; dedicate to a goal

CONSENSUS   unanimity, agreement of opinion or attitude

CONSEQUENTIAL   important

CONSIDERABLE   significant, worth considering

CONSIGN   to commit, entrust

CONSISTENT   containing no contradictions, being harmonious

CONSOLATION   something providing comfort or solace for a loss or hardship

CONSOLIDATE   to combine, incorporate

CONSONANT (adj)   consistent with, in agreement with

CONSTANT   completely uniform and unchanging

CONSTITUENT   component, part; citizen, voter

CONSTRAINED   forced, compelled; confined, restrained

CONSTRAINT   something that forces or compels; something that restrains or confines

CONSTRICT   to inhibit

CONSTRUE   to explain or interpret

CONSUMMATE (adj)   accomplished, complete, perfect

CONSUMMATE (v)   to complete, fulfill

CONTEND   to battle, clash; compete

CONTENTIOUS   quarrelsome, disagreeable, belligerent

CONTINENCE   self-control, self-restraint

CONTRADICT   to deny or oppose

CONTRAVENE   to contradict, deny, act contrary to

CONTRITE   deeply sorrowful and repentant for a wrong

CONTUMACIOUS   rebellious

CONTUSION   bruise

CONUNDRUM   riddle, puzzle, or problem with no solution

CONVALESCENCE   gradual recovery after an illness

CONVENE   to meet, come together, assemble

CONVENTIONAL   typical, customary, commonplace

CONVEX   curved outward

CONVIVIAL   sociable; fond of eating, drinking, and people

CONVOKE   to call together, summon

CONVOLUTED   twisted, complicated, involved

COPIOUS   abundant, plentiful

COQUETTE   woman who flirts

CORNUCOPIA   abundance

CORPOREAL   having to do with the body; tangible, material

CORPULENCE   obesity, fatness, bulkiness

CORRELATION   association, mutual relation of two or more things

CORROBORATE   to confirm, verify

CORRODE   to weaken or destroy

CORRUGATE   to mold in a shape with parallel grooves and ridges

COSMETIC (adj)   relating to beauty; affecting the surface of something

COSMOGRAPHY   science that deals with the nature of the universe

COSMOPOLITAN   sophisticated, free from local prejudices

COSSET   to pamper, treat with great care

COTERIE   small group of persons with a common interest or a similar purpose

COUNTENANCE (n)   facial expression; look of approval or support

COUNTENANCE (v)   to favor, support

COUNTERMAND   to annul, cancel, make a contrary order

COUNTERVAIL   to counteract, exert force against

COVEN   group of witches

COVERT   hidden; secret

COVET   to strongly desire something possessed by another

COWER   to cringe in fear

CRASS   crude, unrefined

CRAVEN   cowardly

CREDENCE   acceptance of something as true or real

CREDIBLE   plausible, believable

CREDULOUS   gullible, trusting

CREED   statement of belief or principle

CRESCENDO   gradual increase in volume of sound

CRINGE   to shrink in fear

CRITERION   standard for judging, rule for testing

CRYPTIC   puzzling

CUISINE   characteristic style of cooking

CULMINATION   climax, final stage

CULPABLE   guilty, responsible for wrong

CULPRIT   guilty person

CUMULATIVE   resulting from gradual increase

CUPIDITY   greed

CURATOR   caretaker and overseer of an exhibition, esp. in a museum

CURMUDGEON   cranky person

CURSORY   hastily done, superficial

CURT   abrupt, blunt

CURTAIL   to shorten

CUTLERY   cutting instruments; tableware

CYGNET   young swan

CYNIC   person who distrusts the motives of others

D

DALLY   to act playfully or waste time

DAUNT   to discourage, intimidate

DEARTH   lack, scarcity, insufficiency

DEBASE   to degrade or lower in quality or stature

DEBAUCH   to corrupt, seduce from virtue or duty; indulge

DEBILITATE   to weaken, enfeeble

DEBUNK   to discredit, disprove

DEBUTANTE   young woman making debut in high society

DECADENCE   decline or decay, deterioration

DECAMP   to leave suddenly

DECAPITATE   to behead

DECATHLON   athletic contest with ten events

DECIDUOUS   losing leaves in the fall; short-lived, temporary

DECLIVITY   downward slope

DECOROUS   proper, tasteful, socially correct

DECORUM   proper behavior, etiquette

DECRY   to belittle, openly condemn

DEFACE   to mar the appearance of, vandalize

DEFAMATORY   slanderous, injurious to the reputation

DEFAME   to disgrace or slander

DEFECT   an imperfection or shortcoming

DEFENDANT   person required to answer a legal action or suit

DEFER   to submit or yield

DEFERENCE   respect, honor

DEFERENTIAL   respectful and polite in a submissive way

DEFICIENT   defective, not meeting a normal standard

DEFILE   to make unclean or dishonor

DEFINITIVE   clear-cut, explicit or decisive

DEFLATION   decrease, depreciation

DEFORM   to disfigure, distort

DEFT   skillful, dexterous

DEFUNCT   no longer existing, dead, extinct

DELECTABLE   appetizing, delicious

DELEGATE (v)   to give powers to another

DELETERIOUS   harmful, destructive, detrimental

DELINEATION   depiction, representation

DELTA   tidal deposit at the mouth of a river

DELUGE (n)   flood

DELUGE (v)   to submerge, overwhelm

DEMAGOGUE   leader or rabble-rouser who usually uses appeals to emotion or prejudice

DEMARCATION   borderline; act of defining or marking a boundary or distinction

DEMEAN   to degrade, humiliate, humble

DEMISE   death

DEMOGRAPHICS   data relating to study of human population

DEMOTE   to reduce to a lower grade or rank

DEMOTION   lowering in rank or grade

DEMUR   to express doubts or objections

DEMYSTIFY   to remove mystery from, clarify

DENIGRATE   to slur or blacken someone's reputation

DENOUNCE   to accuse, blame

DENUDE   to make bare, uncover, undress

DENUNCIATION   public condemnation

DEPICT   to describe, represent

DEPLETE   to use up, exhaust

DEPLORE   to express or feel disapproval of; regret strongly

DEPLOY   to spread out strategically over an area

DEPOSE   to remove from a high position, as from a throne

DEPRAVITY   sinfulness, moral corruption

DEPRECATE   to belittle, disparage

DEPRECIATE   to lose value gradually

DERANGED   to be disturbed or insane

DERIDE   to mock, ridicule, make fun of

DERISIVE   expressing ridicule or scorn

DERIVATIVE   copied or adapted; not original

DERIVE   to originate; take from a certain source

DEROGATE   to belittle, disparage

DESCRY   to discover or reveal

DESECRATE   to abuse something sacred

DESICCATE   to dry completely, dehydrate

DESIST   to stop doing something

DESPONDENT   feeling discouraged and dejected

DESPOT   tyrannical ruler

DESTITUTE   very poor, poverty-stricken

DESULTORY   at random, rambling, unmethodical

DETACHED   separate, unconnected

DETER   to discourage; prevent from happening

DETERMINATE   having defined limits; conclusive

DETESTATION   extreme hatred

DETRACTOR   one who takes something away

DETRIMENTAL   causing harm or injury

DEVIATE   to stray, wander

DEVIATION   departure, exception, anomaly

DEVOID   totally lacking

DEVOUT   deeply religious

DEXTEROUS   skilled physically or mentally

DIABOLICAL   fiendish; wicked

DIALECT   regional style of speaking

DIAPHANOUS   allowing light to show through; delicate

DIATRIBE   bitter verbal attack

DICHOTOMY   division into two parts

DICTUM   authoritative statement; popular saying

DIDACTIC   excessively instructive

DIFFER   disagree

DIFFERENTIATE   to distinguish between two items

DIFFIDENCE   shyness, lack of confidence

DIFFRACT   to cause to separate into parts, esp. light

DIFFUSE   widely spread out

DIGRESS   to turn aside; to stray from the main point

DILAPIDATED   in disrepair, run-down, neglected

DILATE   to enlarge, swell, extend

DILATORY   slow, tending to delay

DILETTANTE   an amateur

DILUVIAL   relating to a flood

DIMINUTIVE   small

DIPLOMACY   discretion, tact

DIRGE   funeral hymn

DISABUSE   to free from a misconception

DISAFFECTED   discontented and disloyal

DISARRAY   clutter, disorder

DISBAND   to break up

DISBAR   to expel from legal profession

DISBURSE   to pay out

DISCERN   to perceive something obscure

DISCLAIM   to deny, disavow

DISCLOSE   to confess, divulge

DISCOMFIT   to cause perplexity and embarrassment

DISCOMPOSE   to disturb the composure or serenity

DISCONCERTING   bewildering, perplexing, slightly disturbing

DISCONSOLATE   unable to be consoled; extremely sad

DISCORDANT   harsh-sounding, badly out of tune

DISCREDIT   to dishonor or disgrace

DISCREDITED   disbelieved, discounted; disgraced, dishonored

DISCREPANCY   difference between

DISCRETE   distinct, separate

DISCRETIONARY   subject to one's own judgment

DISCURSIVE   wandering from topic to topic

DISDAIN   to regard with scorn and contempt

DISDAINFUL   contemptuous, scornful

DISENGAGED   disconnected, disassociated

DISGORGE   to vomit, discharge violently

DISHEVELED   untidy, disarranged, unkempt

DISINCLINED   averse, unwilling, lacking desire

DISINGENUOUS   sly and crafty

DISINTEREST   lack of interest or a disadvantage

DISJOINTED   lacking coherence or order, being separated

DISPARAGE   to belittle, speak disrespectfully about

DISPARATE   dissimilar, different in kind

DISPARITY   contrast, dissimilarity

DISPASSIONATE   free from emotion; impartial, unbiased

DISPEL   to drive out or scatter

DISPENSE   to distribute, administer

DISPENSE WITH   to suspend the operation of, do without

DISPERSE   to break up, scatter

DISPIRIT   to dishearten, make dejected

DISPUTE   to debate, to quarrel

DISQUIETED   feeling anxiety, being disturbed, lacking peace

DISREGARD   to neglect, pay no attention to

DISREPUTE   disgrace, dishonor

DISSEMBLE   to pretend, disguise one's motives

DISSEMINATE   to spread far and wide

DISSENSION   difference of opinion

DISSIMULATE   to disguise or put on a false appearance

DISSIPATE   to scatter; to pursue pleasure to excess

DISSOCIATE   to separate; remove from an association

DISSONANT   harsh and unpleasant sounding

DISSUADE   to persuade someone to alter original intentions

DISTAFF   the female branch of a family

DISTEND   to swell, inflate, bloat

DISTRAUGHT   very worried and distressed

DISTRUST (n)   disbelief and suspicion

DITHER (v)   to move or act confusedly or without clear purpose

DIURNAL   daily

DIVERGE   to move in different directions, to deviate from a source

DIVERSE   differing

DIVERT   to turn from one course to another

DIVEST   to get rid of

DIVINE (v)   to foretell or know by inspiration

DIVISIVE   creating disunity or conflict

DOCILE   tame, willing to be taught

DOCTRINAIRE   rigidly devoted to theories

DOGGED (adj)   persistent, stubborn

DOGMATIC   rigidly fixed in opinion, opinionated

DOLDRUMS   a period of despondency

DOLEFUL   sad, mournful

DOLOR   sadness

DOLT   idiot, dimwit, foolish person

DOMINEER   to rule over something in a tyrannical way

DONOR   benefactor, contributor

DORMANT   at rest, inactive, in suspended animation

DOTAGE   senile condition, mental decline

DOTARD   senile old person

DOTING   excessively fond, loving to excess

DOUGHTY   courageous

DOUR   sullen and gloomy; stern and severe

DOWRY   money or property given by a bride to her husband

DRAFT (v)   to plan, outline; to recruit, conscript

DRAW   to attract, to pull toward

DRIVEL   stupid talk; slobber

DROLL   amusing in a wry, subtle way

DROSS   waste produced during metal smelting; garbage

DUDGEON   angry indignation

DULCET   pleasant sounding, soothing to the ear

DUMB   unable to speak

DUPE (n)   fool, pawn

DUPE (v)   to deceive, trick

DUPLICITY   deception, dishonesty, double-dealing

DURABILITY   strength, sturdiness

DURATION   period of time that something lasts

DURESS   threat of force or intimidation; imprisonment

DWINDLE   to shrink or decrease

DYSPEPTIC   suffering from indigestion; gloomy and irritable

E

EARTHY   crude

EBB (v)   to fade away, recede

EBULLIENT   exhilarated, full of enthusiasm and high spirits

ECLECTIC   selecting from various sources

ECSTATIC   joyful

EDDY   air or wind current

EDICT   law, command, official public order

EDIFICE   building

EDIFY   to instruct morally and spiritually

EDITORIALIZE   to express an opinion on an issue

EFFACE   to erase or make illegible

EFFERVESCENT   bubbly, lively

EFFICACIOUS   effective, efficient

EFFIGY   stuffed doll; likeness of a person

EFFLUVIA   outpouring of gases or vapors

EFFRONTERY   impudent boldness; audacity

EFFULGENT   brilliantly shining

EFFUSIVE   expressing emotion without restraint

EGOCENTRIC   acting as if things are centered around oneself

EGREGIOUS   conspicuously bad

EGRESS   exit

ELATION   exhilaration, joy

ELEGY   mournful poem, usually about the dead

ELEVATED   high in status, exalted

ELICIT   to draw out, provoke

ELOQUENCE   fluent and effective speech

ELUCIDATE   to explain, clarify

EMACIATED   skinny, scrawny, gaunt, esp. from hunger

EMANCIPATE   to set free, liberate

EMBELLISH   to ornament, make attractive with decoration or details; add details to a statement

EMBEZZLE   to steal money in violation of a trust

EMBROIL   to involve in; cause to fall into disorder

EMEND   to correct a text

EMINENT   celebrated, distinguished; outstanding, towering

EMOLLIENT   having soothing qualities, esp. for skin

EMOTIVE   appealing to or expressing emotion

EMPATHY   identification with another's feelings

EMULATE   to copy, imitate

ENCHANT   to charm or attract

ENCIPHER   to translate a message into code

ENCOMIUM   warm praise

ENCORE   additional performance, often demanded by audience

ENCUMBER   to hinder, burden, restrict motion

ENDEMIC   belonging to a particular area, inherent

ENDOGAMOUS   marrying within a specific group due to law or custom

ENDURANCE   ability to withstand hardships

ENERVATE   to weaken, sap strength from

ENGENDER   to produce, cause, bring about

ENIGMATIC   puzzling, inexplicable

ENJOIN   to urge, order, command; forbid or prohibit, as by judicial order

ENMITY   hostility, antagonism, ill-will

ENNUI   boredom, lack of interest and energy

ENORMITY   state of being gigantic or terrible

ENSCONCE   to settle comfortably into a place

ENSHROUD   to cover, enclose with a dark cover

ENTAIL   to involve as a necessary result, necessitate

ENTHRALL   to captivate, enchant, enslave

ENTICE   to lure or tempt

ENTITY   something with its own existence or form

ENTOMOLOGIST   scientist who studies insects

ENTREAT   to plead, beg

ENTRENCHED   established solidly

ENUMERATE   to count, list, itemize

ENUNCIATE   to pronounce clearly

EON   indefinitely long period of time

EPHEMERAL   momentary, transient, fleeting

EPICURE   person with refined taste in food and wine

EPIGRAM   short, witty saying or poem

EPIGRAPH   quotation at the beginning of a literary work

EPILOGUE   concluding section of a literary work

EPITHET   an abusive word or phrase

EPITOME   representative of an entire group; summary

EPOCHAL   very significant or influential; defining an epoch or time period

EQUANIMITY   calmness, composure

EQUESTRIAN (n)   one who rides on horseback

EQUINE   relating to horses

EQUITABLE   fair

EQUITY   justice, fairness

EQUIVOCAL   ambiguous, open to two interpretations

EQUIVOCATE   to use vague or ambiguous language intentionally

ERADICATE   to erase or wipe out

ERODE   to diminish or destroy over a period of time

ERRANT   straying, mistaken, roving

ERRATIC   wandering and unpredictable

ERRONEOUS   in error; mistaken

ERSATZ   fake

ERUDITE   learned, scholarly

ESCALATE   to increase the intensity or scope of

ESCHEW   to abstain from, avoid

ESOTERIC   understood only by a learned few

ESPOUSE   to support or advocate; to marry

ESTIMABLE   admirable

ESTRANGE   to alienate, keep at a distance

ESURIENT   hungry, greedy

ETHEREAL   not earthly, spiritual, delicate

ETHICAL   moral, abiding by an accepted code of conduct

ETHOS   beliefs or character of a group

ETYMOLOGY   origin and history of a word; study of words

EULOGY   high praise, often in a public speech

EUPHEMISM   use of an inoffensive word or phrase in place of a more distasteful one

EUPHONY   pleasant, harmonious sound

EUPHORIA   feeling of well-being or happiness

EURYTHMICS   art of harmonious bodily movement

EUTHANASIA   mercy killing; intentional, easy and painless death

EVADE   to avoid, dodge

EVANESCENT   momentary, transitory, short-lived

EVICT   to put out or force out

EVIDENT   clear, able to be understood

EVINCE   to show clearly, display, signify

EVOKE   to inspire memories; to produce a reaction

EXACERBATE   to aggravate, intensify the bad qualities of

EXALT   to glorify, to elevate

EXASPERATION   irritation

EXCERPT (n)   selection from a book or play

EXCOMMUNICATE   to bar from membership in the church

EXCORIATE   to denounce

EXCRUCIATING   agonizing, intensely painful

EXCULPATE   to clear of blame or fault

EXECRABLE   utterly detestable

EXEMPLARY   serving as an example, commendable

EXHILARATION   state of being energetic or filled with happiness

EXHORT   to urge or incite by strong appeals

EXHUME   to remove from a grave; uncover a secret

EXIGENT   urgent; excessively demanding

EXONERATE   to clear of blame

EXORBITANT   extravagant, greater than reasonable

EXORCISE   to expel evil spirits

EXOTIC   foreign; romantic, excitingly strange

EXPANSIVE   sweeping, comprehensive; tending to expand

EXPATIATE   to wander; to discuss or describe at length

EXPATRIATE (n)   one who lives outside one's native land

EXPATRIATE (v)   to drive someone from his or her native land

EXPEDIENT (adj)   convenient, efficient, practical

EXPIATE   to atone for, make amends for

EXPIRE   to come to an end; die; breathe out

EXPLICABLE   capable of being explained

EXPLICIT   clearly defined, specific; forthright in expression

EXPLODE   to debunk, disprove; blow up, burst

EXPONENT   one who champions or advocates

EXPOUND   to elaborate; to expand or increase

EXPUNGE   to erase, eliminate completely

EXPURGATE   to censor

EXTEMPORANEOUS   unrehearsed, on the spur of the moment

EXTENUATE   to lessen the seriousness, strength, or effect of

EXTINCTION   end of a living thing or species

EXTOL   to praise

EXTORT   to obtain something by threats

EXTRANEOUS   irrelevant, unrelated, unnecessary

EXTRAPOLATE   to estimate

EXTREMITY   outermost or farthest point

EXTRICATE   to free from, disentangle, free

EXTRINSIC   not inherent or essential, coming from without

EXTROVERT   an outgoing person

EXUBERANT   lively, happy, and full of good spirits

EXUDE   to give off, ooze

EXULT   to rejoice

F

FABRICATE   to make or devise; construct

FABRICATED   constructed, invented; faked, falsified

FACADE   face, front; mask, superficial appearance

FACETIOUS   witty in an inappropriate way

FACILE   very easy

FACILITATE   to aid, assist

FACILITY   aptitude, ease in doing something

FACSIMILE   an exact copy

FALLACIOUS   wrong, unsound, illogical

FALLIBLE   capable of failing

FALLOW   uncultivated, unused

FAMINE   extreme scarcity of food

FANATICISM   extreme devotion to a cause

FARCICAL   absurd, ludicrous

FASTIDIOUS   careful with details

FATHOM (v)   to measure the depth of, gauge; to understand

FATUOUS   stupid; foolishly self-satisfied

FAULT   break in a rock formation; mistake or error

FAWN (v)   to flatter excessively, seek the favor of

FAZE   to bother, upset, or disconcert

FEALTY   intense loyalty

FEASIBLE   possible, capable of being done

FECKLESS   ineffective, careless, irresponsible

FECUND   fertile, fruitful, productive

FEDERATION   union of organizations; union of several states, each of which retains local power

FEIGN   to pretend, give a false impression; to invent falsely

FEISTY   excitable, easily drawn into quarrels

FELICITOUS   suitable, appropriate; well-spoken

FELICITY   feeling great happiness

FELL (v)   to chop, cut down

FELL (adj)   cruel

FERVID   passionate, intense zealous

FETID   foul-smelling, putrid

FETTER   to bind, chain, confine

FEUD   a prolonged quarrel between families

FEY   otherworldly; doomed

FIASCO   disaster, utter failure

FICKLE   unreliable

FICTIVE   fictional, imaginary

FIDELITY   loyalty

FIENDISH   excessively bad or cruel

FILCH   to steal

FILIAL   appropriate for a child

FILIBUSTER   use of obstructive tactics in a legislative assembly to prevent adoption of a measure

FINESSE   refinement or skill at a task or in a situation

FINICKY   fussy, difficult to please

FISSION   process of splitting into two parts

FISSURE   a crack or break

FITFUL   intermittent, irregular

FIXITY   being fixed or stable

FLACCID   limp, flabby, weak

FLAG   to loose energy and strength

FLAGRANT   outrageous, shameless

FLAIR   a natural inclination towards something

FLAMBOYANT   flashy, garish; exciting, dazzling

FLAMMABLE   combustible, being easily burned

FLAUNT   to show off

FLEDGLING   young bird just learning to fly; beginner, novice

FLIPPANT   disrespectful, casual

FLORA   plants

FLORID   gaudy, extremely ornate; ruddy, flushed

FLOUNDER   to falter, waver; to muddle, struggle

FLOUT   to treat contemptuously, scorn

FLUCTUATE   to alternate, waver

FLURRIED   to become agitated and confused

FLUSTER   to agitate or confuse

FODDER   raw material; feed for animals

FOIBLE   minor weakness or character flaw

FOIL (v)   to defeat, frustrate

FOIST   to pass off as genuine

FOLIATE   to grow, sprout leaves

FOMENT   to arouse or incite

FORAGE   to wander in search of food

FORBEARANCE   patience, restraint, leniency

FORD (v)   to cross a body of water at a shallow place

FOREBODING   dark sense of evil to come

FORECLOSE   to rule out; to seize debtor's property for lack of payments

FORENSIC   relating to legal proceedings; relating to debates

FORENSICS   study of argumentation and debate

FORESTALL   to prevent, delay; anticipate

FORETHOUGHT   anticipation, foresight

FORFEND   to prevent

FORGO   to go without, refrain from

FORLORN   dreary, deserted; unhappy; hopeless, despairing; pitiful in appearance

FORMULATE   to conceive, devise; to draft, plan; to express, state

FORSAKE   to abandon, withdraw from

FORSWEAR   to repudiate, renounce, disclaim, reject

FORTE (n)   strong point, something a person does well

FORTNIGHT   two weeks

FORTUITOUS   happening by luck, fortunate

FOSTER (v)   to nourish, cultivate, promote

FOUNDATION   groundwork, support; institution established by donation to aid a certain cause

FOUNDER (v)   to fall helplessly; sink

FRACAS   noisy dispute

FRACTIOUS   unruly, rebellious

FRAGMENTATION   division, separation into parts, disorganization

FRANK   honest and straightforward

FRATRICIDE   the killing of a brother or sister

FRAUD   deception, hoax

FRAUDULENT   deceitful, dishonest, unethical

FRAUGHT   full of, accompanied by

FRENETIC   wildly frantic, frenzied, hectic

FRENZIED   feverishly fast, hectic, and confused

FRIVOLOUS   petty, trivial; flippant, silly

FROND   leaf

FRUGAL   thrifty; cheap

FULMINATE   to explode with anger

FULSOME   excessive, overdone, sickeningly abundant

FUNEREAL   mournful, appropriate to a funeral

FUROR   rage, fury

FURTIVE   secret, stealthy

FUSION   process of merging things into one

G

GAINSAY   to deny

GALL (n)   bitterness; careless nerve

GALL (v)   to exasperate and irritate

GALLANT   a very fashionable young man

GAMBOL   to dance or skip around playfully

GAME (adj)   courageous

GARGANTUAN   giant, tremendous

GARNER   to gather and store

GARRULOUS   very talkative

GAUCHE   crude, socially awkward

GAUCHERIE   a tactless or awkward act

GAUNT   thin and bony

GAVEL   mallet used for commanding attention

GENRE   type, class, category

GENTEEL   stylish, elegant in manner or appearance

GERIATRIC   relating to old age or the process of aging

GERMINATE   to begin to grow (as in a seed or idea)

GESTATION   growth process from conception to birth

GIBE (v)   to make heckling, taunting remarks

GIRTH   distance around something

GLIB   fluent in an insincere manner; offhand, casual

GLOBAL   involving the entire world; relating to a whole

GLOWER   to glare, stare angrily and intensely

GLUTTONY   eating and drinking to excess

GNARL   to make knotted, deform

GNOSTIC   having to do with knowledge

GOAD   to prod or urge

GOSSAMER   something light, delicate, or tenuous

GOUGE   scoop out; extort

GRADATION   process occurring by regular degrees or stages; variation in color

GRANDILOQUENCE   pompous talk, fancy but meaningless language

GRANDIOSE   magnificent and imposing; exaggerated and pretentious

GRANULAR   having a grainy texture

GRASP (v)   to perceive and understand; to hold securely

GRATIS   free, costing nothing

GRATUITOUS   free, voluntary; unnecessary and unjustified

GRATUITY   something given voluntarily, tip

GREGARIOUS   outgoing, sociable

GRIEVOUS   causing grief or sorrow; serious and distressing

GRIMACE   facial expression showing pain or disgust

GRIMY   dirty, filthy

GROSS (adj)   obscene; blatant, flagrant

GROSS (n)   total before deductions

GROVEL   to humble oneself in a demeaning way

GRUBBY   dirty, sloppy

GUILE   trickery, deception

GULLIBLE   easily deceived

GUSTATORY   relating to sense of taste

GYRATE   to move in a circular motion

H

HABITAT   dwelling place

HACKNEYED   worn out by overuse

HAIL   to greet with praise

HALLOW   to make holy; treat as sacred

HAMLET   small village

HAPLESS   unfortunate, having bad luck

HARANGUE   a pompous speech

HARBINGER   precursor, sign of something to come

HARDY   robust, vigorous

HARMONY   accord, tranquillity, agreement

HARROWING   extremely distressing, terrifying

HASTEN   to hurry, to speed up

HAUGHTY   arrogant and condescending

HEADLONG   recklessly

HEADSTRONG   reckless; insisting on one's own way

HEATHEN   pagan; uncivilized and irreligious

HECTIC   hasty, hurried, confused

HECTOR   a bully, braggart

HEDONISM   pursuit of pleasure as a goal

HEGEMONY   leadership, domination, usually by a country

HEIGHTEN   to raise

HEINOUS   shocking, wicked, terrible

HEMICYCLE   semicircular form or structure

HEMORRHAGE (n)   heavy bleeding

HEMORRHAGE (v)   to bleed heavily

HERETICAL   opposed to an established religious orthodoxy

HERMETIC   tightly sealed

HETERODOX   unorthodox, not widely accepted

HETEROGENEOUS   composed of unlike parts, different, diverse

HEW   to cut with an ax

HIATUS   a gap or a break

HIDEBOUND   excessively rigid; dry and stiff

HINDER   to hamper

HINDSIGHT   perception of events after they happen

HINTERLAND   wilderness

HOARY   very old; whitish or gray from age

HOLISTIC   emphasizing importance of the whole and interdependence of its parts

HOLOCAUST   widespread destruction, usually by fire

HOMAGE   public honor and respect

HOMOGENEOUS   composed of identical parts

HOMONYM   word identical in pronunciation but different in meaning

HONE   to sharpen

HONOR (v)   to praise, glorify, pay tribute to

HUMANE   merciful, kindly

HUSBAND (v)   to farm; manage carefully and thriftily

HUTCH   pen or coop for animals; shack, shanty

HYDRATE   to add water to

HYGIENIC   clean, sanitary

HYMN   religious song, usually of praise or thanks

HYPERBOLE   purposeful exaggeration for effect

HYPERVENTILATE   to breathe abnormally fast

HYPOCHONDRIA   unfounded belief that one is often ill

HYPOCRITE   person claiming beliefs or virtues he or she doesn't really possess

HYPOTHERMIA   abnormally low body temperature

HYPOTHESIS   assumption subject to proof

HYPOTHETICAL   theoretical, speculative

I

ICONOCLAST   one who attacks traditional beliefs

IDEALISM   pursuit of noble goals

IDIOSYNCRASY   peculiarity of temperament, eccentricity

IGNOBLE   dishonorable, not noble in character

IGNOMINIOUS   disgraceful and dishonorable

IGNORAMUS   an ignorant person

ILK   type or kind

KAPLAN

ILLICIT   illegal, improper

ILLIMITABLE   limitless

ILLUSORY   unreal, deceptive

ILLUSTRIOUS   famous, renowned

IMBUE   to infuse; dye, wet, moisten

IMMACULATE   spotless; free from error

IMMATERIAL   extraneous, inconsequential, nonessential; not consisting of matter

IMMENSE   enormous, huge

IMMERSE   to bathe, dip; to engross, preoccupy

IMMOBILE   not moveable; still

IMMUNE   exempt; protected from harm or disease; unresponsive to

IMMUNOLOGICAL   relating to immune system

IMMURE   to imprison

IMMUTABLE   unchangeable, invariable

IMPAIR   to damage, injure

IMPASSE   blocked path, dilemma with no solution

IMPASSIONED   with passion

IMPASSIVE   showing no emotion

IMPEACH   to charge with misdeeds in public office; accuse

IMPECCABLE   flawless, without fault

IMPECUNIOUS   poor, having no money

IMPEDIMENT   barrier, obstacle; speech disorder

IMPERATIVE   essential; mandatory

IMPERIOUS   arrogantly self-assured, domineering, overbearing

IMPERTINENT   rude

IMPERTURBABLE   not capable of being disturbed

IMPERVIOUS   impossible to penetrate; incapable of being affected

IMPETUOUS   quick to act without thinking

IMPIOUS   not devout in religion

IMPLACABLE   inflexible, incapable of being pleased

IMPLANT   to set securely or deeply; to instill

IMPLAUSIBLE   improbable, inconceivable

IMPLICATE   to involve in a crime, incriminate

IMPLICIT   implied, not directly expressed

IMPOLITIC   unwise

IMPORTUNE   to ask repeatedly, beg

IMPOSE   to inflict, force upon

IMPOSING   dignified, grand

IMPOTENT   powerless, ineffective, lacking strength

IMPOUND   to seize and confine

IMPOVERISH   to make poor or bankrupt

IMPRECATION   curse

IMPREGNABLE   totally safe from attack, able to resist defeat

IMPRESSIONABLE   easily influenced or affected

IMPROMPTU   spontaneous, without rehearsal

IMPROVIDENT   without planning or foresight, negligent

IMPRUDENT   unwise

IMPUDENT   arrogant and rude

IMPUGN   to call into question, attack verbally

IMPULSE   sudden tendency, inclination

IMPULSIVE   spontaneous, unpredictable

INADVERTENTLY   unintentionally

INANE   foolish, silly, lacking significance

INAUGURATE   to begin or start officially; to induct into office

INCANDESCENT   shining brightly

INCARCERATE   to put in jail; to confine

INCARCERATION   imprisonment

INCARNADINE   blood-red in color

INCARNATE   having bodily form

INCENDIARY   combustible, flammable, burning easily

INCENSE (v)   to infuriate, enrage

INCEPTION   beginning

INCESSANT   continuous, never ceasing

INCHOATE   just begun; disorganized

INCIPIENT   beginning to exist or appear; in an initial stage

INCISIVE   perceptive, penetrating

INCLINATION   tendency towards

INCLUSIVE   comprehensive, all-encompassing

INCOGNITO   in disguise, concealing one's identity

INCOMMUNICADO   lacking a means to communicate

INCONCEIVABLE   impossible, unthinkable

INCONGRUOUS   incompatible, not harmonious

INCONSEQUENTIAL   unimportant, trivial

INCONTROVERTIBLE   unquestionable, beyond dispute

INCORRIGIBLE   incapable of being corrected

INCREDULOUS   skeptical, doubtful

INCULCATE   to teach, impress in the mind

INCULPATE   to blame, charge with a crime

INCUMBENT (adj)   holding a specified office, often political; required, obligatory

INCURSION   sudden invasion

INDEFATIGABLE   never tired

INDEFENSIBLE   inexcusable, unforgivable

INDELIBLE   permanent, not erasable

INDENTURE   bound to another by contract

INDICATIVE   showing or pointing out, suggestive of

INDICT   to accuse formally, charge with a crime

INDIGENOUS   native, occurring naturally in an area

INDIGENT   very poor

INDIGNANT   angry, incensed, offended

INDISPUTABLE   not disputed, unquestioned

INDOLENT   habitually lazy, idle

INDOMITABLE   fearless, unconquerable

INDUBITABLE   unquestionable

INDUCE   to persuade; bring about

INDUCT   to place ceremoniously in office

INDULGE   to give in to a craving or desire

INDUSTRY   business or trade; diligence, energy

INEBRIATED   drunk, intoxicated

INEPT   clumsy, awkward

INERT   unable to move, tending to inactivity

INESTIMABLE   too great to be estimated

INEVITABLE   certain, unavoidable

INEXORABLE   inflexible, unyielding

INEXTRICABLE   incapable of being disentangled

INFALLIBLE   incapable of making a mistake

INFAMY   reputation for bad deeds

INFANTILE   childish, immature

INFATUATED   strongly or foolishly attached to, inspired with foolish passion, overly in love

INFER   to conclude, deduce

INFERNAL   hellish, diabolical

INFILTRATE   to pass secretly into enemy territory

INFINITESIMAL   extremely tiny

INFIRMITY   disease, ailment

INFRINGE   to encroach, trespass; to transgress, violate

INFURIATE   to anger, provoke, outrage

INFURIATING   provoking anger or outrage

INGENIOUS   original, clever, inventive

INGENUOUS   straightforward, open; naive and unsophisticated

INGLORIOUS   lacking fame or honor, shameful

INGRAINED   an innate quality, deep-seated

INGRATE   ungrateful person

INGRATIATE   to bring oneself purposely into another's good graces

INGRESS   entrance

INHIBIT   to hold back, prevent, restrain

INIMICAL   hostile, unfriendly

INIQUITY   sin, evil act

INITIATE   to begin, introduce; to enlist, induct

INJECT   to force into; to introduce into conversation

INJUNCTION   command, order

INJURIOUS   causing injury

INKLING   hint; vague idea

INNATE   natural, inborn

INNATENESS   state of being natural or inborn

INNOCUOUS   harmless; inoffensive

INNOVATE   to invent, modernize, revolutionize

INNUENDO   indirect and subtle criticism, insinuation

INNUMERABLE   too many to be counted

INOFFENSIVE   harmless, innocent

INOPERABLE   not operable; incurable by surgery

INQUEST   investigation; court or legal proceeding

INQUISITIVE   curious

INSATIABLE   never satisfied

INSCRUTABLE   impossible to understand fully

INSENTIENT   unfeeling, unconscious

INSIDIOUS   sly, treacherous, devious

INSINUATE   to suggest, say indirectly, imply

INSIPID   bland, lacking flavor; lacking excitement

INSOLENT   insulting and arrogant

INSOLUBLE   not able to be solved or explained

INSOLVENT   bankrupt, unable to pay one's debts

INSTIGATE   to incite, urge, agitate

INSUBSTANTIAL   modest, insignificant

INSUFFICIENCY   lacking in something

INSULAR   isolated, detached

INSUPERABLE   insurmountable, unconquerable

INSURGENT (adj)   rebellious, insubordinate

INSURRECTION   rebellion

INTEGRAL   central, indispensable

INTEGRATED   unified

INTEGRITY   decency, honest; wholeness

INTEMPERATE   not moderate

INTER   to bury

INTERDICT   to forbid, prohibit

INTERJECT   to interpose, insert

INTERLOCUTOR   someone taking part in a dialog

INTERLOPER   trespasser; meddler in others' affairs

INTERMINABLE   endless

INTERMITTENT   starting and stopping

INTERNECINE   deadly to both sides

INTERPOLATE   to insert; change by adding new words or material

INTERPOSE   to insert; to intervene

INTERREGNUM   interval between reigns

INTERROGATE   to question formally

INTERSECT   to divide by passing through or across

INTERSPERSE   to distribute among, mix with

INTERSTICE   a space between things

INTIMATION   clue, suggestion

INTRACTABLE   not easily managed

INTRAMURAL   within an institution like a school

INTRANSIGENT   uncompromising, refusing to be reconciled

INTREPID   fearless

INTRIGUED   interested, curious

INTRINSIC   inherent, internal

INTROSPECTIVE   contemplating one's own thoughts and feelings

INTROVERT   someone given to self-analysis

INTRUSION   trespass, invasion of another's privacy

INTUITIVE   instinctive, untaught

INUNDATE   to cover with water; overwhelm

INURE   to harden; accustom; become used to

INVALIDATE   to negate or nullify

INVARIABLE   constant, not changing

INVECTIVE   verbal abuse

INVEIGH   protest strongly

INVESTITURE   ceremony conferring authority

INVETERATE   confirmed, long-standing, deeply rooted

INVIDIOUS   likely to provoke ill will, offensive

INVINCIBLE   invulnerable, unbeatable

INVIOLABLE   safe from violation or assault

INVOKE   to call upon, request help

IOTA   very tiny amount

IRASCIBLE   easily angered

IRIDESCENT   showing many colors

IRRESOLVABLE   unable to be resolved; not analyzable

IRREVERENT   disrespectful

IRREVOCABLE   conclusive, irreversible

ITINERANT   wandering from place to place, unsettled

ITINERARY   route of a traveler's journey

J

JADED   tired by excess or overuse; slightly cynical

JANGLING   clashing, jarring; harshly unpleasant (in sound)

JARGON   nonsensical talk; specialized language

JAUNDICE   yellowish discoloration of skin

JAUNDICED   affected by jaundice; prejudiced or embittered

JETTISON   to cast off, throw cargo overboard

JIBE   to shift suddenly from one side to the other

JINGOISM   belligerent support of one's country

JOCULAR   jovial, playful, humorous

JUBILEE   special anniversary

JUDICIOUS   sensible, showing good judgment

JUGGERNAUT   huge force destroying everything in its path

JUNCTURE   point where two things are joined

JURISPRUDENCE   philosophy of law

JUVENILE   young or childish acting

JUXTAPOSITION   side-by-side placement

K

KEEN   having a sharp edge; intellectually sharp, perceptive

KERNEL   innermost, essential part; seed grain, often in a shell

KEYNOTE   note or tone on which a musical key is founded; main idea of a speech, program, etc.

KINDLE   to set fire to or ignite; excite or inspire

KINETIC   relating to motion; characterized by movement

KISMET   fate

KNELL   sound of a funeral bell; omen of death or failure

KUDOS   fame, glory, honor

L

LABYRINTH   maze

LACERATION   cut or wound

LACHRYMOSE   tearful

LACKADAISICAL   idle, lazy; apathetic, indifferent

LACKLUSTER   dull

LACONIC   using few words

LAGGARD   dawdler, loafer, lazy person

LAMBASTE   disapprove angrily

LAMENT (v)   to deplore, grieve

LAMPOON (v)   to attack with satire, mock harshly

LANGUID   lacking energy, indifferent, slow

LANGUOR   listlessness

LAP (v)   to drink using the tongue; to wash against

LAPIDARY   relating to precious stones

LARCENY   theft of property

LARDER   place where food is stored

LARGESS   generosity; gift

LARYNX   organ containing vocal cords

LASCIVIOUS   lewd, lustful

LASSITUDE   lethargy, sluggishness

LATENT   present but hidden; potential

LATITUDE   freedom of action or choice

LAUDABLE   deserving of praise

LAVISH   to give plentiful amounts of

LAXITY   carelessness

LEERY   suspicious

LEGERDEMAIN   trickery

LEGIBLE   readable

LEGISLATE   to decree, mandate, make laws

LEGITIMATE   adhering to the law, rightful

LENIENT   easygoing, permissive

LETHARGY   indifferent inactivity

LEVITATE   to rise in the air or cause to rise

LEVITY   humor, frivolity, gaiety

LEXICON   dictionary, list of words

LIBERAL (adj)   tolerant, broad-minded; generous, lavish

LIBERATION   freedom, emancipation

LIBERTARIAN   one who believes in unrestricted freedom

LIBERTINE   one without moral restraint

LIBIDINOUS   lustful

LICENSE   freedom to act

LICENTIOUS   immoral; unrestrained by society

LIEN   right to possess and sell the property of a debtor

LIMPID   clear and simple; serene; transparent

LINEAGE   ancestry

LINGUISTICS   study of language

LINIMENT   medicinal liquid used externally to ease pain

LIONIZE   to treat as a celebrity

LISSOME   easily flexed, limber, agile

LISTLESS   lacking energy and enthusiasm

LITERAL   word for word; upholding the exact meaning of a word

LITERATE   able to read and write; well-read and educated

LITHE   moving and bending with ease; graceful

LITIGATION   lawsuit

LIVID   discolored from a bruise; reddened with anger

LOATHE   to abhor, despise, hate

LOCOMOTION   movement from place to place

LODGED   fixed in one position

LOFTY   noble, elevated in position

LOGO   corporate symbol

LOITER   to stand around idly

LOQUACIOUS   talkative

LOW (v)   to make a sound like a cow, moo

LUCID   clear and easily understood

LUDICROUS   laughable, ridiculous

LUGUBRIOUS   sorrowful, mournful

LULL   to soothe

LUMBER (v)   to move slowly and awkwardly

LUMINARY   bright object; celebrity; source of inspiration

LUMINOUS   bright, brilliant, glowing

LUNAR   relating to the moon

LURID   harshly shocking, sensational; glowing

LURK   to prowl, sneak

LUSCIOUS   very good-tasting

LUXURIANCE   elegance, lavishness

LYRICAL   suitable for poetry and song; expressing feeling

M

MACABRE   gruesome, producing horror

MACHINATION   plot or scheme

MACROBIOTICS   art of prolonging life by special diet of organic, nonmeat substances

MACROCOSM   system regarded as an entity with subsystems

MAELSTROM   whirlpool; turmoil; agitated state of mind

MAGNANIMOUS   generous, noble in spirit

MAGNATE   powerful or influential person

MAGNITUDE   extent, greatness of size

MAINSTAY   chief support

MALADROIT   clumsy, tactless

MALADY   illness

MALAPROPISM   humorous misuse of a word

MALCONTENT   discontented person, one who holds a grudge

MALEDICTION   curse

MALEFACTOR   evil-doer; culprit

MALEVOLENT   ill-willed; causing evil or harm to others

MALFUNCTION (n)   breakdown, failure

MALFUNCTION (v)   to fail to work

MALICE   animosity, spite, hatred

MALINGER   to evade responsibility by pretending to be ill

MALLEABLE   capable of being shaped

MALNUTRITION   undernourishment

MALODOROUS   foul-smelling

MANDATORY   necessary, required

MANIFEST (adj)   obvious

MANIFOLD   diverse, varied, comprised of many parts

MANNERED   artificial or stilted in character

MANUAL (adj)   hand-operated; physical

MANUMISSION   release from slavery

MAR   to damage, deface; spoil

MARGINAL   barely sufficient

MARITIME   relating to the sea or sailing

MARTIAL   warlike, pertaining to the military

MARTINET   strict disciplinarian, one who rigidly follows rules

MARTYR   person dying for his or her beliefs

MASOCHIST   one who enjoys pain or humiliation

MASQUERADE   disguise; action that conceals the truth

MATERIALISM   preoccupation with material things

MATRICULATE   to enroll as a member of a college or university

MATRILINEAL   tracing ancestry through mother's line rather than father's

MAUDLIN   overly sentimental

MAVERICK   a person who resists adherence to a group

MAWKISH   sickeningly sentimental

MEAGER   scanty, sparse

MEANDER   to wander aimlessly without direction

MEANINGFUL   significant

MEDDLER   person interfering in others' affairs

MEDIEVAL   relating to the Middle Ages

MEGALITH   huge stone used in prehistoric structures

MEGALOMANIA   mental state with delusions of wealth and power

MELANCHOLY   sadness, depression

MELODIOUS   having a pleasing melody

MELODY   pleasing musical sounds; tune

MENAGERIE   various animals kept together for exhibition

MENDACIOUS   dishonest

MENDACITY   a lie, falsehood

MENDICANT   beggar

MENTOR   experienced teacher and wise adviser

MERCENARY (adj)   motivated only by greed

MERCENARY (n)   soldier for hire in foreign countries

MERCURIAL   quick, shrewd, and unpredictable

MERETRICIOUS   gaudy, falsely attractive

MERIDIAN   circle passing through the two poles of the earth

MERITORIOUS   deserving reward or praise

METAMORPHOSIS   change, transformation

METAPHOR   figure of speech comparing two different things

METICULOUS   extremely careful, fastidious, painstaking

METRONOME   time-keeping device used in music

METTLE   courageousness; endurance

MICROBE   microorganism

MICROCOSM   tiny system used as analogy for larger system

MIGRATORY   wandering from place to place with the seasons

MILITATE   to operate against, work against

MILLENNIUM   one thousand years

MINATORY   menacing, threatening

MINIMAL   smallest in amount, least possible

MINUSCULE   very small

MIRTH   frivolity, gaiety, laughter

MISANTHROPE   person who hates human beings

MISAPPREHEND   to misunderstand, fail to know

MISCONSTRUE   to misunderstand, fail to discover

MISCREANT   one who behaves criminally

MISERLINESS   extreme stinginess

MISGIVING   apprehension, doubt, sense of foreboding

MISHAP   accident; misfortune

MISNOMER   an incorrect name or designation

MISSIVE   note or letter

MITIGATE   to soften, or make milder

MNEMONIC   relating to memory; designed to assist memory

MOBILITY   ease of movement

MOCK (v)   to deride, ridicule

MODERATE (adj)   reasonable, not extreme

MODERATE (v)   to make less excessive, restrain; regulate

MODICUM   a small amount

MOLLIFY   to calm or make less severe

MOLLUSK   sea animal with a soft body

MOLT (v)   to shed hair, skin, or an outer layer periodically

MOMENTOUS   important

MONASTIC   extremely plain or secluded, as in a monastery

MONOCHROMATIC   having one color

MONOGAMY   custom of marriage to one person at a time

MONOLITH   large block of stone

MONOLOGUE   dramatic speech performed by one actor

MONOTONY   lack of variation; wearisome sameness

MONTAGE   composite picture

MOOT   debatable; previously decided

MORBID   gruesome; relating to disease; abnormally gloomy

MORDACIOUS   caustic, biting

MORDANT   sarcastic

MORES   customs or manners

MORIBUND   dying, decaying

MOROSE   gloomy, sullen, or surly

MORSEL   small bit of food

MOTE   small particle, speck

MOTLEY   many-colored; composed of diverse parts

MOTTLE   to mark with spots

MULTIFACETED   having many parts, many-sided

MULTIFARIOUS   diverse

MUNDANE   worldly; commonplace

MUNIFICENT   generous

MUNITIONS   ammunition

MUTABILITY   changeability

MUTE   unable to speak

MYOPIC   near-sighted

MYRIAD   immense number, multitude

N

NADIR   lowest point

NAIVE   lacking sophistication

NAIVETÉ   a lack of worldly wisdom

NARRATIVE   account, story

NASCENT   starting to develop, coming into existence

NATAL   relating to birth

NEBULOUS   vague, cloudy

NECROMANCY   black magic

NEFARIOUS   vicious, evil

NEGLIGENT   careless, inattentive

NEGLIGIBLE   not worth considering

NEMESIS   a formidable, often victorious opponent

NEOLOGISM   new word or expression

NEONATE   newborn child

NEOPHYTE   novice, beginner

NETHER   located under or below

NETTLE (v)   to irritate

NEUTRALITY   disinterest, impartiality

NEUTRALIZE   to balance, offset

NICETY   elegant or delicate feature; minute distinction

NICHE   recess in a wall; best position for something

NIGGARDLY   stingy

NIGGLING   trifle, petty

NIHILISM   belief that existence and all traditional values
are meaningless

NOBLE   illustrious, moral

NOCTURNAL   pertaining to night; active at night

NOISOME   stinking, putrid

NOMADIC   moving from place to place

NOMENCLATURE   terms used in a particular science or
discipline

NOMINAL   existing in name only; negligible

NON SEQUITUR   conclusion not following from apparent
evidence

NONCHALANT   unconcerned, indifferent

NONDESCRIPT   lacking interesting or distinctive qualities;
dull

NONENTITY   an insignificant person

NOTORIETY   fame; unfavorable fame

NOVICE   apprentice, beginner

NOVITIATE   period of being a beginner or novice

NOXIOUS   harmful, unwholesome

NUANCE   shade of meaning

NULLIFY   to make legally invalid; to counteract the effect of

NUMISMATICS   coin collecting

NUPTIAL   relating to marriage

NUTRITIVE   relating to nutrition or health

O

OBDURATE   stubborn

OBEISANCE   a show of respect or submission

OBFUSCATE   to confuse, obscure

OBJURGATE   scold

OBLIGING   accommodating, agreeable

OBLIQUE   indirect, evasive; misleading, devious

OBLITERATE   demolish completely, wipe out

OBLIVIOUS   unaware, inattentive

OBLOQUY   abusive language; ill repute

OBSCURE (adj)   dim, unclear; not well known

OBSCURITY   place or thing that's hard to perceive

OBSEQUIOUS   overly submissive, brownnosing

OBSEQUY   funeral ceremony

OBSESSIVE   preoccupying, all-consuming

OBSOLETE   no longer in use

OBSTINATE   stubborn

OBSTREPEROUS   troublesome, boisterous, unruly

OBTRUSIVE   pushy, too conspicuous

OBTUSE   insensitive, stupid, dull

OBVIATE   to make unnecessary; to anticipate and prevent

OCCLUDE   to shut, block

ODIOUS   hateful, contemptible

OFFICIOUS   too helpful, meddlesome

OFFSHOOT   branch

OMINOUS   menacing, threatening, indicating misfortune

OMNIPOTENT   having unlimited power

OMNISCIENT   having infinite knowledge

OMNIVOROUS   eating everything; absorbing everything

ONEROUS   burdensome

ONTOLOGY   theory about the nature of existence

OPALESCENT   iridescent, displaying colors

OPAQUE   impervious to light; difficult to understand

OPERATIVE   functioning, working

OPINE   to express an opinion

OPPORTUNE   appropriate, fitting

OPPORTUNIST   one who takes advantage of circumstances

OPPROBRIOUS   disgraceful, contemptuous

OPTIMUM   the most favorable degree

OPULENCE   wealth

ORACLE   person who foresees the future and gives advice

ORATION   lecture, formal speech

ORATOR   lecturer, speaker

ORB   spherical body; eye

ORCHESTRATE   to arrange music for performance; to coordinate, organize

ORDAIN   to make someone a priest or minister; to order

ORIFICE   an opening

ORNITHOLOGIST   scientist who studies birds

OROTUND   pompous

OSCILLATE   to move back and forth

OSSIFY   to turn to bone; to become rigid

OSTENSIBLE   apparent

OSTENTATIOUS   showy

OSTRACISM   exclusion, temporary banishment

OUSTER   expulsion, ejection

OVERABUNDANCE   excess, surfeit

OVERSTATE   to embellish, exaggerate

OVERT   in the open, obvious

OVERTURE   musical introduction; proposal, offer

OVERWEENING   arrogant

OVERWROUGHT   agitated, overdone

P

PACIFIC   calm, peaceful

PACIFIST   one opposed to war

PACIFY   to restore calm, bring peace

PAEAN   a song of praise or thanksgiving

PALATIAL   like a palace, magnificent

PALAVER   idle talk

PALEONTOLOGY   study of past geological eras through fossil remains

PALETTE   board for mixing paints; range of colors

PALISADE   fence made up of stakes

PALL (n)   covering that darkens or obscures; coffin

PALL (v)   to lose strength or interest

PALLIATE   to make less serious, ease

PALLID   lacking color or liveliness

PALPABLE   obvious, real, tangible

PALPITATION   trembling, shaking, irregular beating

PALTRY   pitifully small or worthless

PANACEA   cure-all

PANACHE   flamboyance, verve

PANDEMIC   spread over a whole area or country

PANEGYRIC   elaborate praise; formal hymn of praise

PANOPLY   impressive array

PANORAMA   broad view; comprehensive picture

PARADIGM   ideal example, model

PARADOX   contradiction, incongruity; dilemma, puzzle

PARADOXICAL   self-contradictory but true

PARAGON   model of excellence or perfection

PARAMOUNT   supreme, dominant, primary

PARAPHRASE   to reword, usually in simpler terms

PARASITE   person or animal that lives at another's expense

PARCH   to dry or shrivel

PARE   to trim

PARIAH   outcast

PARITY   equality

PARLEY   discussion, usually between enemies

PAROCHIAL   of limited scope or outlook, provincial

PARODY   humorous imitation

PAROLE   conditional release of a prisoner

PARRY   to ward off or deflect

PARSIMONY   stinginess

PARTISAN (adj)   biased in favor of

PARTISAN (n)   strong supporter

PASTICHE   piece of literature or music imitating other works

PATENT (adj)   obvious, unconcealed

PATENT (n)   official document giving exclusive right to sell an invention

PATERNITY   fatherhood; descent from father's ancestors

PATHOGENIC   causing disease

PATHOS   pity, compassion

PATRICIAN   aristocrat

PATRICIDE   murder of one's father

PATRIMONY   inheritance or heritage derived from one's father

PATRONIZE   to condescend to, disparage; to buy from

PAUCITY   scarcity, lack

PAUPER   very poor person

PAVILION   tent or light building used for shelter or exhibitions

PECCADILLO   minor sin or offense

PECULATION   theft of money or goods

PEDAGOGUE   teacher

PEDANT   one who pays undue attention to book learning and rules; one who displays learning ostentatiously

PEDESTRIAN (adj)   commonplace

PEDIATRICIAN   doctor specializing in children and their ailments

PEDIMENT   triangular gable on a roof or facade

PEER (n)   contemporary, equal, match

PEERLESS   unequaled

PEJORATIVE   having bad connotations; disparaging

PELLUCID   transparent; translucent; easily understood

PENANCE   voluntary suffering to repent for a wrong

PENCHANT   inclination

PENDING (prep)   during, while awaiting

PENITENT   expressing sorrow for sins or offenses, repentant

PENSIVE   thoughtful

PENULTIMATE   next to last

PENUMBRA   partial shadow

PENURY   extreme poverty

PERAMBULATE   walk about

PERCIPIENT   discerning, able to perceive

PERDITION   complete and utter loss; damnation

PEREGRINATE   to wander from place to place

PEREMPTORY   imperative; dictatorial

PERENNIAL   present throughout the years; persistent

PERFIDIOUS   faithless, disloyal, untrustworthy

PERFUNCTORY   done in a routine way; indifferent

PERIHELION   point in orbit nearest to the sun

PERIPATETIC   moving from place to place

PERIPHRASTIC   containing too many words

PERJURE   to tell a lie under oath

PERMEABLE   penetrable

PERNICIOUS   very harmful

PERPETUAL   endless, lasting

PERPETUITY   continuing forever

PERPLEXING   puzzling, bewildering

PERSONIFICATION   act of attributing human qualities to objects or abstract qualities

PERSPICACIOUS   shrewd, astute, keen-witted

PERT   lively and bold

PERTINACIOUS   persistent, stubborn

PERTINENT   applicable, appropriate

PERTURBATION   disturbance

PERUSAL   close examination

PERVASIVE   present throughout

PERVERT (v)   to cause to change in immoral way; to misuse

PESTILENCE   epidemic, plague

PETTISH   fretful

PETULANCE   rudeness, peevishness

PHALANX   massed group of soldiers, people, or things

PHILANDERER   pursuer of casual love affairs

PHILANTHROPY   love of humanity; generosity to worthy causes

PHILISTINE   narrow-minded person, someone lacking appreciation for art or culture

PHILOLOGY   study of words

PHLEGM   coldness or indifference

PHLEGMATIC   calm in temperament; sluggish

PHOBIA   anxiety, horror

PHOENIX   mythical, immortal bird that lives for 500 years, burns itself to death, and rises from its ashes

PHONETICS   study of speech sounds

PHONIC   relating to sound

PICAYUNE   petty, of little value

PIDDLING   trivial

PIETY   devoutness

PILFER   to steal

PILLAGE   to loot, especially during a war

PILLORY   ridicule and abuse

PINNACLE   peak, highest point of development

PIOUS   dedicated, devout, extremely religious

PIQUE   fleeting feeling of hurt pride

PITHY   profound, substantial; concise, succinct, to the point

PITTANCE   meager amount or wage

PLACATE   to soothe or pacify

PLACID   calm

PLAGIARIST   one who steals words or ideas

PLAINTIFF   injured person in a lawsuit

PLAINTIVE   expressing sorrow

PLAIT   to braid

PLANGENT   loud sound; wailing sound

PLASTIC   flexible; pliable

PLATITUDE   stale, overused expression

PLAUDIT   applause

PLEBEIAN   crude, vulgar; low-class

PLENITUDE   abundance, plenty

PLETHORA   excess, overabundance

PLIANT   pliable, yielding

PLUCK   to pull strings on musical instrument

PLUCKY   courageous, spunky

PLUMMET   to fall, plunge

PLURALISTIC   including a variety of groups

PLY (v)   to use diligently; to engage; to join together

PNEUMATIC   relating to air; worked by compressed air

POACH   to steal game or fish; cook in boiling liquid

PODIUM   platform or lectern for orchestra conductors or speakers

POIGNANT   emotionally moving

POLAR   relating to a geographic pole; exhibiting contrast

POLARIZE   to tend towards opposite extremes

POLEMIC   controversy, argument; verbal attack

POLITIC   shrewd and practical; diplomatic

POLYGLOT   speaker of many languages

POMPOUS   self-important

PONDEROUS   weighty, heavy, large

PONTIFICATE   to speak in a pretentious manner

PORE (v)   to study closely or meditatively

POROUS   full of holes, permeable to liquids

PORTENT   omen

PORTLY   stout, dignified

POSIT   to put in position; to suggest an idea

POSTERIOR   bottom, rear

POSTERITY   future generations; all of a person's descendants

POTABLE   drinkable

POTENTATE   monarch or ruler with great power

POVERTY   lacking money or possessions

PRAGMATIC   practical; moved by facts rather than abstract ideals

PRATTLE   meaningless, foolish talk

PRECARIOUS   uncertain

PRECEPT   principle; law

PRECIPICE   edge, steep overhang

PRECIPITATE (adj)   sudden and unexpected

PRECIPITATE (v)   to throw down from a height; to cause to happen

PRECIPITOUS   hasty, quickly, with too little caution

PRÉCIS   short summary of facts

PRECISION   state of being precise; exactness

PRECLUDE   to rule out

PRECOCIOUS   unusually advanced at an early age

PRECURSOR   forerunner, predecessor

PREDATOR   one that preys on others, destroyer, plunderer

PREDESTINE   to decide in advance

PREDICAMENT   difficult situation

PREDICATE (v)   to found or base on

PREDICTIVE   relating to prediction, indicative of the future

PREDILECTION   preference, liking

PREDISPOSITION   tendency, inclination

PREEMINENT   celebrated, distinguished

PREFACE   introduction to a book; introductory remarks to a speech

PREMEDITATE   to consider, plan beforehand

PREMONITION   forewarning; presentiment

PREPONDERANCE   majority in number; dominance

PREPOSSESSING   attractive, engaging, appealing

PREPOSTEROUS   absurd, illogical

PRESAGE   to foretell, indicate in advance

PRESCIENT   having foresight

PRESCRIBE   to set down a rule; to recommend a treatment

PRESENTIMENT   premonition, sense of foreboding

PRESTIDIGITATION   sleight of hand

PRESUMPTUOUS   rude, improperly bold

PRETENTIOUS   showy, self-important

PRETEXT   excuse, pretended reason

PREVALENT   widespread

PREVARICATE   to lie, evade the truth

PRIMEVAL   ancient, primitive

PRIMORDIAL   original, existing from the beginning

PRISTINE   untouched, uncorrupted

PRIVATION   lack of usual necessities or comforts

PROBITY   honesty, high-mindedness

PROCLIVITY   tendency, inclination

PROCRASTINATION   putting off something that must be done

PROCRASTINATOR   one who continually and unjustifiably postpones

PROCURE   to obtain

PRODIGAL   wasteful, extravagant, lavish

PRODIGIOUS   vast, enormous, extraordinary

PROFANE   impure; contrary to religion; sacrilegious

PROFICIENT   expert, skilled in a certain subject

PROFLIGATE   corrupt, degenerate

PROFUNDITY   great depth

PROFUSE   lavish, extravagant

PROGENITOR   originator, forefather, ancestor in a direct line

PROGENY   offspring, children

PROGNOSIS   prediction of disease outcome; any prediction

PROGNOSTICATE   to predict

PROGRESSIVE   favoring progress or change; moving forward

PROLIFERATION   propagation, reproduction; enlargement, expansion

PROLIFIC   productive, fertile

PROLIX   tedious; wordy

PROLOGUE   introductory section of a literary work or play

PROMONTORY   piece of land or rock higher than its surroundings

PROMULGATE   to make known publicly

PROPAGATE   to breed

PROPENSITY   inclination, tendency

PROPINQUITY   nearness

PROPITIATE   to win over, appease

PROPITIOUS   favorable, advantageous

PROPONENT   advocate, defender, supporter

PROPRIETY   appropriateness

PROSAIC   relating to prose; dull, commonplace

PROSCRIBE   to condemn; to forbid, outlaw

PROSE   ordinary language used in everyday speech

PROSECUTOR   person who initiates a legal action or suit

PROSELYTIZE   to convert to a particular belief or religion

PROSTRATE   lying face downward, lying flat on the ground

PROTAGONIST   main character in a play or story, hero

PROTEAN   readily assuming different forms or characters

PROTESTATION   declaration

PROTOCOL   ceremony and manners observed by diplomats

PROTRACT   to prolong, draw out, extend

PROTRUSION   something that sticks out

PROVIDENT   prudent, frugal

PROVIDENTIAL   prudent, lucky

PROVINCIAL   rustic, unsophisticated, limited in scope

PROVOCATION   cause, incitement to act or respond

PROWESS   bravery, skill

PROXIMITY   nearness

PROXY   power to act as substitute for another

PRUDE   one who is excessively proper or modest

PRUDENT   careful, cautious

PRURIENT   lustful, exhibiting lewd desires

PRY   to intrude into; force open

PSEUDONYM   pen name; fictitious or borrowed name

PSYCHIC (adj)   having to do with the mind; perceptive of nonmaterial, spiritual forces

PUDGY   chubby, overweight

PUERILE   childish, immature, silly

PUGILISM   boxing

PUGNACIOUS   quarrelsome, eager and ready to fight

PULCHRITUDE   beauty

PULVERIZE   to pound, crush, or grind into powder; destroy

PUMMEL   to pound, beat

PUNCTILIOUS   careful in observing rules of behavior or ceremony

PUNDIT   an authority or critic

PUNGENT   strong or sharp in smell or taste

PUNITIVE   having to do with punishment

PURGATION   process of cleansing, purification

PURGE (v)   to cleanse or free from impurities

PURITANICAL   adhering to a rigid moral code

PURPORT   to profess, suppose, claim

PUSILLANIMOUS   cowardly

PUTRID   rotten

Q

QUACK (n)   faker; one who falsely claims to have medical skill

QUADRILATERAL   four-sided polygon

QUADRUPED   animal having four feet

QUAFF   to drink heartily

QUAGMIRE   marsh; difficult situation

QUALIFY   to provide with needed skills; modify, limit

QUANDARY   dilemma, difficulty

QUARANTINE   isolation period, originally 40 days, to prevent spread of disease

QUATERNARY   consisting of or relating to four units or members

QUELL   to crush or subdue

QUERULOUS   inclined to complain, irritable

QUERY (n)   question

QUIBBLE   to argue about insignificant and irrelevant details

QUICKEN   to hasten, arouse, excite

QUIESCENCE   inactivity, stillness

QUIESCENT   inactive, at rest

QUINTESSENCE   most typical example; concentrated essence

QUIVER (v)   to shake slightly, tremble, vibrate

QUIXOTIC   overly idealistic, impractical

QUOTIDIAN   occurring daily; commonplace

R

RACONTEUR   witty, skillful storyteller

RADICAL (adj)   fundamental; drastic

RAGING   violent, wild

RAIL (v)   to scold with bitter or abusive language

RAILLERY   lighthearted jesting

RALLY (v)   to assemble; recover, recuperate

RAMBLE (v)   to roam, wander; to babble, digress

RAMIFICATION   implication, outgrowth, or consequence

RAMPANT   unrestrained

RAMSHACKLE   likely to collapse

RANCID   spoiled, rotten

RANCOR   bitter hatred

RANT   to harangue, rave, forcefully scold

RAPACIOUS   greedy; predatory

RAPPORT   relationship of trust and respect

RAPPROCHEMENT   having a cordial relationship

RAPT   deeply absorbed

RAREFY   to make thinner, purer, or more refined

RASH (adj)   careless, hasty, reckless

RATIFY   to approve formally, confirm

RATIOCINATION   methodical, logical reasoning

RATION (n)   portion, share

RATION (v)   to supply; to restrict consumption of

RATIONAL   logical, reasonable

RATIONALE   line of reasoning

RAUCOUS   harsh-sounding; boisterous

RAVAGE   to destroy, devastate

RAVENOUS   extremely hungry

RAVINE   deep, narrow gorge

RAW   vulgar, coarse

RAZE   to tear down, demolish

REACTIONARY (adj)   marked by extreme conservatism, esp. in politics

REBARBATIVE   irritating; repellent

REBUFF (n)   blunt rejection

REBUKE (v)   to reprimand, scold

REBUT   to refute by evidence or argument

RECALCITRANT   resisting authority or control

RECANT   to retract a statement, opinion, etc.

RECAPITULATE   to review with a brief summary

RECEPTIVE   open to others' ideas; congenial

RECIDIVISM   tendency to repeat previous behavior

RECIPROCATE   to show or feel in return

RECLUSIVE   shut off from the world

RECONDITE   relating to obscure learning; known to only a few

RECOUNT (v)   to describe facts or events

RECREANT   disloyal; cowardly

RECRUIT (v)   to draft, enlist; to seek to enroll

RECTIFY   to correct

RECTITUDE   moral uprightness

RECURRENCE   repetition

REDRESS (n)   relief from wrong or injury

REDUNDANCY   unnecessary repetition

REFECTORY   room where meals are served

REFLECTION   image, likeness; opinion, thought, impression

REFORM (v)   to change, correct

REFRACT   to deflect sound or light

REFRACTORY   obstinately resistant

REFUGE   escape, shelter

REFURBISH   to renovate

REFUTE   to contradict, discredit

REGAL   magnificent, splendid, fit for royalty

REGARD   high esteem

REGIMEN   government rule; systematic plan

REGRESS   to move backward; revert to an earlier form or state

REHABILITATE   to restore to good health or condition; reestablish a person's good reputation

REITERATE   to say again, repeat

REJOINDER   response

REJUVENATE   to make young again; renew

RELEGATE   to assign to a class, especially to an inferior one

RELENT   to become gentler in attitude

RELINQUISH   to renounce or surrender something

RELISH (v)   to enjoy greatly

REMEDIABLE   capable of being corrected

REMEDY (v)   to cure, correct

REMINISCENCE   remembrance of past events

REMISSION   lessening, relaxation

REMIT   to send (usually money) as payment

REMONSTRATE   to protest or object

REMOTE   distant, isolated

REMUNERATION   pay or reward for work, trouble, etc.

RENASCENT   reborn, coming into being again

RENEGADE   traitor, person abandoning a cause

RENEGE   to go back on one's word

RENITENT   resisting pressure, obstinate

RENOUNCE   to give up or reject a right, title, person, etc.

RENOWN   fame, widespread acclaim

RENT   (adj) torn apart

REPAST   meal or mealtime

REPEAL   to revoke or formally withdraw (often a law)

REPEL   to rebuff, repulse; disgust, offend

REPENT   to regret a past action

REPENTANT   apologetic, guilty, remorseful

REPLETE   abundantly supplied

REPLICATE   to duplicate, repeat

REPOSE   relaxation, leisure

REPREHEND   to criticize

REPREHENSIBLE   blameworthy, disreputable

REPRESS   to restrain or hold in

REPRESSION   act of restraining or holding in

REPRISE   repetition, esp. of a piece of music

REPROACH (v)   to find fault with; blame

REPROBATE   morally unprincipled person

REPROVE   to criticize or correct

REPUDIATE   to reject as having no authority

REPULSE   to repel, fend off; sicken, disgust

REQUIEM   hymns or religious service for the dead

REQUITE   to return or repay

RESCIND   to repeal, cancel

RESIDUE   remainder, leftover, remnant

RESILIENT   able to recover quickly after illness or bad luck; able to bounce back into shape

RESOLUTE   determined; with a clear purpose

RESOLVE (n)   determination, firmness of purpose

RESOLVE (v)   to conclude, determine

RESONATE   to echo

RESPIRE   to breathe

RESPITE   interval of relief

RESPLENDENT   splendid, brilliant

RESTITUTION   act of compensating for loss or damage

RESTIVE   impatient, uneasy, restless

RESTORATIVE   having the power to renew or revitalize

RESTRAINED   controlled, repressed, restricted

RESUSCITATE   to revive, bring back to life

RETAIN   to hold, keep possession of

RETARD (v)   to slow, hold back

RETICENT   not speaking freely; reserved

RETINUE   group of attendants with an important person

RETIRING   shy, modest, reserved

RETORT   cutting response

RETRACT   to draw in or take back

RETRENCH   to regroup, reorganize

RETRIEVE   to bring, fetch; reclaim

RETROACTIVE   applying to an earlier time

RETROGRADE   having a backward motion or direction

RETROSPECTIVE   looking back to the past

REVELRY   boisterous festivity

REVERE   to worship, regard with awe

REVERT   to backslide, regress

REVILE   to criticize with harsh language, verbally abuse

REVITALIZE   to renew; give new energy to

REVOKE   to annul, cancel, call back

REVULSION   strong feeling of repugnance or dislike

RHAPSODY   emotional literary or musical work

RHETORIC   persuasive use of language

RHYTHM   regular pattern or variation of sounds and stresses

RIBALD   humorous in a vulgar way

RIDDLE (v)   to make many holes in; permeate

RIFE   widespread, prevalent; abundant

RIFT   an open space; to divide

RIGHTEOUS   morally right

RIPOSTE   a retort

RISQUÉ   bordering on being inappropriate or indecent

ROBUST   strong and healthy; hardy

ROCOCO   very highly ornamented

ROIL   to disturb or cause disorder

ROOT (v)   to dig with a snout (like a pig)

ROOTED   to have an origin or base

ROSTRUM   stage for public speaking

ROTUND   round in shape; fat

RUE   to regret

RUFFLED   irritated

RUMINATE   to contemplate, reflect upon

RUSTIC   rural

S

SACCHARINE   excessively sweet or sentimental

SACROSANCT   extremely sacred; beyond criticism

SAGACIOUS   shrewd, wise

SALACIOUS   lustful

SALIENT   prominent or conspicuous

SALLOW   sickly yellow in color

SALUBRIOUS   healthful

SALUTATION   greeting

SANCTION   permission, support; law; penalty

SANCTUARY   haven, retreat

SANGUINE   ruddy; cheerfully optimistic

SAP (v)   to weaken gradually

SAPIENT   wise

SARDONIC   cynical, scornfully mocking

SATIATE   to satisfy

SAUNTER   to amble; walk in a leisurely manner

SAVANT   learned person

SAVORY   agreeable in taste or smell

SCABBARD   sheath for sword or dagger

SCABROUS   dealing with indecent things; blemished

SCALE (v)   to climb to the top of

SCANTINESS   barely enough, meager

SCARCITY   not enough, insufficient

SCATHING   harshly critical; painfully hot

SCENARIO   plot outline; possible situation

SCHISM   a division or separation; disharmony

SCINTILLA   very small amount

SCINTILLATE   to sparkle, flash

SCION   descendent, child

SCOFF   to deride, ridicule

SCORE (n)   notation for a musical composition

SCORE (v)   to make a notch or scratch

SCRIVENER   professional copyist

SCRUPULOUS   restrained; careful and precise

SCRUTINY   careful observation

SCURRILOUS   vulgar, low, indecent

SECANT   straight line intersecting a curve at two points

SECEDE   to withdraw formally from an organization

SECLUDED   isolated and remote

SECTARIAN   narrow-minded; relating to a group or sect

SECULAR   not specifically pertaining to religion

SEDENTARY   inactive, stationary; sluggish

SEDITION   behavior promoting rebellion

SEISMOLOGY   science of earthquakes

SEMINAL   relating to the beginning or seeds of something

SENESCENT   aging, growing old

SENSUAL   satisfying or gratifying the senses; suggesting sexuality

SENTENTIOUS   having a moralizing tone

SENTIENT   aware, conscious, able to perceive

SEPULCHRAL   typical of a place of burial

SEQUEL   anything that follows

SEQUESTER   to remove or set apart; put into seclusion

SERAPHIC   angelic, pure, sublime

SERENDIPITY   habit of making fortunate discoveries by chance

SERENITY   calm, peacefulness

SERPENTINE   serpent-like; twisting, winding

SERRATED   saw-toothed, notched

SERVILE   submissive, obedient

SHARD   piece of broken glass or pottery

SHEEPISH   timid, meek, or bashful

SHIRK   to avoid a task due to laziness or fear

SIDLE   to cause to turn sideways; to move along one side

SIGNIFY   denote, indicate; symbolize

SIMIAN   apelike; relating to apes

SIMPER   to smirk, smile foolishly

SIMPLE   lacking in knowledge or intelligence

SIMULATED   fake, made to look real

SINCERE   genuine, true

SINECURE   well-paying job or office that requires little or no work

SINGE   to burn slightly, scorch

SINUOUS   winding; intricate, complex

SKEPTICAL   doubtful, questioning

SKULK   to move in a stealthy or cautious manner; sneak

SLAKE   to calm down or moderate

SLIGHT   to treat as unimportant; insult

SLIPSHOD   careless, hasty

SLOTH   sluggishness, laziness

SLOUGH   to discard or shed

SLOVENLY   untidy, messy

SLUGGARD   lazy, inactive person

SMELT (v)   to melt metal in order to refine it

SMUTTY   obscene, indecent

SNIPPET   tiny part, tidbit

SOBRIETY   seriousness

SOBRIQUET   nickname

SODDEN   thoroughly soaked; saturated

SOJOURN   visit, stay

SOLACE   comfort in distress; consolation

SOLARIUM   room or glassed-in area exposed to the sun

SOLECISM   grammatical mistake

SOLICITOUS   concerned, attentive; eager

SOLIDARITY   unity based on common aims or interests

SOLILOQUY   literary or dramatic speech by one character, not addressed to others

SOLIPSISM   belief that the self is the only reality

SOLSTICE   shortest or longest day of the year

SOLUBLE   capable of being solved or dissolved

SOMBER   dark and gloomy; melancholy, dismal

SOMNAMBULIST   sleepwalker

SOMNOLENT   drowsy, sleepy; inducing sleep

SONIC   relating to sound

SONOROUS   producing a full, rich sound

SOPHIST   person good at arguing deviously

SOPHISTRY   deceptive reasoning or argumentation

SOPHOMORIC   immature and overconfident

SOPORIFIC   sleepy or tending to cause sleep

SORDID   filthy; contemptible and corrupt

SOVEREIGN   having supreme power

SPARTAN   austere, severe, grave; simple, bare

SPAWN   to generate, produce

SPECIOUS   deceptively attractive

SPECULATION   contemplation; act of taking business risks for financial gain

SPECULATIVE   involving assumption; uncertain; theoretical

SPLENDID   grand, illustrious

SPONTANEOUS   on the spur of the moment, impulsive

SPORADIC   infrequent, irregular

SPORTIVE   frolicsome, playful

SPRIGHTLY   lively, animated, energetic

SPUR (v)   to prod

SPURIOUS   lacking authenticity; counterfeit, false

SPURN   to reject or refuse contemptuously; to scorn

SQUABBLE   quarrel

SQUALID   filthy; morally repulsive

SQUANDER   to waste

STACCATO   marked by abrupt, clear-cut sounds

STAGNANT   immobile, stale

STAID   self-restrained to the point of dullness

STALK (v)   to hunt, pursue

STALWART   strong, unwavering

STAND (n)   group of trees

STARK   bare, empty, vacant

STASIS   motionless state; standstill

STATELY   grand, unapproachable

STEADFAST   immovable

STEADY   stable, unfaltering

STENTORIAN   extremely loud

STIFLE   to smother or suffocate; suppress

STIGMA   mark of disgrace or inferiority

STILTED   stiff, unnatural

STINT (n)   period of time spent doing something

STINT (v)   to be sparing or frugal

STIPEND   allowance; fixed amount of money paid regularly

STOCKADE   enclosed area forming defensive wall

STOIC   indifferent to or unaffected by emotions

STOLID   having or showing little emotion

STRATAGEM   trick designed to deceive an enemy

STRATIFY   to arrange into layers

STRIATE   striped, grooved

STRICTURE   something that restrains; negative criticism

STRIDENT   loud, harsh, unpleasantly noisy

STRINGENT   imposing severe, rigorous standards

STRIPLING   an adolescent boy

STULTIFY   to impair or reduce to uselessness

STUNTED   having arrested growth or development

STUPEFY   to dull the senses of; stun, astonish

STYLIZE   to fashion, formalize

STYMIE   to block or thwart

SUAVE   smoothly gracious or polite; blandly ingratiating

SUBDUED   suppressed, stifled

SUBJECTION   dependence, obedience, submission

SUBJUGATE   to conquer, subdue; enslave

SUBLIMATE   to repress impulses

SUBLIME   awe-inspiring; of high spiritual or moral value

SUBLIMINAL   subconscious; imperceptible

SUBMISSIVE   tending to be meek and submit

SUBPOENA   notice ordering someone to appear in court

SUBSEQUENT   following in time or order

SUBSTANTIAL   important, real

SUBTERFUGE   trick or tactic used to avoid something

SUBTERRANEAN   hidden, secret; underground

SUBTLE   hard to detect or describe; perceptive

SUBVERT   to undermine or corrupt

SUCCINCT   terse, brief, concise

SUCCULENT   juicy; full of vitality or freshness

SUFFERABLE   bearable

SUFFRAGIST   one who advocates extended voting rights

SULLEN   brooding, gloomy

SULLY   to soil, stain, tarnish; taint

SUMPTUOUS   lavish, splendid

SUPERABUNDANCE   excessive

SUPERANNUATED   too old, obsolete, outdated

SUPERCILIOUS   arrogant, haughty, overbearing, condescending

SUPEREROGATORY   nonessential

SUPERFICIAL   hasty; shallow and phony

SUPERFLUOUS   extra, more than necessary

SUPERSEDE   to take the place of; replace

SUPERVISE   to direct or oversee the work of others

SUPPLANT   to replace, substitute

SUPPLE   flexible, pliant

SUPPLICANT   one who asks humbly and earnestly

SUPPOSITION   assumption

SURFEIT   excessive amount

SURLY   rude and bad-tempered

SURMISE   to make an educated guess

SURMOUNT   to conquer, overcome

SURPASS   to do better than, be superior to

SURPLUS   excess

SURREPTITIOUS   characterized by secrecy

SURVEY (v)   to examine in a comprehensive way

SUSCEPTIBLE   vulnerable, unprotected

SUSPEND   to defer, interrupt; dangle, hang

SUSTAIN   support, uphold; endure, undergo

SUSTENANCE   supplying the necessities of life

SWARTHY   having a dark complexion

SYBARITE   person devoted to pleasure and luxury

SYCOPHANT   self-serving flatterer, yes-man

SYLLABUS   outline of a course

SYMBIOSIS   cooperation, mutual helpfulness

SYMPOSIUM   meeting with short presentations on related topics

SYNCHRONOUS   happening at the same time

SYNCOPATION   temporary irregularity in musical rhythm

SYNOPSIS   plot summary

SYNTHESIS   blend, combination

SYNTHETIC   artificial, imitation

T

TABLEAU   vivid description, striking incident or scene

TACIT   silently understood or implied

TACITURN   uncommunicative, not inclined to speak much

TACTFUL   skillful in dealing with others

TACTILE   relating to the sense of touch

TAINT   to spoil or infect; to stain honor

TAINTED   stained, tarnished; corrupted, poisoned

TALISMAN   something producing a magical effect

TALON   claw of an animal, esp. a bird of prey

TANDEM   acting as a group or in partnership

TANG   sharp flavor or odor

TANGENTIAL   digressing, diverting

TANGIBLE   able to be sensed; perceptible, measurable

TANTAMOUNT   equivalent in value or significance; amounting to

TARNISHED   corroded, discolored; discredited, disgraced

TAWDRY   gaudy, cheap, showy

TAXONOMY   science of classification

TECHNOCRAT   strong believer in technology; technical expert

TEETER   to waver or move unsteadily

TEMERITY   recklessness

TEMPERANCE   restraint, self-control, moderation

TEMPERED   moderated, restrained

TEMPESTUOUS   stormy, raging, furious

TEMPORAL   relating to time; chronological

TENABLE   defensible, reasonable

TENACIOUS   stubborn, holding firm

TENDENTIOUS   biased

TENET   belief, doctrine

TENSILE   capable of withstanding physical stress

TENUOUS   weak, insubstantial

TEPID   lukewarm; showing little enthusiasm

TERMINAL (adj)   concluding, final; fatal

TERMINAL (n)   depot, station

TERRESTRIAL   earthly; down-to-earth, commonplace

TERSE   concise, brief, free of extra words

TESTAMENT   statement of belief; will

TESTIMONIAL   statement testifying to a truth; something given in tribute to a person's achievement

TETHER (v)   to bind, tie

THEOCRACY   government by priests representing a god

THEOLOGY   study of God and religion

THEORETICAL   abstract

THERAPEUTIC   medicinal

THESAURUS   book of synonyms and antonyms

THESIS   theory or hypothesis; dissertation or long written composition

THRALL   a person in servitude, enslaved

THRENODY   a sad poem or song

THWART   to block or prevent from happening; frustrate

TIDINGS   news

TIMOROUS   timid, shy, full of apprehension

TINGE   to color slightly

TIRADE   long violent speech; verbal assault

TITAN   person of colossal stature or achievement

TOADY   flatterer, hanger-on, yes-man

TOLERANCE   capacity to respect different values; capacity to endure or resist something

TOME   book, usually large and academic

TONAL   relating to pitch or sound

TOPOGRAPHY   art of making maps or charts

TORPID   lethargic; unable to move; dormant

TORRID   burning hot; passionate

TORSION   act of twisting and turning

TORTUOUS   having many twists and turns; highly complex

TOTTERING   barely standing

TOXIN   poison

TRACTABLE   obedient, yielding

TRAMMEL   to impede or hamper

TRANQUIL   to calm or steady

TRANSCEND   to rise above, go beyond

TRANSCENDENT   rising above, going beyond

TRANSCRIPTION   copy, reproduction; record

TRANSFIGURATION   a change; an exalting change

TRANSFORMATION   a change in form or appearance

TRANSGRESS   to trespass, violate a law

TRANSIENT (adj)   temporary, short-lived, fleeting

TRANSITORY   short-lived, existing only briefly

TRANSLATION   a change from one state to another; converting one language into another

TRANSLUCENT   partially transparent

TRANSMUTE   to change in appearance or shape

TRANSPIRE   to happen, occur; become known

TRAVESTY   parody, exaggerated imitation, caricature

TREMULOUS   trembling, quivering; fearful, timid

TRENCHANT   acute, sharp, incisive; forceful, effective

TREPIDATION   fear and anxiety

TRIBUTE   a gift or statement showing respect or gratitude

TRIFLING   of slight worth, trivial, insignificant

TRITE   shallow, superficial

TROUNCE   to beat severely, defeat

TROUPE   group of actors

TRUCULENT   savage and cruel; fierce; ready to fight

TRUISM   something that is obviously true

TRUNCATE   to cut off, shorten by cutting

TRYING   difficult to deal with

TRYST   agreement between lovers to meet; rendezvous

TUMULT   state of confusion; agitation

TUNDRA   treeless plain found in Arctic or subarctic regions

TURBID   muddled; unclear

TURBULENCE   commotion, disorder

TURGID   swollen, bloated

TURPITUDE   inherent vileness, foulness, depravity

TYRANNICAL   oppressive; dictatorial

TYRO   beginner, novice

U

UBIQUITOUS   being everywhere simultaneously

UMBRAGE   offense, resentment

UNADULTERATED   absolutely pure

UNANIMITY   state of total agreement or unity

UNAPPEALING   unattractive, unpleasant

UNAVAILING   hopeless, useless

UNBENDING   inflexible, unyielding

UNBRIDLED   unrestrained

UNCONSCIONABLE   unscrupulous; shockingly unfair or unjust

UNCTUOUS   greasy, oily; smug and falsely earnest

UNDAUNTED   resolute even in adversity

UNDERMINE   to sabotage, thwart

UNDOCUMENTED   not certified, unsubstantiated

UNDULATING   moving in waves

UNEQUIVOCAL   absolute, certain

UNFAILING   not likely to fail, constant, infallible

UNFETTERED   free, unrestrained

UNFROCK   to strip of priestly duties

UNGRACIOUS   rude, disagreeable

UNHERALDED   unannounced, unexpected

UNIDIMENSIONAL   having one size or dimension

UNIFORM (adj)   consistent and unchanging; identical

UNIMPEACHABLE   beyond question

UNINITIATED   not familiar with an area of study

UNKEMPT   uncombed, messy in appearance

UNOBTRUSIVE   modest, unassuming

UNPOLISHED   lacking sophistication

UNRUFFLED   poised, calm

UNSCRUPULOUS   dishonest

UNSOILED   clean, pure

UNSOLICITED   unrequested

UNSTINTING   generous

UNSULLIED   clean

UNSWAYABLE   unable to change

UNTOWARD   not favorable; unruly

UNTRAMMELED   unhampered

UNWARRANTED   groundless, unjustified

UNWITTING   unconscious; unintentional

UNYIELDING   firm, resolute

UPBRAID   to scold sharply

UPROARIOUS   loud and forceful

UPSURGE   sudden rise

URBANE   courteous, refined, suave

USURP   to seize by force

USURY   practice of lending money at exorbitant rates

UTILITARIAN   efficient, functional, useful

UTOPIA   perfect place

V

VACILLATE   to waver, show indecision

VACUOUS   empty, void; lacking intelligence, purposeless

VAGRANT   poor person with no home

VALIANT   brave, courageous

VALIDATE   to authorize, certify, confirm

VALOROUS   brave, valiant

VANQUISH   to conquer, defeat

VAPID   tasteless, dull

VARIABLE   changeable, inconstant

VARIEGATED   varied; marked with different colors

VAUNTED   boasted about, bragged about

VEHEMENTLY   strongly, urgently

VENAL   willing to do wrong for money

VENDETTA   prolonged feud marked by bitter hostility

VENERABLE   respected because of age

VENERATION   adoration, honor, respect

VENT (v)   to express, say out loud

VERACIOUS   truthful, accurate

VERACITY   accuracy, truth

VERBATIM   word for word

VERBOSE   wordy

VERDANT   green with vegetation; inexperienced

VERDURE   fresh, rich vegetation

VERIFIED   proven true

VERISIMILITUDE   quality of appearing true or real

VERITY   truthfulness; belief viewed as true and enduring

VERMIN   small creatures offensive to humans

VERNACULAR   everyday language used by ordinary people; specialized language of a profession

VERNAL   related to spring

VERSATILE   adaptable, all-purpose

VERVE   energy, vitality

VESTIGE   trace, remnant

VETO (v)   to reject formally

VEX   to irritate, annoy; confuse, puzzle

VIABLE   workable, able to succeed or grow

VIADUCT   series of elevated arches used to cross a valley

VICARIOUS   substitute, surrogate; enjoyed through imagined participation in another's experience

VICISSITUDE   change or variation; ups and downs

VIE   to compete, contend

VIGILANT   attentive, watchful

VIGNETTE   decorative design; short literary composition

VILIFY   to slander, defame

VIM   energy, enthusiasm

VINDICATE   to clear of blame; to support a claim

VINDICATION   clearance from blame or suspicion

VINDICTIVE   spiteful, vengeful, unforgiving

VIRGINAL   pure, chaste

VIRILE   manly, having qualities of an adult male

VIRTUE   conforming to what is right

VIRTUOSO   someone with masterly skill; expert musician

VIRULENT   extremely poisonous; malignant; hateful

VISCOUS   thick, syrupy and sticky

VITIATE   reduce in value or effectiveness

VITRIOLIC   burning, caustic; sharp, bitter

VITUPERATE   to abuse verbally

VIVACIOUS   lively, spirited

VIVID   bright and intense in color; strongly perceived

VOCIFEROUS   loud, vocal and noisy

VOID (adj)   not legally enforceable; empty

VOID (n)   emptiness, vacuum

VOID (v)   to cancel, invalidate

VOLATILE   explosive

VOLITION   free choice, free will; act of choosing

VOLLEY (n)   flight of missiles, round of gunshots

VOLUBLE   speaking much and easily, talkative; glib

VOLUMINOUS   large; of great quantity; writing or speaking at great length

VORACIOUS   having a great appetite

VORTEX   swirling, resembling a whirlpool

VULGAR   obscene; common, of low class

VULNERABLE   defenseless, unprotected; innocent, naive

W

WAIVE   to refrain from enforcing a rule; to give up a legal right

WALLOW   to indulge oneself excessively, luxuriate

WAN   sickly pale

WANE   to dwindle, to decrease

WANTON   undisciplined, unrestrained, reckless

WARRANTY   guarantee of a product's soundness

WARY   careful, cautious

WASPISH   rude, behaving badly

WAVER   to show indecision

WAX   to increase

WAYWARD   erratic, unrestrained, reckless

WEATHER (v)   to endure, undergo

WEIGHTY   important, momentous

WELTER (n)   a confused mass; a jumble

WHET   to sharpen, stimulate

WHIMSY   playful or fanciful idea

WILY   clever, deceptive

WINDFALL   sudden, unexpected good fortune

WINSOME   charming, happily engaging

WITHDRAWN   unsociable, aloof; shy, timid

WIZENED   withered, shriveled, wrinkled

WOE   deep suffering or grief

WRAITH   a ghost

WRANGLE   loud quarrel

WRIT   written document, usually in law

WRY   amusing, ironic

X

XENOPHOBIA   fear or hatred of foreigners or strangers

Y

YOKE (v)   to join together

Z

ZEALOT   someone passionately devoted to a cause

ZENITH   highest point, summit

ZEPHYR   gentle breeze

ZOOLOGIST   scientist who studies animals

A Special Note for International Students

About 250,000 international students pursue advanced academic degrees at the master's or Ph.D. level at U.S. universities each year. This trend of pursuing higher education in the United States, particularly at the graduate level, is expected to continue. Business, management, engineering, and the physical and life sciences are popular areas of study for international students. If you are an international student planning on applying to a graduate program in the United States, you will want to consider the following:

- If English is not your first language, you will probably need to take the Test of English as a Foreign Language (TOEFL®) or show some other evidence that you're proficient in English prior to gaining admission to a graduate program. Graduate programs will vary on what is an acceptable TOEFL score. For degrees in business, journalism, management, or the humanities, a minimum TOEFL score of 600 (250 on the computer-based TOEFL) or better is expected. For the hard sciences and computer technology, a TOEFL score of 550 (213 on the computer-based TOEFL) is a common minimum requirement.

- You may also need to take the Graduate Record Exam (GRE®) or the Graduate Management Admissions Test (GMAT®) as part of the admission process.

- Since admission to many graduate programs and business schools is quite competitive, you may want to select three or four programs you would like to attend and complete applications for each program.

- Selecting the correct graduate school is very different from selecting an undergraduate school. You should research the qualifications and interests of faculty members teaching and doing research in your chosen field. Also, select a program that meets your current or future employment needs, rather than simply a program with a big name.

- Begin the application process at least a year in advance. Be aware that many programs offer only August or September start dates. Find out application deadlines and plan accordingly.

- Finally, you will need to obtain an 1-20 Certificate of Eligibility in order to obtain an F-1 Student Visa to study in the United States.

Kaplan English Programs*

If you need more help with the complex process of graduate school admissions, or assistance preparing for the TOEFL, GRE, or GMAT, you may be interested in Kaplan's programs for international students. Kaplan English Programs were designed to help students and professionals from outside the United States meet their educational and career goals. At locations throughout the United States, international students take advantage of Kaplan's programs to help them improve their academic and conversational English skills, raise their scores on the TOEFL, GRE, GMAT, and other standardized exams, and gain admission to top programs.

General Intensive English

Kaplan's General Intensive English classes are designed to help you improve your skills in all areas of English and to increase your fluency in spoken and written English. Classes are available for beginning to advanced students, and the average class size is 12 students.

TOEFL and Academic English

This course provides you with the skills you need to improve your TOEFL score and succeed in an American university or graduate program. It includes advanced reading, writing, listening, grammar, and conversational English. You will also receive training for the TOEFL using Kaplan's exclusive computer-based practice materials.

GRE for International Students

The Graduate Record Exam (GRE) is required for admission to many graduate programs in the United States. Nearly one-half million people take the GRE each year. A high score can help you stand out from other test takers. This course, designed especially for non-native English speakers, includes the skills you need to succeed on each section of the GRE, as well as access to Kaplan's exclusive computer-based practice materials and extra verbal practice.

GMAT for International Students

The Graduate Management Admissions Test (GMAT) is required for admission to many graduate programs in business in the United States. Hundreds of thousands of American students have taken this course to prepare for the GMAT. This course, designed especially for non-native English speakers, includes the skills you need to succeed on each section of the GMAT, as well as access to Kaplan's exclusive computer-based practice materials and extra verbal practice.

*Kaplan is authorized under federal law to enroll nonimmigrant alien students.
Kaplan is accredited by ACCET (Accrediting Council for Continuing Education and Training).

Other Kaplan Programs

Since 1938, more than 3 million students have come to Kaplan to advance their studies, prepare for entry to American universities, and further their careers. In addition to the above programs, Kaplan offers courses to prepare for the SAT®, LSAT®, MCAT®, DAT®, USMLE®, NCLEX®, and other standardized exams at locations throughout the United States.

To get more information or to apply to any of Kaplan's programs, contact us at:

Kaplan English Programs
700 S. Flower, Suite 2900
Los Angeles, CA 90017 USA
Phone (if calling from within the United States): 800-818-9128
Phone (if calling from outside the United States): (213) 452-5800
Fax: (213) 892-1364
Website: www.kaplanenglish.com
Email: world@kaplan.com

How Did We Do? Grade Us.

Thank you for choosing a Kaplan book. Your comments and suggestions are very useful to us. Please answer the following questions to assist us in our continued development of high-quality resources to meet your needs.

The title of the Kaplan book I read was: _____

My name is: _____

My address is: _____

_____

My email address is: _____

	Poor				Outstanding
What overall grade would you give this book?	A	B	C	D	F
How relevant was the information to your goals?	A	B	C	D	F
How comprehensive was the information in this book?	A	B	C	D	F
How accurate was the information in this book?	A	B	C	D	F
How easy was the book to use?	A	B	C	D	F
How appealing was the book's design?	A	B	C	D	F

What were the book's strong points? _____

How could this book be improved? _____

Is there anything that we left out that you wanted to know more about?

Would you recommend this book to others? ☐ YES   ☐ NO

Other comments: _____

_____

_____

Do we have permission to quote you? ☐ YES   ☐ NO

Thank you for your help.
Please tear out this page and mail it to:

Content Manager
Kaplan Publishing
1 Liberty Plaza, 24th floor
New York, NY 10106
or fax to 212-618-2497

Thanks!

KAPLAN